Strategies of Genius

Volume I

Aristotle
Sherlock Holmes
Walt Disney
Wolfgang Amadeus Mozart

by

Robert B. Dilts

Meta Publications
P.O. Box 1910
Capitola, California 95010
(831) 464 - 0254
FAX (831) 464 - 0517

Original artwork by Robert B. Dilts.

Library of Congress Card Number 94-77-813
I.S.B.N. 0-916990-32-X

Contents

Dedication

To my coauthors of
Neuro-Linguistic Programming Volume I
- John Grinder, Richard Bandler,
Judith DeLozier and Leslie Lebeau -
who participated in the birth of this vision and mission,
and to David Gordon, Todd Epstein, Gino Bonissone
and the many others who have shared the vision
with me since then.

Acknowledgments

I would like to acknowledge:

My parents Patricia and Robert who transferred to me their joy and interest in science, literature, art, music and the preciousness of life.

My brothers Mike, Dan and John and my sister Mary who shared with me the fascination and excitement of exploring this incredible and beautiful planet.

My wife Anita, and my children Andrew and Julia whose understanding and patience with me has been almost super-human. There is no way I could have completed such a work without their support.

Todd and Teresa Epstein who have backed my creative efforts over the years, and published early versions of some of these strategies through Dynamic Learning Publications.

Michael Pollard and Ami Sattinger who labored with me as Realist and Critic to put these ideas into book form.

And all of the people over the years who have sent me material and supported me and encouraged me in my mission.

Preface

In the preface to **Neuro-Linguistic Programming Volume I** my coauthors and I attempted to define the scope and purpose of the field that we had participated in creating together. We pointed out that:

> *"NLP could be described as an extension of linguistics, neurology, or psychology; separations that although may in fact be fictitious in nature are in fact expedient for human learning and the development of knowledge that is practical and impactful on our lives...[NLP is] not just useful models and patterns formalized from various activities, but an extension of how those patterns and models came into being, thus a field both informative and practical, but most significant...unique in its purpose and methodology."*

We sought to identify a broad and challenging future for the field as a cognitive science, and expressed our belief that, through NLP, *"...learning and experiences from entirely divergent fields have the opportunity to combine knowledge and experience into configurations that allow further growth, understanding and impact upon ourselves as a species."*

In the book, we defined a system of distinctions and a methodology for studying the "structure of subjective experience." We identified a set of tools that could be used to discover and describe the mental programming of an individual in the form of cognitive "strategies." The book covered principles of *elicitation, utilization, design* and *installation* of such strategies. As illustrations of these principles, we suggested some ways in which this new technology of the mind could be applied to the areas of health, learning, business management and psychotherapy.

In the conclusion to **Neuro-Linguistic Programming Volume I**, we promised:

> "...the next book in the series, **Neuro-Linguistic Programming Volume II**, in which we will apply the model that has been developed here to present and analyze the strategies that we have found to be the most effective and well-formed for achieving the outcomes for which they were created. In Volume II we will present the strategies that have proven to be the most efficient and elegant for achieving successful results in areas and disciplines, ranging from learning physics, to playing chess, to making decisions, to learning to play a musical instrument, to creating entirely new models of the world for yourself. In the second volume we will also explore more specifically how to apply Neuro-Linguistic Programming to your work and everyday life."

For a number of reasons we were unable to follow through with this commitment. But that pledge and the vision behind it has stayed with me these many years since *NLP Volume I* was first conceived and written. In many ways, this series on the *Strategies of Genius* is intended to be the fulfillment of that promise of an *NLP Volume II*.

On another level, this work is the fulfillment of a vision that began almost twenty years ago, a full five years before the publishing of *NLP Volume I*. In a class at the University of California at Santa Cruz, called *Pragmatics of Human Communication,* I had a conversation with John Grinder about the possibility of mapping the sequences in which exceptional people unconsciously employed their senses while they were thinking. I was at that time a junior in college and John Grinder was a professor of linguistics.

The discussion planted a seed in me about a larger study of the cognitive patterns of well known geniuses, that would on the one hand honor their brilliance, and at the same time demystify it and make it have more practical applications. Part of the idea was that these strategies could be coded into basic yet simple enough elements that aspects of them could even be taught to children in preparation for challenges they would face in their adult lives.

That seed was to grow into this work on the *Strategies of Genius*.

This book is the first volume of *Strategies of Genius*. In it I will explore the cognitive processes of four very different but important individuals who have contributed in a positive way to our modern world; Aristotle, Sherlock Holmes, Walt Disney and Wolfgang Amadeus Mozart. The behavioral areas in which all of these individuals operated were quite different from one another, and one of them is actually a character from fiction. However they all have something in common: unique and powerful strategies for analyzing and problem solving or creating, which continue to fascinate and entertain us to this day.

Volume II of this work is entirely devoted to Albert Einstein. The mere scope and magnitude of Einstein's contributions to our perceptions of ourselves and our universe warrants an entire volume.

Future volumes will include studies of Leonardo da Vinci, Sigmund Freud, John Stewart Mill, Nicola Tesla and some more recent 'geniuses' such as Gregory Bateson, Moshe Feldenkrais and Milton H. Erickson, M.D.

The choice of the individuals studied in this work did not come out of any deliberate plan. Rather they were people who had sparked or inspired something in me personally or seemed to represent something deeply fundamental. Often, key material used for analysis was serendipitously given to me by someone who knew I was interested in a certain individual or was researching the strategies of geniuses. The project unfolded organically in a way similar to the processes used by these geniuses themselves.

While the chapters on the various geniuses in this book make references to one another, it is not necessary to read them consecutively, and readers may want to skip around a bit. Obviously the different geniuses studied in each chapter operated in different fields and had different approaches that may be of more or less interest to the reader. Aristotle, for instance, was a philosopher, so his ideas are necessarily more philosophical than pragmatic in nature. If you find some of his ideas too challenging or not as relevant, you may want to skip to one of the other chapters first and then return to Aristotle later on. The same approach can be applied to any of the chapters.

I mentioned earlier that this study has been germinating in me for almost twenty years. Over those years, my understanding of the strategies of genius has matured as I have. My hope is that, through this work, I can convey some of the immense possibilities and scope of the rich tapestry of the human mind and "subjective experience." I hope that you enjoy the journey.

"I want to know how God created this world. I am not interested in this or that phenomenon, in the spectrum of this or that element; I want to know his thoughts; the rest are details."

*- **Albert Einstein***

"In the beginning God created the Heaven and the Earth. And the Earth was without form and void; and darkness was upon the face of the deep. And the spirit of God moved upon the face of the waters. And God said, Let there be light: and there was light. And God saw the light, that it was good: and God divided the light from the darkness. And God called the light Day, and the darkness he called Night. And the evening and the morning were the first day.

"And God said, Let there be a firmament in the midst of the waters, and let it divide the waters from the waters. And God made the firmament, and divided the waters which were under the firmament from the waters which were above the firmament: and it was so. And God called the firmament Heaven. And the evening and morning were the second day.

"And God said, Let the waters under the heaven be gathered together unto one place, and let the dry land appear: and it was so. And God called the dry land Earth; and the waters called he the Seas: and God saw that it was good...And the earth brought forth grass, and herbs yielding seed after his kind, and the tree yielding fruit, whose seed was in itself after his kind: and God saw that it was good. And the evening and the morning were the third day.

"And God said, Let there be lights in the firmament of the heaven to divide the day from the night; and let them be for signs and seasons, and for days and years: And let them be for lights in the firmament of the heaven to give light upon the earth: and it was so. And God made two great lights: the greater light to rule the day, and the lesser light to rule the night: he made the stars also...and God saw that it was good. And the evening and the morning were the fourth day.

"And God said, Let the waters bring forth abundantly the moving creature that hath life, and fowl that may fly above the earth in the open firmament of heaven. And God created great whales, and every living creature that moveth, which the waters brought forth abundantly, after their kind, and every winged fowl after his kind: and God saw that it was good. And God blessed them saying, Be fruitful and multiply, and fill the waters and the seas, and let the fowl multiply in the earth. And the morning and the evening were the fifth day.

"And God said, Let the earth bring forth the living creature after his kind, cattle and creeping thing, and beast of the earth after his kind: and it was so...And God saw that it was good. And God said, Let us make man in our image, after our likeness...So God created man in his own image, in the image of God created he him; male and female created he them. And God blessed them and God said unto them, Be fruitful and multiply, and replenish the earth and subdue it: and have dominion over the fish of the sea, and over the fowl of the air, and over every living thing that moveth over the earth. And God said, Behold, I have given you every herb bearing seed, which is upon the face of all the earth, and every tree, in which is the fruit of a tree yielding seed; to you it shall be for meat. And to every beast of the earth, and to every fowl of the air, and to every thing that creepeth upon the earth wherein there is life, I have given every green herb for meat: and it was so. And God saw everything that he had made, and, behold, it was very good. And the evening and the morning were the sixth day.

"Thus the heavens and the earth were finished, and all the host of them. And on the seventh day God ended his work which he had made; and he rested on the seventh day from all his work which he had made."

*- **Genesis** 1:1 - 2:3*

INTRODUCTION

The powerful and moving words of Genesis tell a story of creation on a number of levels. In addition to describing what was created, they describe a process for *how* it was created. They give us a description of 'God's thoughts' in the form of a strategy for creation that has a specific structure. It is a strategy involving a set of steps which unfold over time in a kind of a feedback loop. Creation begins through the act of making a distinction - creating a difference. This first act leads to another, and then another, and then another - each idea leading to the potential for the next. Each act of creation involves the reiteration of a cycle involving three fundamental processes:

1. Conceptualization - *"And God said, Let there be..."*

2. Implementation - *"And God made..."*

3. Evaluation - *"And God saw that it was good."*

Each cycle leads to a successively more refined and personal expression of ideas. With each cycle the idea takes on more and more of a life of its own - the idea itself is able to 'bring forth', 'multiply' and sustain other ideas. The ultimate expression reflects the process of the creator so much that it is able to 'replenish' all of the other creations as well as multiply itself.

In a way, this series on the 'strategies of genius' tells the same story. It is a study of the process behind the creation of ideas that have influenced our world in some way. The focus of these volumes is not on the ideas themselves, but rather on the strategies that led to the ideas and their concrete expressions.

Einstein's comment that he strove to know 'God's thoughts' epitomizes the essence of genius and the vision behind this work. The content of an act of creation or genius is not the goal. The goal is what more we can learn about the 'mind of God' through the process.

One of my own personal symbols for what genius is about is represented by Michelangelo's painting on the ceiling of the Sistine Chapel in Rome. The painting shows Adam lying on the Earth reaching up toward heaven and the hand of God stretching down from the sky. Their fingers are outstretched toward one another, just ready to touch. To me, the miracle is in that spark in between the two fingers. That is what genius is all about. This is what I seek to explore in this book - that interaction between the sacred and the profane; between the map and the territory; between vision and action.

Vision

Action

Neuro-Linguistic Programming

"Human history is in essence a history of ideas."
H. G. Wells - **The Outline of History**

It has been said that human history is nothing more than a record of the deeds and ideas of great men and women. Since the dawn of recorded history it has been the goal of historians, philosophers, psychologists, sociologists and the other chroniclers of our species to identify and record the critical elements that generated those deeds and ideas.

A fundamental goal of psychology, in particular, has been to attempt to define those key elements which have contributed most to the evolution of ideas. Ever since we humans first began to turn our attention inward to examine our own thought processes, one of the hopes and promises of psychological inquiry has been to map out those critical features of 'mind' that will allow our own thoughts to soar with the giants of history.

Neuro-Linguistic Programming (NLP) provides a new set of tools that can allow us to take major steps toward this promising but elusive goal. The mission of NLP has been to define and extend the leading edge of human knowledge - and in particular the leading edge of human knowledge about humans. This work, the study of strategies of genius, is a part of that mission. My goal has been to model the strategies of people who have not only contributed to our knowledge of the world around us, but also to our knowledge about ourselves, and to discover how to use those strategies to further contribute to the evolution of human beings.

NLP is a pragmatic school of thought - an *'epistemology'* - that addresses the many levels involved in being human. NLP is a multi-dimensional process that involves the development of behavioral competence and flexibility, but also involves strategic thinking and an understanding of the mental and cognitive processes behind behavior. NLP provides tools and skills for the development of states of individual excellence, but it also establishes a system of empowering beliefs and presuppositions about what human beings are, what communication is and what the process of change is all about. At another level, NLP is about self-discovery, exploring identity and mission. It also provides a framework for understanding and relating to the 'spiritual' part of human experience that reaches beyond us as individuals. NLP is not only about competence and excellence, it is about wisdom and vision. All of these elements are required for genius.

The three most influential components involved in producing human experience are neurology, language and programming. The neurological system regulates how our bodies function, language determines how we interface and communicate with other people and our programming determines the kinds of models of the world we create. Neuro-Linguistic Programming describes the fundamental dynamics between mind (neuro) and language (linguistic) and how their interplay effects our body and behavior (programming).

One of the great contributions of NLP is that it gives us a way to look past the behavioral content of what people do to the more invisible forces behind those behaviors; to the structures of thought that allowed these geniuses to accomplish what they accomplished. NLP provides a structure and a language to be able to put into a set of chunks or steps the relevant mental processes used by a Leonardo or an Einstein so that those mental processes can be taught to others.

The other tremendous contribution of NLP is that by looking at the underlying structure of behavior it allows us to transcend the content to the degree that we can apply the thinking process of genius in one field to another whole area of content. We can discover elements of how Einstein thought about physics, his *strategy* for thinking about physics, and apply it to thinking about society or to thinking about a personal problem. Likewise, we can extract key elements of Mozart's strategy for writing music and shift from the content of music to solving an organizational problem or teaching children how to read.

The belief system of NLP is that it is the thinking process behind the accomplishment that is the most important element of creating something like genius. And the same thing that makes an effective strategy for cooking can be applied to a strategy for making movies or a strategy for writing books.

As my colleagues and I stated in **Neuro-Linguistic Programming Vol. I**:

> *By identifying [mental] sequences that lead to specific outcomes we can, in essence, replicate (or "clone") any behavior - whether that of a businessperson, scientist, healer, athlete, musician or anyone that does something well. With the tools provided by NLP, we believe anyone can be transformed into a modern "renaissance" person.*

In essence, all of NLP is founded on two fundamental premises:

1. *The Map is Not the Territory.* As human beings, we can never know reality. We can only know our perceptions of reality. We experience and respond to the world around us primarily through our sensory representational systems. It is our 'neuro-linguistic' maps of reality that determine how we behave and that give those behaviors meaning, not reality itself. It is generally not reality that limits us or empowers us, but rather our map of reality.

2. *Life and 'Mind' are Systemic Processes.* The processes that take place within a human being and between human beings and their environment are systemic. Our bodies, our societies, and our universe form an ecology of complex systems and sub-systems all of which interact with and mutually influence each other. It is not possible to completely

isolate any part of the system from the rest of the system. Such systems are based on certain 'self-organizing' principles and naturally seek optimal states of balance or homeostasis.

All of the models and techniques of NLP are based on the combination of these two principles. In the belief system of NLP it is not possible for human beings to know objective reality. Wisdom, ethics and ecology do not derive from having the one 'right' or 'correct' map of the world, because human beings would not be capable of making one. Rather, the goal is to create the richest map possible that respects the systemic nature and ecology of ourselves and the world in which we live.

Individual Models of the World

The domain of what NLP addresses is best described as "subjective experience." Subjective experience encompasses what has been variously called "thought," "mind," or "intelligence," and in its broadest sense refers to the totality of the activity in our nervous systems. It is through our own personal subjective experience that we know the world around us. In their first book, **The Structure of Magic Vol. I**, Richard Bandler and John Grinder (the co-creators of NLP) pointed out:

> *A number of people in the history of civilization have made this point - that there is an irreducible difference between the world and our experience of it. We as human beings do not operate directly on the world. Each of us creates a representation of the world in which we live - that is, we create a map or model which we use to determine our behavior. Our representation of the world determines to a large degree what our experience of the world will be, how we will perceive the world, what choices we will see available to us as we live in that world... No two*

*human beings have exactly the same experiences. The
model that we create to guide us in the world is based
in part upon our experiences. Each of us may, then,
create a different model of the world we share and thus
come to live in a somewhat different reality.*

Thus, it is our mental model of reality, rather than reality
itself that will determine how we will act. Until someone
mentally created a map of the "atom" or the "virus" or a
"round world" those aspects of "reality" could not affect the
actions of our ancestors or ourselves.

Bandler and Grinder go on to point out that the difference
between people who respond effectively as opposed to those
who respond poorly in the world around them is largely a
function of their internal model of the world.

*[P]eople who respond creatively and cope effectively...are
people who have a rich representation or model of their
situation, in which they perceive a wide range of
options in choosing their action. The other people
experience themselves as having few options, none of
which are attractive to them...What we have found is
not that the world is too limited or that there are no
choices, but that these people block themselves from
seeing those options and possibilities that are open to
them since they are not available in their models of the
world.*

As I pointed out earlier, NLP starts from the presupposi-
tion that "the map is not the territory." Everyone has their
own unique map or model of the world, and no one map is
any more "true" or "real" than any other. Rather, the people
who are most effective are the ones who have a map of the
world that allows them to perceive the greatest number of
available choices and perspectives. A person who is a "ge-

nius," then, simply has a richer and wider way of perceiving, organizing and responding to the world. NLP provides a set of processes for enriching the choices that you have and perceive as available in the world around you.

It is the goal of this book to use NLP to find, in the words of anthropologist Gregory Bateson, "the difference that makes the difference." We want to make a model of the models of the world of a number of great people throughout history. Used in this way, we can say that NLP is a "meta model." That is, a model ABOUT models.

Modeling

"There is properly no history, only biography."
Emerson - **Essays**

Modeling is the process of taking a complex event or series of events and breaking it into small enough chunks that it can be repeated in a manageable way. The field of Neuro-Linguistic Programming has developed out of the modeling of human thinking skills. The NLP modeling process involves finding out about how the brain ("Neuro") is operating by analyzing language patterns ("Linguistic") and non-verbal communication. The results of this analysis are then put into step-by-step strategies or programs ("Programming") that may be used transfer the skill to other people and content areas.

In fact, NLP began when Richard Bandler and John Grinder modeled patterns of language and behavior in the works of Fritz Perls (the founder of Gestalt therapy), Virginia Satir (a founder of family therapy and systemic therapy) and Milton H. Erickson, M.D. (founder of the American Society of Clinical Hypnosis). The first 'techniques' of NLP were derived from key verbal and non-verbal patterns Grinder and Bandler observed in the behavior of these exceptional therapists. The implication of the title of their first book, *The Structure of Magic*, was that what seemed magical and unexplainable often had a deeper structure that, when illuminated, could be understood, communicated and put into practice by people other than the few exceptional 'wizards' who had initially performed the 'magic'. NLP is the process by which the relevant pieces of these people's behavior was discovered and then organized together into a working model.

NLP has developed techniques and distinctions with which to identify and describe patterns of people's verbal and non-verbal behavior - that is, key aspects of what people say and what they do. The basic objectives of NLP are to model special or exceptional abilities and help make them transferable to others. The purpose of this kind of modeling is to put what has been observed and described into action in a way that is productive and enriching.

The modeling tools of NLP allow us to identify specific, reproducible patterns in the language and behavior of effective role models. While most NLP analysis is done by actually watching and listening to the role model in action, much valuable information can be gleaned from written records as well.

In this book I will attempt to model the thinking processes of a number of historical individuals, who have been identified as geniuses of one kind or another, by analyzing their language patterns as they have been passed down to us through their writings. I will also examine the products of their genius when appropriate for what they might tell us about the creative process that produced them. The synthesis of this information will be put into "programs" or strategies that we may, hopefully, use to enhance our own processes of creativity and intelligence.

Levels of Modeling

In modeling an individual there are a number of different aspects, or levels, of the various systems and sub-systems in which that person operated that we may explore. We can look at the historical and geographical *environment* in which the individual lived - i.e., *when* and *where* the person operated. We can examine the individual's specific *behaviors* and actions - i.e., *what* the person did in that environment. We may also look at the intellectual and cognitive strategies and *capabilities* by which the individual selected and guided his or her actions in the environment - i.e., *how* the person generated these behaviors in that context. We could further explore the beliefs and values that motivated and shaped the thinking strategies and capabilities that the individual developed to accomplish his or her behavioral goals in the environment - i.e., *why* the person did things the way he or she did them in those times and places. We could look more deeply to investigate the individual's perception of the self or identity he or she was manifesting through that set of beliefs, capabilities and actions in that environment - i.e., the *who* behind the why, how, what, where and when.

We might also want to examine the way in which that identity manifested itself in relationship to the individual's family, colleagues, contemporaries, Western Society and Culture, the planet, God - i.e., who the person was in relation to *who else*. In other words, how did the behaviors, abilities, beliefs, values and identity of the individual influence and interact with larger systems of which he or she was a part in a personal, social and ultimately *spiritual* way?

One way to visualize the relationships between these elements is as a network of generative systems that focus or converge on the identity of the individual as the core of the modeling process.

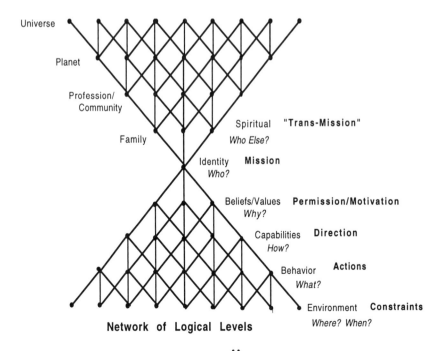

Network of Logical Levels

In summary, modeling the process of genius may involve exploring the interactions of a number of different levels of experience, including:

Spiritual	Vision & Purpose
A. *Who I Am* - Identity	Mission
B. *My Belief System* -	Values, Meta Programs Permission & Motivation
C. *My Capabilities* -	States, Strategies Direction
D. *What I Do* -	Specific Behaviors Actions
E. *My Environment* -	External Context Reactions

- Environment determines the external opportunities or constraints a person has to react to. Relates to the *where* and *when* of genius.
- Behaviors are the specific actions or reactions made by a person within the environment. Relates to the *what* of genius.
- Capabilities guide and give direction to behavioral actions through a mental map, plan or strategy. Relates to the *how* of genius.
- Beliefs and values provide the reinforcement (motivation and permission) that supports or inhibits capabilities. Relates to the *why* of genius.
- Identity involves a person's role, mission and/or sense of self. Relates to the *who* of genius.
- Spiritual involves the larger system of which one is a part and the influence of that system on healing. Relates to the *who else and what else* of genius.

Therefore, as part of the modeling process, we can identify several different levels of strategy.

Strategies

A strategy is a <u>particular area of modeling</u> in which you are specifically looking for a mental map that was used by the individual whom you are modeling in order to orchestrate or organize his or her activities to accomplish an effective result.

Neuro-Linguistic Programming provides a set of tools and distinctions that allow us to map out cognitive processes underlying the works of creative and exceptional people. Rather than focus on the content of the work of the particular individual to be modeled, NLP looks for the deeper structures that produced those results. In particular, NLP searches for the way in which someone uses such basic *neurological* processes as the senses (i.e., *seeing, hearing, feeling, smelling and tasting),* how these processes are shaped and reflected by *language*, and how the two combine to produce a particular *program* or strategy. According to the NLP model it is the way in which we organize our sensory and linguistic functions into a programmed sequence of mental activity that determines to a large degree how we will perceive and respond to the world around us.

Historically, Neuro-Linguistic Programming was brought into existence in California at the same time another important technological and social revolution was being born - the personal computer. As has been true in other periods in history, developments in our understanding of the mind mirror developments in technology (and vice versa). Much of the NLP approach to the mind is based on viewing the brain as functioning similar to a computer in some ways. In fact, much of the NLP terminology (and the name itself) incorporates the language of computer science.

A strategy is like a program in a computer. It tells you what to do with the information you are getting, and like a computer program, you can use the same strategy to process a lot of different kinds of information. A computer program might tell the computer, "take this piece of data and take that piece of data, to add them together and put the answer in a particular place in memory." The program is independent of the content being processed through it. It doesn't care what content is being put together and moved. Some programs are more efficient than others; some allow you to do more with the information than others; some are designed to take a lot of information and reduce it to very tightly chunked information. Other computer programs are designed to take some information and make projections with it. Some programs are designed to find patterns and features within information.

The same thing is going to be true of human strategies. As an analogy, they are the mental software used by the bio-computer of the brain. In a way, the most powerful personal computer in the world is the one that sits up between your ears. The problem with it is that it didn't come with a user's manual, and sometimes the software isn't very "user friendly." The goal of psychology, and in particular NLP, is to discover the "programming language" of the human nervous system so we can get ours and others' to do what we want them to do more elegantly, effectively and ecologically. We can be 'software wizards' and encode in a new language some of the software used by people who have learned to operate that computer very well.

Micro, Macro and Meta Strategies

Strategies occur at different levels - there are micro-strategies, macro-strategies and meta-strategies.

- A micro-strategy focuses on how exactly a particular person is thinking within a specific moment in order to accomplish a particular task. If somebody is engaging in a process of remembering a particular piece of information, lets say a telephone number, what do they do with that information in order to store it and recover it from within their brain or bio-computer? On this micro-level you might want to know exactly what size that person is visualizing the telephone number in his or her mind. Is there a particular color in which that person pictures the number? Does the person verbally repeat the number internally? Does the person have a feeling somewhere in his or her body? This would be a micro-strategy. It would be like assembly language or machine code in a computer.

- <u>A macro-strategy</u> would be more like modeling "success" or "leadership." An overall strategy for success or leadership is not going to be a micro-strategy but rather a higher level program that will incorporate many micro strategies. It might be something that takes place over a much longer period of time. Sometimes it is the more general steps of a process that are important for reaching a particular result, and how specifically you get from A to B to C on a micro-level is not important or may require significant variation. What is important is that you get from A to C regardless of the micro steps. The way you personally get there is up to you. So a macro-strategy would have to do with the more general operations and steps of a thinking process.

- <u>A meta-strategy or a meta-model</u> is basically a model for making models; a strategy for finding strategies, or a model for modeling. In a sense, a major part of what you are going to be learning in this book is a meta-model and a set of meta-strategies - strategies and models for finding the strategies of exceptional individuals and making practical models out of those strategies.

In summary, the purpose of modeling is not to make the one 'real' map or model of something, but rather to enrich our perceptions in a way that allows us to be both more effective and more ecological in how we interact with reality. A model is not intended to be reality, but instead to represent certain aspects of that reality in a practical and concrete way.

The goal of this book is to show how the tools of NLP can be used to analyze important historical figures to produce practical and effective "strategies of genius" that can be learned and applied in other contexts. My particular interest - in relation to my own mission - is to apply these genius' strategies to human issues. In other words, to explore how can we apply these strategies so that we can become more intelligent about our own human processes. As my colleagues and I said in **NLP Volume I**:

> *"Understood and used with the elegance and pragmatism with which NLP was created we may not only discover how Freud made Einstein's theories possible, but a way to influence and predict the very elements that would make human beings capable of being humane, by subjectively valuing what creations, creating can offer."*

Perhaps if we could take Mozart's ability to structure notes into music, Einstein's ability to restructure our perceptions of the universe or Leonardo's ability to form his imagination into a drawing or painting and apply them to restructure the way people interact in social organizations, we might be able to really advance the course of human history. That is my dream; my vision for this work.

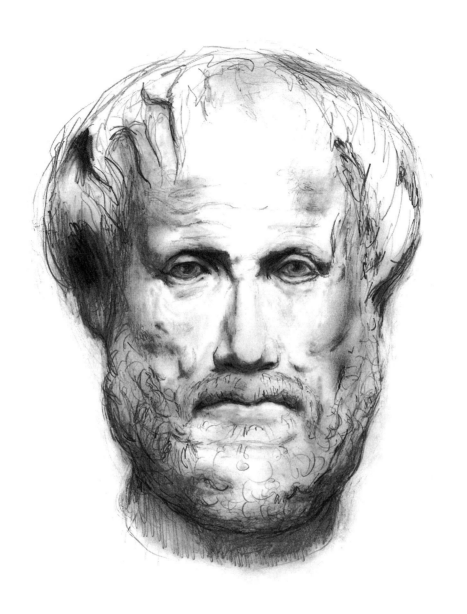

Aristotle

Chapter 1

Aristotle

Creating A Framework
For Genius

Overview of Chapter 1

- **Building Blocks of Genius**

    Getting to 'First Principles'
    Asking Basic Questions
    The Strategy for Finding the 'Middle'
    'Syllogisms' as Expressions of 'First Principles'

    The S.O.A.R. Model

    Basic Types of Causes

    Formal Causes
    Antecedent Causes
    Constraining Causes
    Final Causes

    The Role of Time Perception

    Evaluating One's Premises

- **Aristotle's Model of the Mind**

    The T.O.T.E. Model

Overview of Chapter 1 (continued)

Macro Strategies and the T.O.T.E.

Micro Strategies and the Five Senses

The Role of Memory and Imagination

Common Sensibles

- Modeling Micro Strategies - The R.O.L.E. Model

- Language as a Tool of Thinking and Modeling

- Modeling the Micro Structure of Aristotle's Thinking Strategy

- Applications of Aristotle's Strategies

  The S.C.O.R.E. Model: Implementing Aristotle's Strategies for Defining 'Problem Space'

  Implementing Aristotle's Strategy for Exploring and Organizing a Problem Space

  Finding a System of Causes in a Problem Space

- Summary

- Bibliography

ARISTOTLE
The Building Blocks of Genius

The first genius whose strategy I would like to model for this study is the Greek philosopher Aristotle (385-322 BC). Considered to be the 'father of modern science', Aristotle is undoubtedly one of the most influential geniuses of Western civilization. His scope of thought covered an incredible variety of subjects including physics, logic, ethics, politics, rhetoric, biology, poetics, metaphysics and psychology. In most cases, Aristotle's discoveries and contributions were so fundamental that they stood as the definitive works in each of these fields for centuries.

Clearly, there was something very special about Aristotle's strategy for organizing his observations of the world around him that allowed him to accomplish such a tremendous intellectual feat. Aristotle's mental processes allowed him to creatively explore and usefully organize information from many diverse areas of life (Plato referred to him as "the mind"). It was the rediscovery of Aristotle's way of thinking that is credited with bringing Western civilization out of the dark ages into the renaissance.

From the NLP point of view, Aristotle had his own very effective strategy for modeling. He was in fact a 'modeler'. He looked into the most essential areas of human experience and made very powerful models of them. He wasn't a 'specialist' in any area; and yet he was able to reach a deep level of knowledge about the different aspects of the world he examined.

What is of greatest interest to us, as 'meta' modelers of Aristotle, is the way in which he thought about his experiences. By applying the modeling procedures of NLP to Aristotle's writings, we can map out some of the specific elements of Aristotle's strategy in a way that may contribute some new and practical insight into his impressive genius and how we can apply it to our lives today.

It is interesting that one of the topics that Aristotle never did specifically address was the topic we are attempting to cover in this book - 'genius'. It is an intriguing question to wonder how Aristotle would have approached understanding this phenomenon. Obviously, Aristotle is no longer around to provide an answer, but he has left many clues and cues in his writings about the type of strategy he would have employed. It seems only fitting to begin our inquiry into the strategies of genius, and their application, by 'unpacking' Aristotle's strategy for inquiry and analysis and applying it to our exploration.

Getting to 'First Principles'

Perhaps the most important part of Aristotle's genius was his ability to discover basic and fundamental patterns or 'laws' in whatever field of experience he chose to explore. As he explains in his book ***Physics***:

> *"When the objects of an inquiry in any department, have principles, conditions, or elements, it is through acquaintance with these that knowledge, that is to say scientific knowledge, is attained. For we do not think that we know a thing until we are acquainted with its primary conditions or first principles, and have carried our analysis as far as its simplest elements...*

> *"Now what is to us plain and obvious at first is rather confused masses, the elements and principles of which become known to us later by analysis. Thus we must advance from generalities to particulars...[as] a child begins by calling all men 'father', and all women 'mother', but later on distinguishes each of them."*

In the language of NLP, the process Aristotle is describing is that of 'chunking'. It seems that Aristotle's strategy to get to 'first principles' is to "advance from generalities to particulars" by starting with the largest 'chunks' which are available to sensory perception and to go through an analytical process that chunks this experience down into its "simplest," most basic, content free elements.

If we follow Aristotle's lead, our goal in this study of the strategies of genius would be to 'chunk down' the information we have about genius in order to find its "primary conditions or first principles" by identifying its "simplest elements." In other words, a 'strategy of genius' would define the 'basic conditions' and 'first principles' of the processes related to genius in terms of its primary elements. Of course, it is **how, specifically,** one distills these "rather confused masses" of information into their "simplest elements" and first principles that is our challenge.

Asking Basic Questions

According to Aristotle, the discovery of these basic elements and principles "become known" through the "analysis" (from the Greek *analytica* meaning "to unravel") of our perceptions. In his book ***Posterior Analytics*** Aristotle gives some specific descriptions of his analytical approach. Like his teacher and mentor (and fellow genius) Plato, Aristotle's process of analysis began by asking basic questions. Clearly, the kind of questions one asks will determine the kinds of answers one finds. According to Aristotle:

> *"The kinds of question we ask are as many as the kinds of things which we know, They are in fact four: - (1) whether the connection of an attribute with a thing is a fact, (2) what is the reason of the connection, (3) whether a thing exists, (4) what is the nature of the thing.*

"Thus, when our question concerns a complex of thing and attribute and we ask whether the thing is thus or otherwise qualified - whether, e.g. the sun suffers eclipse or not - then we are asking as to the fact of a connection...On the other hand, when we know the fact we ask the reason; as, for example, when we know the sun is being eclipsed and that an earthquake is in progress, it is the reason of eclipse or earthquake into which we enquire. Where a complex is concerned, then, those are the two questions we ask; but for some objects of inquiry we have a different kind of question to ask, such as whether there is or is not a centaur or a God....On the other hand, when we have ascertained the thing's existence, we inquire as to its nature, asking, for instance, 'what, then, is God?' or 'what is man?'

"These, then are the four kinds of questions, and it is in the answers to these questions that our knowledge consists."

To apply Aristotle's strategy to the study of genius, we must continually pose these four basic questions (in this case, the 'thing' we are exploring is 'genius'). Rearranging the order of Aristotle's questions slightly, we must ask:

1. Does 'genius' in fact exist?
2. If so, what is the nature of 'genius? What are its 'attributes'?
3. When we have identified what we think are the 'attributes' of genius we must then ask, "Are those attributes in fact connected to 'genius'?"
4. If so, what is the reason or cause for the connection?

Aristotle's purpose in asking these four questions was not really to end up with four different answers, but rather to converge upon a single answer - a 'first principle'. According to Aristotle, "to know a thing's nature is to know the reason why it is."

> "[T]he nature of the thing and the reason of the fact are identical: the question 'What is eclipse?' and its answer 'The privating of the moon's light by the interposition of the earth' are identical with the question 'What is the reason of eclipse?' or 'Why does the moon suffer eclipse?' and the reply 'because the failure of light through the earth's shutting it out'."

This implies a powerful relationship between knowledge and application in Aristotle's system. It indicates that there is an equivalence between 'attributes' and 'reasons'. In other words, if we say something like "Genius is knowing the right questions to ask" then we should also be able to say, "Knowing the right questions to ask is the reason for genius." A true 'first principle, then, is one that has this dual ability; not only is it 'instructive' it is also 'instrumental'. That is, not only does such a principle allow us to understand something, it also informs us how it is brought about and influenced.

These basic elements that were both 'attributes' and 'reasons' for something were what Aristotle called the 'middle' - something in between general knowledge and specific instances. Even though Aristotle maintained that we must "advance from generalities to particulars," we cannot simply stop with the particulars. As Aristotle put it, *"perception must be of a particular, whereas scientific knowledge involves the recognition of the commensurate universal."* Once we have 'chunked' something down into its particulars, we must then 'chunk back up' again to find the 'middle'. According to Aristotle, *"all questions are a search for a 'middle'"* which connects the "universal" to "a particular".

> *"[I]n all our inquiries we are asking either whether there is a 'middle' or what the 'middle' is: for the 'middle' here is precisely the cause, and it is the cause that we seek in all our inquiries. Thus, 'Does the moon suffer eclipse?' means 'Is there or is there not a cause producing eclipse of the moon?', and when we have learnt that there is, our next question is, 'What, then, is this cause?'"*

By Aristotle's reasoning, the question 'Does Aristotle possess genius?' means "Is there or is there not a cause producing genius in Aristotle?" If we answer the first question by saying, "Aristotle possessed genius because he asked basic questions," we are simultaneously implying, "Asking basic questions is the cause of Aristotle's genius." The 'cause' (asking basic questions) is the 'middle' or link between the general property of 'genius' and the 'particular' instance of 'Aristotle'. Defining a 'first principle' is establishing such a cause.

The Strategy for Finding the 'Middle'

Once we begin asking such questions, we need a method for arriving at relevant and meaningful answers. We might well wonder, "How exactly does one go about this business of finding causes, first principles, basic conditions and the 'commensurate universal' within the particulars?" In *Posterior Analytics* Aristotle provides a specific description of his strategy for 'chunking back up' from the particulars to find more 'universal' attributes.

> *"We must start by observing a set of similar - i.e. specifically identical - individuals, and consider what element they have in common."*

To illustrate, Aristotle gives the following example:

"If we were inquiring what the essential nature of pride is, we should examine instances of proud men we know to see what, as such, they have in common; e.g. if Alcibiades was proud, or Achilles and Ajax were proud, we should find what they had in common, that it was intolerance of insult; it was this which drove Alcibiades to war, Achilles to wrath, and Ajax to suicide."

Alcibiades, Achilles and Ajax are "specifically identical individuals" because they were all Athenian military leaders that took fairly rash actions that were motivated by 'pride'. In his illustration, Aristotle chooses three individuals to use as examples. While he does not himself state that this particular number of examples is significant, it would seem that if there were fewer, one could not be sure if the set was large enough to produce a similarity that was basic enough. If one tries to compare too many examples, it becomes confusing and unwieldy.

Once we have found what is similar in our first set of examples, Aristotle tells us:

"We must then apply the same process to another set of individuals which belong to one species and are generically but not specifically identical with the former set."

Continuing with his illustration about the examination of 'pride' Aristotle explains:

"We should next examine other cases [of proud men], Lysander, for example, or Socrates."

Lysander and Socrates are of the same species (men) and "generically identical" to Alcibiades, Achilles and Ajax because they are also known as 'proud'. They are not specifically identical, however, in that Lysander was a Spartan military leader and Socrates was a philosopher.

As the next step in his strategy, Aristotle finds whatever similarities there are between the individuals of the second group:

> *"When we have established what the common element is in all members of this second species, we should again consider whether the results established possess any identity, and persevere until we reach a single formula, since this will be the definition of the thing. But if we reach not one formula but two or more, evidently the definiendum cannot be one thing but must be more than one."*

What Aristotle means by "identity" is some quality that is shared by both groups of individuals that we are comparing. As he explains:

> *"If [Socrates and Lysander] have in common indifference alike to good and ill fortune, I take these two results and inquire what common element have equanimity amid the vicissitudes of life and the impatience of dishonor. If they have none, there will be two genera of pride."*

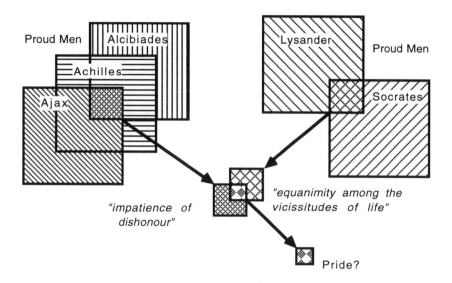

Aristotle's Strategy for Finding First Principles.

In summary, Aristotle's strategy for analysis involves an 'inductive' process made up of the following steps:

1) Collecting together a group of similar examples of something that each share the quality to be analyzed;
2) Comparing the examples and looking for some quality that they all have in common;
3) A second group of different examples that also share the quality is then collected together and compared in the same manner;
4) The quality that unified the first group is compared with the quality that unified the second group in order find what quality, if any, they might share.

If the unifying quality of *group 1* has something in common with the unifying quality of *group 2* we have gotten another step closer to a 'first principle'.

Presumably the process could continue on with other groups until we have discovered the one quality that all examples of the phenomenon have in common. Each successive comparison should lead us to smaller and smaller chunks composed of simpler and more content free elements. The group of examples is a fairly large 'chunk' size. The quality which unifies this group is smaller and simpler. The quality which is common to the unifying elements of both *group 1* and *group 2* should be a smaller and simpler chunk still, and so on.

To apply Aristotle's strategy to the study of 'genius' instead of 'pride' we would first identify a set of 'specifically identical individuals' who all share that characteristic. For instance, we might select a set of scientists who are considered to have possessed the quality of 'genius' - such as Albert Einstein, Nicola Tesla, Gregory Bateson; even Aristotle himself. We would then consider what 'elements' they have in common.

Then, we would repeat the process with another set of individuals who are 'generically but not specifically identical'. For instance, we might choose individuals who are also considered geniuses but who were creative or artistic people instead of scientists - Wolfgang Amadeus Mozart, Leonardo da Vinci and Walt Disney, for example. We would then seek to find what these three had in common.

The next step would be to find out if the common attributes or elements of the scientists also had something in common with the shared attributes of the creative or artistic individuals. If they don't, we may end up concluding that scientific and artistic genius are in fact two separate 'genera' of genius. If the two groups do share common attributes we will have found a potential 'basic condition or first principle' of genius. We might then repeat the process with another set of 'geniuses' such as therapists or healers - like Milton H. Erickson, M.D., Sigmund Freud and Moshe Feldenkrais.

In many ways the structure of this series on genius has been based on just this strategy.

'Syllogisms' as Expressions of 'First Principles'

Of course, finding the common elements and causes, is only a first step. We must also be able to express our conclusions and assess their relevance and usefulness. Aristotle's recognition as a genius did not come merely from what he knew, but from what he was able to express about what he knew. In fact, his ability to express first principles was as important as his ability to find them. Aristotle's strategy for identifying the relationship between the general and the particular by finding the 'middle' or the cause was the basis of his famous 'syllogisms'. Aristotle formulated the 'syllogism' as a linguistic structure to express the principles which resulted from his analysis. In **Prior Analytics** Aristotle explained:

> "A syllogism is discourse in which, certain things being stated, something other than what is stated follows of necessity from their being so."

In essence, a syllogism provides the bridge between knowledge and its application by focusing on the consequences of that knowledge. Expressed in this way, knowledge becomes an 'instrument' or what Aristotle called *organon* (meaning "tool").

Once a principle has been identified through the 'inductive' strategy described earlier, it may be applied 'deductively' through the structure of the syllogism. A 'syllogism' defines the relationship between 'things' and the 'attributes' that accompany them. Specifically, a syllogism relates the attributes of a general class to the 'particular' members of that class, as in the classic example:

e.g.   *All Men die.*
         Socrates is a Man.
         Socrates will die.

The 'middle' term is the attribute or cause that unites the class and its individual members. According to Aristotle, *"I call that term the middle which is itself contained in another and contains another in itself."*

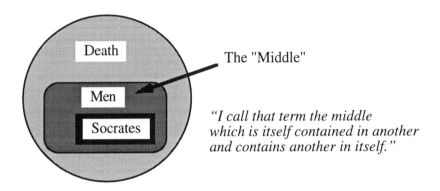

Definition of the "Middle" Term in a Syllogism

In the Socrates example, being a 'man' is one of the attributes that relates the particular individual 'Socrates' to the primary condition of 'dying'. Stated generally, the structure of a syllogism would be something like:

> A phenomenon or class of things has a certain attribute or cause.
> A particular situation or individual possesses that attribute or cause.
> That particular situation or individual will be an example or manifestation of the phenomenon or class of things.

Linguistically, a syllogism typically has three "terms"; the two 'extremes' **A** (the general phenomenon) and **C** (the specific individual or instance), and the 'middle' **B** which connects C to A. For instance, with regard to the example of the 'eclipse' Aristotle explained, *"Let A be the eclipse, C the moon, and B the earth's acting as a screen. To ask whether the moon is eclipsed or not is to ask whether or not B has occurred."*

Thus, in order to become a 'tool', the results of an inquiry need to be put into a structure such that:

> B is an attribute or cause of the general
>   phenomenon A.
> C is a specific instance possessing the attribute
>   or cause B.
> C is an example or expression of A.

In terms of our study of genius, if 'asking fundamental questions' is an 'attribute' and 'cause' (B) of 'genius' (A), we could form a syllogism of the following structure:

> Asking fundamental questions (B) is an attribute
>   of genius (A).
> Aristotle (C) asked fundamental questions (B).
> Aristotle (C) was a genius (A).

Structured in this way, Aristotle believed knowledge could be applied and put into action.

The S.O.A.R. Model

In many ways, Aristotle's process reflects some of today's most advanced artificial intelligence models. In particular, it is remarkably similar to the S.O.A.R. model. S.O.A.R. is a general problem solving model and learning system that was originally developed by Allen Newell, Herbert Simon, and Clifford Shaw in the 1950's. It was first used to create the computer chess playing programs by teaching the computer how to become a chess expert by learning from its experience through remembering how it solved problems. These expert chess programs have been the most successful application of artificial intelligence to date.

S.O.A.R. stands for State-Operator-And-Result. It defines the basic steps involved in the process of change in any system. A 'state' is defined in relationship to some larger 'problem space'. 'Operators' stimulate change in the state by altering some aspect of it 'resulting' in a new state. The desired state is reached through a path of 'transition states' which culminate in the goal.

"According to the model, all the mental activity being devoted to a given task takes place within a cognitive arena called the problem space. A problem space in turn consists of a set of states, which describe the situation at any given moment, and a set of operators, which describe how the problem solver can change the situation from one state to another. In chess, for example, the problem space would be [the set of parameters which define] "a chess game" [such as the two opponents, the chess board, etc.], a state would consist of a specific configuration of pieces on the chess board, and an operator would consist of a legal move, such as "Knight to King-4." The task of the problem solver is to search for the sequence of operators that will take it from a given initial state (say, with the

pieces lined up for the start of the chess game) to a given solution state (the opponent's king in a checkmate)." (Waldrop, 1988)

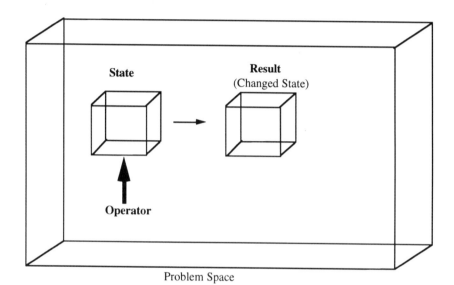

Problem Space

Basic Elements of the S.O.A.R. Model

Once the relevant parameters have been defined the problem solver must formulate a guidance strategy in order to find the sequence of operators that will lead from the starting state to the goal state. This takes place through a set of prioritized condition-action rules in the form of "**IF** you perceive a certain state, **THEN** apply a certain sequence of operators." If an impasse is reached such that progress is not able to be made to the goals state, the problem is 'chunked' down into sub-goals and sub-operations until a new path is found. These new 'chunks' are then remembered as other condition-action rules. Following this course, the problem solver moves from a Trial-and-Error guidance strategy (novice), through Hill Climbing (doing what seems best at the time) to one involving Means-Ends analysis (expert).

The S.O.A.R. structure lies at the core of the NLP modeling process. The S.O.A.R. distinctions give us the meta strategy or meta model from which to identify and define effective macro and micro strategies. The S.O.A.R. provides a very basic framework with which to model effective performance in many diverse areas of activity. In a computer, for example, the computer hardware creates a *problem space* which can produce many different *states*. Computer software instructions serve as *operators* which produce changes in these states in order to produce specific results.

Another example could be that of preparing a meal. The kitchen defines a problem space in which various stages or states of food preparation take place. The cooking tools and utensils are the operators which produce changes in the state of the food. Each 'operation' leads to a result which is then operated on again, until the final meal is produced. A third example can be derived from the opening passage from Genesis quoted at the beginning of this book. 'Heaven and Earth' define a problem space that God operates on to produce a set of successively more refined states, resulting in the creation of 'man and woman'.

Aristotle's approach to knowledge acquisition was very similar to the S.O.A.R. model. Physics, logic, rhetoric, politics, etc. are all 'problem spaces'. Aristotle set out to define those problem spaces by identifying the *"principles, conditions and elements"* from which they were made. The phenomena which make up each field would be the various states within the problem space. Like the basic learning process of the S.O.A.R., Aristotle 'chunked down' from "generalities to particulars" successively elaborating more details. The "middle terms" and "causes" that Aristotle sought are similar to the operators which determine and influence the states within the problem space. Aristotle's syllogisms are like the 'condition-action' rules through which knowledge is accumulated in the S.O.A.R. structure.

Thus, our modeling of the meta strategies of various geniuses must include how they perceived and conceptualized the problem space in which they were operating. It must also include how they identified and 'chunked' the relevant desired states and transition states within that space. Finally, and most importantly, we must identify the operators they used to create their paths through the problem space to achieve their desired states.

Basic Types of Causes

The common 'elements', 'middle terms' and "causes" Aristotle was constantly seeking are essentially the 'operators' of the S.O.A.R. model. When we ask, "What was the 'cause' of Einstein's genius, or Mozart's genius, or Leonardo's genius, or Aristotle's genius," we are essentially asking "Which operators or operations enabled them to achieve the intellectual and artistic feats for which they are known?" A basic issue for this study, then, relates to the types of operations or causes that might be relevant.

According to Aristotle (*Posterior Analytics*) there were four basic types of causes: 1) "formal" causes, 2) "antecedent," "necessitating" or "precipitating" causes, 3) "efficient" or "constraining" causes and 4) "final" causes.

Formal Causes

Formal causes essentially relate to fundamental definitions and perceptions of something. The "formal cause" of a phenomenon is that which gives the definition of its essential character. We call a bronze statue of a four legged animal with a mane, hooves and a tail a "horse" because it displays the form or 'formal' characteristics of a horse. We say, "The acorn grew into an oak tree," because we define something that has a trunk, branches and a certain shape of leaves as being an 'oak tree'."

Formal causes actually say more about the perceiver than the phenomenon being perceived. Identifying formal causes involves uncovering our own basic assumptions and mental maps about a subject. When an artist like Picasso puts the handlebars of a bicycle together with the bicycle seat to make the head of a 'goat' he is tapping into 'formal causes' because he is dealing with the essential elements of the form of something.

This type of cause is related to what Aristotle called "intuition." Before we can begin to scientifically investigate something like physics, ethics, pride or genius, we have to have the idea that such phenomena might possibly exist. Even choosing our examples of 'prideful' people implies that we have the intuition that these individuals are examples of what we are looking for. As Aristotle pointed out:

> *"[I]t will be intuition that apprehends the primary premises - a result which follows from the fact that demonstration cannot be the originative source of demonstration, nor, consequently, scientific knowledge of scientific knowledge...intuition will be the originative source of scientific knowledge."*

Identifying the formal causes of genius, for instance, would involve examining our basic definitions, assumptions and intuitions about genius. For example, we could say, "Aristotle was a genius because we define people who have influenced our society in such a basic and widespread fashion as 'geniuses'." Modeling the formal causes of genius for a particular person would involve identifying that person's basic assumptions about the area or areas in which his or her genius was expressed.

Antecedent Causes

Antecedent or precipitating causes relate to past events, actions or decisions that influence the present state of a thing or event through a linear chain of 'action and reaction'. This is probably the most common form of causal explanation that we use to describe things. For instance, we say, "The acorn grew into an oak tree because the man planted it, watered it and fertilized it." "The man cut down the tree because he had recently bought a new axe." Or "The tree fell because the man chopped a deep cut in its trunk with his axe."

Past   *Present*

Antecedent or Precipitating Cause

Seeking the precipitating causes of genius would involve looking for the chain of events in various geniuses' personal histories that lead to the development of their exceptional abilities - such as their genetics or their experiences. For example, we could say, "Aristotle's genius was caused by his training at the Academy in Athens with Socrates and Plato, and by the interest in biology and science that he inherited from his father who was a court physician."

Constraining Causes

Constraining causes involve ongoing relationships, presuppositions and boundary conditions (or lack of boundaries) within a system which maintain it's state (regardless of the chain of events that brought it there). For instance, applying this kind of cause, we might say, "The acorn grew into an oak tree because there was no significant competition for water and light from the trees surrounding it." "The man cut down the tree because the weather constrained him from traveling deeper into the woods to select another tree." "The tree fell because the gravitational field of the Earth pulled the tree toward its center and held it against the ground."

Present

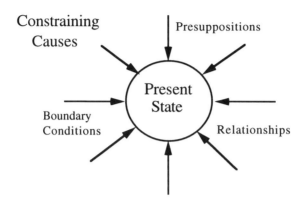

Efficient or Constraining Causes

Seeking the constraining causes of genius would involve examining the conditions surrounding a person at the time his or her genius was being expressed - such as the prevailing social conditions and the reaction and support they received from others around them. For example, we could say, "Aristotle was a genius because he was given both the opportunities and the focus to follow his interests by the Athenian system of government and by his position as a tutor to Alexander the Great. He had no significant competitors because only a few people had even begun to think scientifically during that age and education was still rare except for the upper class. Many of his key works were recorded from his lectures and written and edited by his students." Constraining causes tend to be more 'systemic' in nature, and may be defined in terms of potential constraints which were not present as well as those which were.

Final Causes

Final causes relate to future objectives, goals or visions which guide or influence the present state of the system giving current actions meaning, relevance or purpose. Final causes involve the motives or 'ends' for which something exists. In this sense, final causes often relate to a thing's role or 'identity' with respect to the larger system of which it is a part. In his biological researches especially, Aristotle focused on this type of causation - the intentional aim or end of nature - which he held to be distinct from the mechanical causation also operative in inorganic phenomena. Thus, while Aristotle tended to seek antecedent causes in cases of mechanical and non-living phenomena, he found final causes more relevant for mental and biological phenomena, claiming, *"mind always does whatever it does for the sake of something, which something is its end."*

He noted that, if one burns an acorn, he destroys it in a mechanical way but that, if he gives it a chance, it turns *itself* into an oak. Thinking in terms of this kind of cause we might say, "The acorn grew into a tree because its nature is to become a tree." "The man cut down the tree because he wanted to be warm and needed wood to make a fire." "The tree fell because it was destined to provide support to other creatures on this planet."

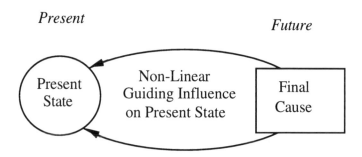

Final Cause

Seeking the final causes of genius would involve considering the intended goals, purposes and desired results that guided or inspired the thoughts and actions of the individuals we are studying. It would also involve considering the individuals' perceptions of their own identity within the environmental and social systems they were operating. For example, we could say, "Aristotle's genius was caused by his constant desire to discover and share the first principles which united and brought balance to all of the phenomena of the natural world."

Clearly, any one of these causes taken to be the whole explanation by itself is likely to lead to an incomplete picture. In today's science we look mostly for mechanical causes, or what Aristotle referred to as 'antecedent' causes. When we study a phenomenon scientifically we tend to look for the linear cause-and-effect chain which brought it about. For instance, we say "Our universe was caused by the 'big bang' which happened billions of years ago." Or we say, "AIDS is caused by a virus that enters the body and interferes with the immune system." Or "This organization is successful because it took those particular steps at those particular times." These understandings are certainly important and useful but do not necessarily tell us the whole story of these phenomena.

Identifying the formal causes of the "universe," a "successful organization" or "AIDS" would involve examining our basic assumptions and intuitions about the phenomena. What exactly do we mean when we talk about our "universe" or about "success," an "organization" or about "AIDS?" What are we presupposing about their structure and their "nature?" (These were the type of questions that lead Albert Einstein to reformulate our whole perception of time, space and the structure of the universe.)

Identifying constraining causes would involve examining what holds a particular phenomenon's current structure in place, regardless of what brought it there. Why is it, for instance, that many people who have the AIDS virus do not manifest any physical symptoms? If the universe has been expanding after the 'big bang', what determines the current rate at which it is expanding? What constraints will cause the universe to stop expanding? What are the current constraints or lack of constraints that could cause an organization to fail or suddenly take off, regardless of its history?

Searching for final causes, would involve exploring the potential aims or ends of these phenomena with respect to the rest of nature. For instance, is AIDS simply a scourge, is it a lesson, or is it an evolutionary process? Is God "playing dice" with universe, or is it heading toward something? What are the visions and goals that make an organization successful?

These same kinds of considerations are relevant to our study of genius. Attempting to find the *formal causes* of genius leads us to view it as a function of the definitions and assumptions we apply to a person's life and actions. Looking for *precipitating causes* leads us to see genius as a result of special events and experiences within a person's life. Seeking *constraining causes* leads us to perceive genius as something brought out by unique or extraordinary conditions within which the person was living. Considering *final causes* leads us to perceive genius as a result of a person's motives or destiny.

The Role of Time Perception

It seems clear that Aristotle's various types of causes imply different relationships between phenomena in 'time'. Antecedent causes relate to the 'past' while final causes relate to the 'future'. Constraining causes relate to the 'present'. Formal causes are the only ones not directly related to time.

For Aristotle, the perception of 'time', like other concepts, was a 'tool' to be used in different ways. In fact, in his book, *Physics*, he even somewhat humorously questions the existence of time:

> *"[T]he following considerations would make one suspect that [time] either does not exist at all or barely, and in an obscure way. One part of it has been and is not, while the other is going to be and is not yet. Yet time - both infinite time and any time you like to take - is made up of these. One would naturally suppose that what is made up of things which do not exist could have no share in reality."*

Certainly, one of the key outcomes of the modeling process is to organize sequences of relevant cognitive and behavioral influences with respect to time. The way in which one organizes and places events in time can greatly influence the effects they are perceived to have.

In the same way that Aristotle distinguished between the relevance of different types of causes with respect to organic versus mechanical process, he appears to have had different ways in which he perceived the influence of time with regard to different types of phenomena. For mechanical causation, Aristotle tended to apply the traditional view of time as something linear. Antecedent causes, for instance, formed a linear sequence of reactions. He explains:

"We apprehend time only when we have marked it by motion, marking it by 'before' and 'after'; and it is only when we have perceived 'before' and 'after' in motion that we say that time has elapsed. Now we mark them by judging that A and B are different, and that some third thing is intermediate to them. When we think of the extremes as different from the middle and the mind pronounces that the 'nows' are two, one before and one after, it is then that we say there is time...For what is bounded by the 'now' is thought to be time...For time is just this - number of motion in respect of 'before' and 'after'...there is a correspondence with the point; for the point also both connects and terminates the length - it is the beginning of one length and the end of another."

This perception of time as "points" on "lengths" of a line for quantifying events, such that the present or "now" is "after" the past (A) and "before" the future (B), has been picked up and used by scientists and planners ever since. It fact, "time lines" have become the primary mode of thinking about time in Western Society.

In the basic model of NLP, there are two fundamental perspectives one can have with respect to time: perceiving something "in time" or "through time."[1]

---

[1] The notion of the "in time" and "through time" time lines first developed in NLP in 1979 with the advent of the so called "meta program" patterns. Exploration of other forms of time perception took place in the early 1980's by individuals such as Richard Bandler and myself. Specific applications of time lines in the form of techniques began in the mid to late 1980's; most notably by Tad James and Wyatt Woodsmall (1987), Steve and Connirae Andreas (1987) and my own work involving the physicalization of time lines (1987).

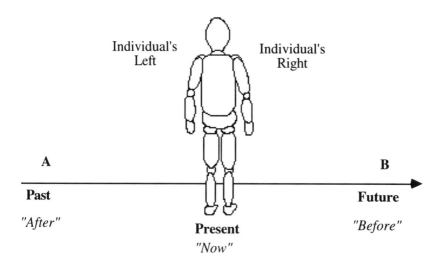

Individual's Left

Individual's Right

A   B

Past   **Future**

"After"   **Present**   *"Before"*

                             "Now"

"Through Time" Time Line

When one perceives an event "through time" one takes a vantage point that is outside of the sequence of events, disassociated from whatever is being observed or modeled. From this perspective, the 'time line' is typically viewed such that the 'before' and 'after' are lines extending off to the left and right, with the 'now' being somewhere in the middle.

Perceiving an event "in time" involves taking a vantage point associated within the event that is unfolding. From this perceptual position, the 'now' is one's current physical position with the future represented as a line extending off in the direction one is facing and the past trailing behind - such that one is walking into the future and leaving the past behind.

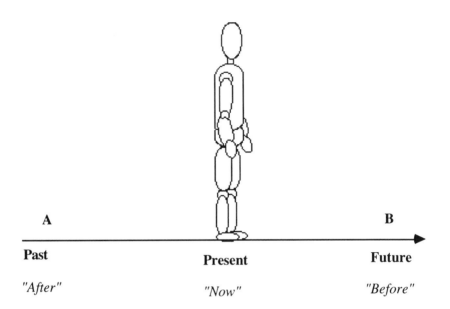

A		B
Past	**Present**	**Future**
"After"	*"Now"*	*"Before"*

"In Time" Time Line

The two perspectives (which may be represented either visually or through the use of actual physical space) create different perceptions of the same event. The "through time" perspective is effective for quantitative analysis, but is more passive because it is disassociated. The "in time" perspective is more active and involved but makes it easier to "lose sight of the whole."

In Aristotle's view, though, these linear methods of perceiving and measuring time were only one way; that were primarily of value with respect to mechanical causes. He considered the influence of time with respect to biological and mental phenomena in a different way:

"[There is a] common saying that human affairs form a circle, and that there is a circle in all other things that have a natural movement of coming into being and passing away. This is because all other things are discriminated by time, and end and begin as though conforming to a cycle; for even time itself is thought to be a circle...So to say that things that come into being form a circle is to say that there is a circle of time; and to say that it is measured by circular movement."

Thus, time that relates to mechanical processes based on the perception of 'before' and 'after' bounded by the 'now' may be represented by the classical 'time line'. However, time that relates to more organic processes involving the *"natural movement of coming into being and passing away"* may be best represented in the form of circles and "cycles."

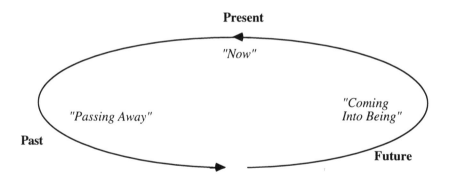

"Circular" or Cyclic Time Line

These different ways of perceiving time will tend to focus our attention on different types of causes. The 'through time' time line, for instance, leads us to perceive antecedent or precipitating causes. An 'in time' perspective emphasizes

constraining causes. A cyclic time line would tend to bring
out final and formal causes.

Similarly, different types of time lines tend to be more
appropriate for different levels of processes. For instance,
preparing to enact physical behaviors can be best done via an
'in time' time line. Planning a course of action or considering
one's capabilities requires the broader perspective of the
'through time' time line. Processes related to beliefs and
identity are often best represented in the form of cycles, as
they tend to involve recurring patterns rather than one time
linear events.

In our study of genius, it appears that it will be important
to consider the relevance of time from all of these different
perspectives. A "through time" time line will enable us to
identify and describe specific and discrete sequences of steps.
An "in time" time line will aid us to more easily step into the
shoes of the geniuses we are modeling and see their actions
in history as they experienced them. Perceiving events in the
"circle" or "cycle" of time will help us to recognize recurrent
patterns, view processes as whole and to identify how the
different steps relate to the "natural movement" of the whole.

Evaluating One's Premises

Searching for different types of causes leads us to reaching different types of conclusions; and considering events with respect to different ways of representing time will alter our perceptions of them. Thus, it seems clear that one needs some way to assess or evaluate the conclusions that one arrives at through one's explorations. According to Aristotle, the key to the effectiveness of our conclusions about a principle is the strength and 'universality' of the relationship between a phenomenon and the attributes or causes that we have discovered. This relationship is what Aristotle called the "premise" of the conclusion.

> *"Every premise states that something either **is** or **must be** or **may be** the attribute of something else; of premises of these three kinds some are affirmative, others negative."*

In the first case, we can state what something is or what it is not. For example, we can say that a human being *is* an animal, and a human being *is not* a vegetable.

With respect to the second type of premise, we can state that a human being *must have* the capacity for language, and a human being *must not have* a tail.

In the third type of premise, we can say that some human beings *may be able to* sculpt statues, or some human beings *may not be able to* speak Greek.

These different types of premises are essentially the first two terms of a 'syllogism' - (A) the general phenomenon and (B) the 'middle' or the causes and attributes associated with that phenomenon. The validity of these two terms determines the validity of any conclusions drawn from them.

The first test for these various premises was in what Aristotle called their "convertibility":

"It is necessary then that in universal attribution the terms of the negative premise should be convertible, e.g. if no pleasure is good, then no good will be pleasure;

the terms of the affirmative must be convertible, not however universally, but in part, e.g. if every pleasure is good, some good must be pleasure;

the particular affirmative must convert in part (for if some pleasure is good, then some good will be pleasure); but the particular negative need not convert, for if some animal is not man, it does not follow that some man is not animal."

From Aristotle's point of view, then, the evaluation of a 'first principle' essentially involved looking for 'counter examples' or exceptions to the rule, which challenged its 'universality' by utilizing the process of 'conversion'.

However, the validity of the conversion had to be backed up by observation. Aristotle believed the only effective 'proof' of a first principle was through "demonstration." Once a principle was formed, it had to be applied and validated through experience. In other words, the map must be shown to be useful by the degree to which it helps us navigate the territory. As Aristotle claimed in **On the Generation of Animals**, *"credit must be given to observation rather than to theories, and to theories only insofar as they are confirmed by the observed facts."*

The value of the process of conversion is that it tells us where to look to find possible counter examples. Thus, if we say, "All birds have wings," then we should not find any birds that do not have wings. But we may find animals with wings that are not birds. If we say, "No birds are featherless," then we should not find any featherless creature that is a bird.

The essential structure of finding counter examples through the principle of conversion involves checking the strength of the relationship implied by the premise. For instance, a premise will be something like:

All **A** have **B**
or
A causes **B**

To seek counter examples we would first ask:

Is there any **A** that does *not* have **B**?
or
Is there any **A** that does *not* cause **B**?

Next we would 'convert' the terms and ask:

Is there anything that has **B** that is *not* **A**?
or
Is there any **B** that is *not* caused by **A**?

For an attribute to be truly definitive, we should find no counter examples. For instance, not all birds fly, but all birds have wings. However, not all animals with wings are birds; insects, bats and some dinosaurs also have or had wings. But if we say that all animals with wings *and* beaks are birds, it will be more unlikely that we will find counter examples; i.e., animals that are not birds that have wings and beaks.

We can apply this same assessment process to our study of the strategies of genius. After posing a hypothesis (based on finding 'common elements' within a number of examples) in the form of a premise, we would then look for any potential counter examples. So, if we find that "All geniuses ask basic questions," then we should see if there are any examples of geniuses that do not ask fundamental questions. Did Mozart, for example, ask fundamental questions? If so, which ones? We should also find out if there are people who ask fundamental questions who are not geniuses. The fewer counter examples there are, the more 'universal' the attribute or cause is.

Finding a counter example, by the way, does not mean that our premise is 'wrong', it generally means that the system or phenomenon we are exploring or studying is more complex than we are perceiving it to be, or that we have not yet reached its simplest elements.

Aristotle's Model of the Mind

Seeking universal causes and attributes presupposes that we must know which elements to look for as possible causes or attributes. And according to Aristotle's prescriptions, we must look for the "simplest elements." What are the simplest elements making up the 'causes' and 'attributes' of genius? Clearly they have to do with the 'mind'. And while Aristotle did not write about genius specifically, he had much to say about the nature of the mind.

In many ways, in fact, Aristotle was the first person to do NLP. Certainly he was the originator of many of the basic principles behind NLP. He was one of the first people in history to try to define and categorize the various aspects of the "mind" and the thinking process. In his book *On The Soul*, for instance, Aristotle maintained the way you know that something is alive, and thus has a 'soul' or 'psyche', is because it can sense things and it can move under its own power. He wrote:

> *"The soul of animals is characterized by two faculties,*
> *(a) the faculty of discrimination which is the work of*
> *thought and sense, and (b) the faculty of originating*
> *local movement."*

The way you know something has a psyche is because it can sense features of its world, make discriminations about what it senses and it can originate movement in itself in relationship to the sensory discriminations it makes.

These basic distinctions fit well with the information processing model proposed by NLP - that the brain is like a microcomputer and functions via inputs and outputs. Movements are originated and directed by the mental discriminations we make about our inputs.

Unlike modern behaviorists, however, Aristotle did not think of this process as being a simple reflexive action. As we mentioned earlier, he claimed that *"mind always does whatever it does for the sake of something, which something is its end."* Thus, for Aristotle, all psychological experience was organized towards some end. As a result, sensing and discriminating differences in what we sense is always done in relationship to some goal. All sensing is given meaning in terms of this relationship to a 'goal'. In other words, for Aristotle, psyche meant the ability to have a goal, to be able to sense your relationship to your goal and to be able to vary your behavior in order to achieve the goal.

William James (the American psychologist who is usually considered the father of cognitive psychology) similarly defined the mind as having the ability to have a fixed future goal and very broad choices with which to get to that goal.

"The pursuance of future ends and the choice of means for their attainment are thus the mark and criterion of the presence of mentality in a phenomenon."

In the language of NLP, both Aristotle and William James were describing the T.O.T.E. process (Miller, et al, 1960) which says intelligent behavior is a function of having tests and operations that lead you in the direction of some fixed future goal - a "final cause." Like the S.O.A.R., the T.O.T.E. model is fundamental to the NLP modeling process. It also complements the S.O.A.R. by defining the basic way in which operators are placed into action. A particular T.O.T.E. defines a distinctive pathway through the problem space. In this sense, the T.O.T.E. is the basic structure by which defines a person's macro strategy.

The T.O.T.E. Model

T.O.T.E. stands for Test-Operate-Test-Exit. It defines the basic feedback loop through which we systematically change states. According to the T.O.T.E. Model, we generally operate on a state to change it in order to reach a goal. We continually test the ongoing state against some evidence or criteria to find out if we have achieved that goal. Depending on the result of this test we adjust our operations accordingly. That is, first you test your relationship to your goal. If you are not reaching your goal, you operate by varying your behavior in some way. Then you test the result of that movement again, and if you have been successful you exit to the next step. If not, you vary your behavior again and repeat the process.

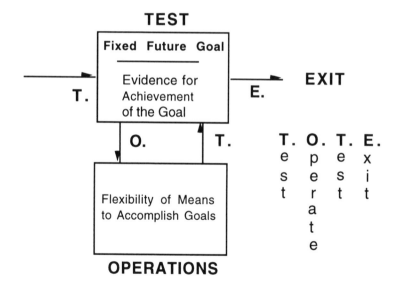

Diagram of the Basic T.O.T.E. Feedback Loop

Thus, in terms of the T.O.T.E. model, intelligent behavior is organized around the ability to establish:

1) A fixed future goal.
2) The sensory evidence necessary to accurately determine your progress toward the goal.
3) A variable set of means to get to your goal and the behavioral flexibility to implement these choices.

In relation to Aristotle's definition of the 'soul of animals', a living creature organizes its activity around the T.O.T.E. It 'discriminates' by testing its progress towards its goals or 'ends' through evidence provided by the process of sensory perception. If it is not achieving its goal or end, it 'moves' or operates to do something to try to reach that goal.

This is a profoundly different concept than the models of Skinner and Pavlov, who defined the process behind behavior as being that of reflexes and stimulus-response chains. For Aristotle mind is not reflex. The 'psyche' operates at a different level than that of simply receiving a stimulus that makes one respond; rather, stimuli are more or less irrelevant unless they relate to the goal or 'final cause'. In Aristotle's model, behavior is not stimulus driven, it is goal driven.

Aristotle's view certainly matches my own observations of my son when he was first learning how to move his body at a few months old. 'Stimuli' were irrelevant to him unless they fit in with some inner goal or purpose that he had. Rather than reflexively and mindlessly reacting to external stimuli, his movements centered around things that he was internally interested in. For example, there were some toys he exhibited preferences for from the outset and others he completely ignored initially. He only began to interact with them when he became interested in them as a result of relating them to some sort of inner goal or end that he had. Then he would interact with them through this T.O.T.E. feedback loop. When he wanted to get something, he 'tested' by looking at his hand in relationship to it, 'operated' by sort of swiping his hand at it, missed, 'tested' again, swiped his hand again this time a little closer, and basically continued to test and operate until he got it. Then he 'exited' on to his next interest. Rather than stimulus-response, it was a goal driven feedback loop.

Studies of very young infants (Bower, 1985) in the first weeks and months of life, also tend to confirm Aristotle's view of behavior. In a typical experiment a child is sat in front of an "attractive" toy, such as a mobile. The toy moves intermittently depending on the child's activity. To stop the mobile the child has to lower his or her foot, breaking a light beam and preventing the mobile from turning. To start it again, the child has to lift his or her foot out of the light beam. Most babies become interested in the stopping and starting of the mobile, analyze the situation quite rapidly, and then notice the movement is caused by something they've done with their foot. They play around with both feet, and quickly realize what to do to make the event - the starting and stopping of the mobile - occur.

In the past, theorists assumed that the child was most interested in the event: the 'reinforcement' or reward which encouraged the child to learn; i.e. the mobile. But researchers became convinced it wasn't the event, it was figuring out how to control what was going on that was important to the child. Learning itself was reinforcing - the reinforcement was realizing how to interact with and influence the outside world.

By adjusting the experimental parameters researchers were able to test whether the child really was interested in his or her own control rather than the event itself. For instance, if the child's control is made less than perfect, so that by moving his or her foot the child doesn't always stop or start the mobile, then the child will carry on and on until he or she has solved the problem. Once the child has the solution he or she can become bored quite rapidly, except occasionally to check that he or she still has power over the event.

There are two important points in this example; 1) the successful exercise of the "faculties" of "discrimination" and "originating local movement" is inherently self-reinforcing, and 2) the way an individual learns to influence the world is by interacting and adapting his or her own reactions in response to feedback.[2]

Macro Strategies and the T.O.T.E.

The T.O.T.E. provides the basic structure and distinctions for identifying and defining macro strategies for effective performances. The general structure of a computer program, for instance, could be described in terms of a specific T.O.T.E. A spell checking program, for example, has the goal of insuring correct spelling. It goes through all of the words in a body of text testing to see that each one meets the criteria it has been provided to determine correct spellings. If it detects an incorrectly spelled word, it operates to inform the writer and change the word.

In establishing the macro strategy for preparing a meal, the goal may be defined in terms of the particular kind of meal to be produced - say a holiday dinner. The food is tested for compatibility and taste, etc., then operated on accord-

---

[2] This tells us something important about using stimulus-response teaching methods or learning methods and not acknowledging the goal of the students. 'Rewarding' a student by giving him or her a good grade is likely to be ineffective unless the student wants to get a good grade. Giving money as a 'reinforcement' to someone won't motivate him or her unless the person's objective is to get more money. For instance, Mother Teresa would pursue her mission just as dilligently whether she was paid or not. According to the T.O.T.E. model there is no such thing as a real external reinforcement in the Skinnerian sense. Nothing is a reinforcement unless it is perceived in relationship to a goal coming from inside the person or animal.

ingly. There is even a macro strategy in the example provided by the opening quotation from Genesis. Each day is a kind of T.O.T.E. in which God sets out to accomplish a particular goal in his creation ("And God said, Let there be..."), operates to achieve it ("And God made...") and then evaluates it ("And God saw that it was good").

Modeling the 'macro strategies' of genius, involves identifying the way in which the individuals we are studying used the various elements of the T.O.T.E.:

1) What goals did they strive to achieve?
2) What types of evidence and evidence procedures did they use to get feedback in order to determine their progress toward their goals?
3) What set of means and operations did they employ to reach their goals?

Answering these questions will give us the 'macro strategy' of the individual. For example, based on what we have examined so far about Aristotle, we could define his macro strategy in the following way:

1) Aristotle's goal was to find the "first principles" in all aspects of the natural world.

2) Aristotle's evidence involved having premises that were both logical ('convertible' and without obvious counter examples) and 'demonstrable'.

3) Aristotle's operations involved a) exploring a problem space by asking basic questions, b) finding the 'middle' (basic causes and attributes which connected general principles to specific examples) through an inductive process that involved finding common elements shared by different examples of a particular phenomenon and c) forming the results into a syllogism that could be tested and demonstrated.

Micro Strategies And The Five Senses

Identifying micro strategies involves filling in the cognitive and behavioral details of how, specifically, a particular macro strategy is carried out. In the model of NLP, micro strategies relate to the way in which one uses his or her sensory 'representational systems', such as mental imagery, internal self talk, emotional reactions, etc., in order to carry out a task or T.O.T.E.

Like NLP, Aristotle identified the basic elements of cognitive process as intimately associated with our sensory experience. Aristotle's basic premise then was that, in order to fulfill their various goals, animals had to move and in order to move they needed sensory contact with the outside world to guide that movement in relation to their goals. This sensory contact formed the basis for what would become 'thought' and 'skill'. As he describes it in *Posterior Analytics*:

> *"[A]ll animals...possess a congenital discriminative capacity which is called sense-perception. But though sense-perception is innate in all animals, in some the sense-impression comes to persist, in others it does not. So animals in which this persistence does not come to be have either no knowledge at all outside the act of perceiving, or no knowledge of objects of which no impression persists; animals in which it does come into being have perception and can continue to retain the sense-impression in the soul: and when such persistence is frequently repeated a further distinction at once arises between those which out of the persistence of such sense-impressions develop a power of systematizing them and those which do not.*

> *"So out of sense-perception comes to be what we call memory, and out of frequently repeated memories of the same thing develops experience; for a number of memories constitutes a single experience. From*

experience again - i.e. from the universal now stabilized
in its entirety within the soul, the one beside the many
which is the single identity within them all - originate
the skill of the craftsman, and the knowledge of the
man of science, skill in the sphere of being.

Aristotle outlines the fundamental process of 'thinking' as
being an inductive process by which 1) "sense-perceptions"
leave impressions in the 'soul'; 2) the impressions which
persist become "memories"; 3) the frequent repetition of
memories of a particular phenomenon become systematized
or chunked into a "single experience" or "universal"; 4)
collections of these universals form the foundation for "skill"
and "knowledge." Our basic mental capacities, then, come
from our abilities to use our senses in order to perceive, and
then to represent and remember what we have perceived.

While in NLP we would substitute the term 'nervous
system' for the 'soul', much of what Aristotle describes
mirrors the essential conceptualization of mental process in
NLP. For instance, the "universal" which is made up of a
number of memories - *"the one beside the many which is the*
single identity within them all" - reflects the basic idea
behind the concept of logical levels in NLP. Groups of
behaviors form the basis for a capability; groups of capabilities form the basis for our belief and value systems; groups of
beliefs and values form the basis for our sense of identity. All
of these levels of perception, however, are founded on the
micro level through sensory perception.

In **On The Soul**, Aristotle categorized the senses into the
five basic classes of sight, hearing, touch, smell and taste.
Aristotle's five senses correspond directly with the five 'representational systems' employed in the in NLP modeling
process - Visual, Auditory, Kinesthetic, Olfactory and Gustatory. According to Aristotle, the five senses provided the
psyche with information about qualities in the outside world
that fell into a certain range:

> *"[T]he field of each sense is according to the accepted view determined as the range between a single pair of contraries, white and black for sight, acute and grave for hearing, bitter and sweet for taste; but in the field of what is tangible we find several such pairs, hot cold, dry moist, hard soft, etc. This problem finds a partial solution, when it is recalled that in the case of the other senses more than one pair of contraries are to be met with, e.g. in sound not only acute and grave but loud and soft, smooth and rough, etc.; there are similar contrasts in the field of color."*

These "pairs of contraries" correspond to what in NLP are called the "sub-modalities." Sub-modalities are the particular perceptual qualities that may be registered by each of the five primary sensory modalities. Our visual modality, for instance, can perceive such qualities as color, brightness, shape, depth, etc.; our auditory modality is capable of registering volume, pitch, tempo, etc.; Our kinesthetic system perceives such qualities as pressure, temperature, texture, etc., and so on. Each sub-modality registers qualities that may range between two opposites: color<=>black-and-white, bright<=>dim, loud<=>quiet, high<=>low, hot<=>cold, heavy<=>light, etc.

For Aristotle, it was the relationship between these qualities that determined how we responded to the objects or situations we are experiencing.

> *"[W]hen an object of touch is equally hot and cold or hard and soft we cannot perceive; what we perceive must have a degree of the sensible quality lying beyond the neutral point. This implies that the sense itself is a 'mean' between any two opposite qualities which determine the field of that sense...it is indifferent what in each case the substance is; what alone matters is*

*what quality it has, i.e., in what ratio its constituents
are combined."*

Sensing, then, is noticing the relationship between these
polarities - registering differences and ratios of difference.
Aristotle implied that it was these "ratios" of perceptual
qualities, not the objects themselves, that determined how
we respond to something - i.e., it is the information about
sensory qualities of things that are most important to our
minds or 'psyches', not the things themselves. As Aristotle
put it, *"[I]t is not the stone which is present in the soul but its
form."* In other words, the 'form' is more important than the
'content' - our perceptual model of the world is more important than the objective reality of the world. And these 'submodality' qualities are the fundamental "formal cause" of our
mental models of the world.

According to Aristotle it was the ratio between these
polarities that determined what was pleasurable and what
was painful, and thus what was to be approached or avoided
and how much it was to be approached or avoided. If
something was too much at either end of the polarity it
became uncomfortable. There was a certain range of balance
in which one experienced comfort. For example, a fire is, in
and of itself, neither good nor bad, pleasurable nor painful.
If one gets too close to the fire the ratio of hot-to-cold is too
much on the hot side and it becomes uncomfortable. If one
gets too far away from the fire, and it is cold weather, the
ratio of hot-to-cold gets too much on the cold side and it also
becomes uncomfortable.

Perception of pain and pleasure has to do with the ratio,
the balance point of the senses. Thus, in Aristotle's view, we
are constantly seeking to keep these ratios in balance. In
other words, pain and pleasure are a communication about
the degree of balance within the system.

A key consideration in modeling micro strategies with
NLP relates to the functioning of the senses and their 'sub-

modalities' in a person's thinking process. These qualities have obvious significance in relationship to artistic processes such as painting and music where the dynamic balancing of qualities such as colors and tones are the essence of aesthetics. However, these qualities can have tremendous significance in other fields as well. Consider the impact of the ability to represent 'perspective' in regard to bringing about the European Renaissance. Further, it is not difficult to imagine that it would be a very different experience to try to conceptualize Einstein's theory of relativity by visualizing it in the form of flat, still, black and white mental images than to use three dimensional imagery that is moving and in color.

Aristotle also related these sensory qualities directly with the perception of pain and pleasure. Certainly, geniuses take pleasure in what they do. Their attraction to their work may come as a result of the cognitive micro structure with which they represent their particular subject matter. For instance, through NLP, these subtle perceptual qualities have been found to be at the basis of phenomena such as phobias, compulsions and addictions. Very effective techniques for treating these kind of problems have been developed that involve teaching a person to directly manipulate their internal experiences in order to adjust the 'ratios' of key qualities.

These qualities can even be shown to play a significant role in a person's ability to distinguish "imagination" from "reality" and "memory" from "fantasy."

The Role of Memory and Imagination

In addition to these sensory qualities, another fundamental element of the micro structure of "thinking" and "mental strategies" is the ability to recall and associate perceptions with other perceptions. In Aristotle's model of behavior, the 'psyche' used internal mental replications of sensory experiences to determine what to approach and avoid. Memory allowed an animal to consider a larger scope of experience that included things which were not able to be sensed in the here and now. "Thoughts" operated more off of the impressions left by the senses than ongoing sensory input. These impressions took the form of "imagination" and "memory."

Aristotle believed that the mind was *"in its essential nature activity."* Therefore, perception, and memory were the results of this 'activity' or 'movement'. As he maintained:

> *"The process of movement [sensory stimulation - RD] involved in the act of perception stamps in, as it were, a sort of impression of the percept, just as persons do who make an impression with a seal."*

Aristotle also believed that, *"imagination must be a movement resulting from an actual exercise of the power of sense."* As a result, it could also leave impressions in memory that could become associated together with those traces left by actual sensation. These associations of sensory impression were the basis for all thought.

To Aristotle, the process of "thinking" began when "impressions" became connected together through the 'law of association' which he described in his work **On Memory**: According to Aristotle:

> *"Acts of recollection, as they occur in experience, are due to the fact that one movement has by nature another that succeeds it in regular order. If this order be necessary, whenever a subject experiences the former of two movements thus connected, it will invariably, experience the latter; if, however, the order be not necessary, but customary, only in the majority of cases will the subject experience the latter of the two movements.*
>
> *"But it is a fact that there are some movements, by a single experience of which persons take the impress of custom more deeply than they do by experiencing*

others many times; hence upon seeing some things but once we remember them better than others which we may have seen frequently. Whenever, therefore, we are recollecting, we are experiencing certain of the antecedent movements until finally we experience the one after which customarily comes that which we seek."

The process that Aristotle is defining here is similar to what is called "anchoring" in NLP. When two experiences occur together in a close enough time frame they can become linked or "anchored" together, so that one of the experiences will become a trigger for the other. As Aristotle mentions, an association may, and often does, take place in a single trial. When a series of sensory representations become associated with each other in a particular sequence it forms the basis of a cognitive "strategy."

Clearly, the ability to remember and form associations will be a fundamental influence on the phenomena of genius. For example, Mozart's phenomenal and practically instantaneous memory for music is often cited as both an 'attribute' and a 'cause' of his musical genius. One important question relating to the study of strategies of genius involves whether or not such capabilities are "innate" or "genetic" or can be developed.

In the NLP view it is believed that, while certain individuals may possess genetic proclivities, these abilities can be enhanced via particular skills and techniques. It is therefore relevant to explore, if possible, the micro processes by which geniuses facilitate their ability to remember and associate sensory experiences together. For instance, in the model of NLP, there are certain micro behavioral cues that are generally overlooked in the study of genius, which serve as *'accessing cues'*. 'Accessing cues' serve to help people recall experiences and make associations. An accessing cue may range from idiosyncratic cues like snapping ones fingers, mumbling "hmmm" or scratching one's head, to deeper and more universal cues like unconscious lateral eye movements and breathing patterns.

Observing and tracking these subtle cues can provide clues to how an individual is thinking, and can be used to help facilitate associative processes. For example, one of the most effective NLP strategies is the 'spelling strategy' in which an individual facilitates the process of visually representing and remembering a spelling word by moving his or her eyes up (and typically to the left) while learning or recalling a particular word.

In summary, Aristotle believed sensory input from the outside world would leave impressions which could become associated with one another, or with constructed impressions caused by an internal activation of the sensory system (i.e., imagination). These associations formed mental 'ideas' or replicas of sequences of sensory input and internally generated experience. Associations of present sensations to future consequences formed the basis of "calculations" and "deliberations." These associations in turn trigger the animal to move toward or away from objects in its surroundings. On another level, given an appropriate number and frequency of individual memories, a 'universal' perception would emerge from clusters of similar experiences as a principle which united the experiences together in a 'single experience'. As Aristotle states in *Posterior Analytics*:

> *"We conclude that these states of knowledge are neither innate in a determinate form, nor developed from other higher states of knowledge, but from sense-perception...for though the act of sense-perception is of the particular, its content is universal - is 'a man', for example, not the particular man Callias...*
>
> *"Thus it is clear that we must get to know the primary premises by induction; for the method by which even sense-perception implants the universal is inductive."*

Common Sensibles

According to Aristotle the process of inductively identifying universals from particular sense-perceptions took place through the "common sense" - the place in the 'psyche' where all of the senses met. One of the functions of the "common sense" was to register something which repeated in a number of experiences - a pattern. Patterns or 'universals' were perceived in terms of a set of content-free qualities that Aristotle called the "common sensibles," which were the discriminations that were shared by all the senses.

> *"'Common sensibles' are movement, rest, number, figure, magnitude, unity; these are not peculiar to any one sense but are common to all."*

It is significant that Aristotle's "common sensibles" are not a function of any particular sensory modality. They are on a different level than the "pairs of contraries" or so called 'submodalities' in NLP, which are perceived by the individual senses (color, depth, shape, etc., for vision; tone, tempo, pitch, etc., for hearing; and temperature, pressure, texture, etc., for feeling).[3] The "common sensibles" identified relationships between the perceptions and impressions left by the senses.

For example, 'intensity' is something you can register in any sense. You can have intensity of color, sound, taste, smell or touch. The same with 'number'; you can see three things, hear three things, feel three things, etc. Location and movement are also perceptible via all the senses. You can see, hear, feel or smell that something coming from a particular location or moving in a particular direction. These qualities

---

[3] In fact, Aristotle's concept of the "common sensibles" points at some important new directions for NLP research and analysis in the future.

are not a function of only one sense. They are something that can be shared by all the senses and facilitate the transfer of information between the senses. According to Aristotle, common sensibles allowed us to do our higher level mental processing.

For example, Bower (1985) - the researcher who conducted the learning experiments with babies cited earlier - determined that children have to solve quite complex conceptual problems from an early age. These problems involved issues such as: Is a stopped object the same as a moving object? Can a toy move and be transformed into something else at the same time? Can an object go inside, on top of, behind another object, and then reappear unchanged? To solve these problems, which the infant rapidly does, it is not preoccupied with the specific sensory qualities of objects - i.e. colors, textures, shapes and smells. According to Bower:

> "The more intangible properties of the object - movement, place or position - are far more important in the child's thinking. These 'formal' (rather than sensory) properties of stimulation were the kind of features which could be presented and interpreted by several senses. Consider, for example, the movement of the mother's breast to the infant. Movement might be sensed through smell or touch. Symmetry is another example of a formal property of stimulation. If straight ahead, a sound source produces exactly the same stimulation in each ear. If it is to the right, the right ear is stimulated earlier and more intensely then the left ear, and if to the left the opposite happens. Symmetry works equally well for detecting smells, vibration or something visual.
>
> "Like movement and position, symmetry of stimulation is independent of any sense - it is a formal property of stimulation. I thought maybe the child's perceptual

*world was keyed to perceive these formal properties
rather than respond to specific details."*

Bower's "formal properties of stimulation" are what Aristotle called the "common sensibles." Bower began to wonder if
he could use these formal properties to help transfer information from one sense to another in order to help sensorially
impaired children such as those who were born blind. He
reports:

*"Training infants to transfer perceptual information
from sense to sense seemed almost impossible. What
we needed was a device which could change formal
properties that would normally be easily seen -
symmetry, movement, place - into sounds. Once this
was done the device could be used on sighted children
in the dark, or blind children to find out if they could
'see' through sound."*

Bower and his colleagues eventually came up with a device
called the 'sonic guide'. It was worn as a headband by the
child, and gave an ultrasonic pulse. The pitch of the audible
signal indicated the distance of the objects from which the
echo came. High pitch meant distant objects; low pitch near
ones. The amplitude of the signal coded for the size of the
irradiated object (loud=large, quiet=small). The texture of
the object was given by the clarity of the signal. When he
first began applying the device, Bower was expecting slow,
gradual learning to be necessary. So he was astounded by
the results of the first session.

The child was a sixteen-week-old congenitally blind infant.
A silent object was moved slowly to and from the infant's
face. In the fourth presentation his eyes started to converge
as the object approached, and diverge as the object moved
away. In the seventh presentation he used his hand to reach
out for the object. Then they tested him on objects moving to

the right and the left. He tracked them with his head and eyes, and swiped at the objects.

Bower subsequently used the sonic guide on several congenitally blind infants of which the most remarkable was a young girl who started using the guide when she was about seven months. At that stage she was learning to crawl, but she was frightened of moving very far. After several sessions with the guide she became much freer. At two years old, she was walking up and down stairs, which is challenging enough for a normal sighted child. The guide gave her a very complicated signal from the stairs, but she actually seemed to like the complex input and loved running up and down the stairs. When the guide was removed she learned to stamp her own feet - sending out sound waves to get echoes back in order to orient herself.

Interestingly, when Bower tried the guide on older children he found they couldn't benefit as much from the signals. It appeared that once a child has learned that sound is a (property of *objects*), that child seemed to lose the ability to use it as a medium for perceiving the more abstract qualities necessary to transfer information between the senses.

After many experiments with the sonic guide, Bower reached the conclusion that a newborn child is most sensitive to the formal properties of stimulation or 'common sensibles' - such as symmetry, movement and position - and that these formal properties can indeed be transferred from sense to sense - visual information transferred to sound and so on. Initially, it seems the senses are not so specialized as to focus on sensory details associated only with specific senses. During perceptual development the senses become 'educated' by experience and begin to focus more on 'objects' and 'things', losing some of their sensitivity to common sensibles. According to Bower:

> "Our adult perceptual world is very sensory, full of colors, smells, sounds, and so on. But the newborn's

*world is not sensory, it is 'perceptual'. The child picks
up the formal characteristics associated with sensory
experience, without picking up the sensory experiences
themselves...I think children are responding to forms
of stimulation, and the sense which gives the best form
is the sense they will specialize in."*

The ability to communicate from one sense to another
appears to be a basic property of genius. For example,
Mozart's musical genius didn't come simply from his ability
to recognize and play specific notes and manipulate qualities
of sound such as tempo, volume and tone. His gift involved
perceiving and representing deep patterns, relationships and
"universals" through sound. When we examine his process
later in this book, we will find that Mozart had a remarkable
ability to link sounds with all of the other senses. For
Mozart, music involved emotions, the mind's eye and even
the sense of taste as much as it did his ears. Mozart's
description of his strategy for composition suggests that
music was a kind of multi-sensory mental 'sonic guide' in
which feelings, imagery and even taste blended together.
Perhaps, unlike most adults, Mozart and other geniuses
retained their direct access to the 'common sensibles' and
their ability to share information easily between the senses
and to perceive 'forms' rather than 'things'.

According to Bower, we lose access to the common sensibles
because we learn to associate sensory qualities with 'things'
as opposed to their 'formal characteristics' and relationships.
We even tend to 'objectify' the sensory qualities themselves,
perceiving colors, smells and sounds as 'things' rather than
ratios between "pairs of contraries" as Aristotle suggested.
(Even many NLP techniques treat 'sub-modalities' as if they
are a checklist of 'things' rather than ratios.) For instance,
we talk about an internal image being "bright" or "distant" as
if it were a 'thing' associated with a particular image. To
determine if an image is 'bright' it is necessary to first

determine, "Bright compared to what?" An image is neither inherently 'bright' nor 'dim', 'colorful' nor 'dull', 'distant' nor 'close'; it is "distant, colorful or bright compared to something else" - such as its background or another image.

An enlightening experiment was done by gestalt psychologists with a group of dogs. The dogs were trained to approach something when shown a 'white' square and avoid it when shown a 'gray' square. When the dogs had learned this particular discrimination task successfully, the experimenters switched to using the 'gray' square in contrast to a 'black' square. The dogs immediately shifted to approaching the object in response to the 'gray' square (which had previously triggered avoidance), and avoiding the object when shown the black square (which had not been 'conditioned' to anything). Presumably, rather than perceive the 'gray' and an absolute stimulus, the dogs were responding to the deeper ratio 'lighter versus darker' as opposed to 'gray', 'white' or 'black' as being 'things'.

Bower suggests that we lose the sensitivity to deeper relationships and 'formal characteristics' as we become 'educated' to focus on the 'particulars' of experience as opposed to the 'universals'. The process of 'objectifying' a group of sensory qualities is related to what Aristotle called the "incidental objects of sense." "Incidental objects of sense" resulted from combining the information provided by different senses to perceive 'things' which were made up of clusters of sensory qualities. In *On The Soul* Aristotle explains:

"We speak of an incidental object of sense where e.g. the white object which we see is the son of Diares; here because 'being the son of Diares' is incidental to the directly visible white patch...perceived or seen by us...The senses perceive each other's special objects incidentally...because all form a unity: this incidental perception takes place whenever sense is directed at one and the same moment to two disparate qualities in

one and the same object, e.g. to the bitterness and yellowness of bile, and the assertion of the identity of both cannot be the act of either of the senses; hence the illusion of sense, e.g. the belief that if a thing is yellow it is bile."

"Incidental objects of sense" are a kind of fundamental 'sensory syllogism' through which individuals build maps of the world from their sensory experiences. For example, "If something is yellow and bitter then it is bile," or "If an object is small, yellow, moves quickly and emits a high pitched tone then it is a canary," etc. In a way, this process has to do with very basic 'formal causes' related to our perception. According to Aristotle, the 'common sense' associated qualities from different senses together form what we might call 'beliefs' or 'maps' of 'reality'. And that it was from these deep 'syllogisms' that Aristotle felt we built our models of the world.

Yet while this process allows us to organize, make sense of and bring coherency to our experiences, it is also the source of the "illusion of sense" or, as Bower implies, an 'objectification' of sense that begins to narrow and limit our awareness and use of the deeper 'formal characteristics' of sense or 'common sensibles'. In NLP terms, we begin to confuse the 'map' and the 'territory' and lose access to possible choices.

Bower's comment that "the sense which gives the best form is the sense they will specialize in" points to the concept of the 'most highly valued representational system' in NLP. Originally described by William James (1879), the notion of a person "specializing" in or "highly valuing" a particular sensory modality relates to the fact that different people tend to rely on certain sensory modalities more so than others. According to James, *"In some individuals the habitual 'thought-stuff,' if one may so call it, is visual; in others it is auditory, articulatory, or motor: in most, perhaps, it is evenly mixed."* A more 'visually oriented' person, for instance, will tend to depend heavily on his or her sense of sight to learn, organize or plan, etc. If an individual has specialized to a very high degree, he or she may even experience difficulties learning or managing tasks that involve an emphasis on other senses. A highly 'visual' person, for instance, may excel in mathematics or drawing, but may experience difficulties with music or athletics. Individuals who are highly 'auditorally oriented' may have exceptional verbal skills but lack visually oriented skills, such as the mental spatial manipulation of objects, or their 'kinesthetic' abilities, such as physical coordination. Similarly, people who have highly specialized in touch or 'feeling' may learn manual skills easily but experience difficulties in academic subjects (which are more visual and verbal).

One of the key issues in micro modeling relates to how individuals use their senses and whether they have specialized with respect to particular senses.

Modeling Micro Strategies - The R.O.L.E. Model

The R.O.L.E. model (Dilts, 1987, 1991, 1993) is a micro modeling structure in NLP which summarizes and incorporates Aristotle's basic distinctions relating to the mind or 'psyche'. **R.O.L.E.** stands for **R**epresentational System-**O**rientation-**L**ink-**E**ffect. It may be used to define the micro level cognitive structure of a particular T.O.T.E. Each step in the T.O.T.E. involves the representation of some information which will be oriented to a certain part of the problem space and linked to other representations. The way in which information is represented, oriented and linked will produce a particular effect in terms of the overall process.

Step 1　　　　　　　　　**Step 2**

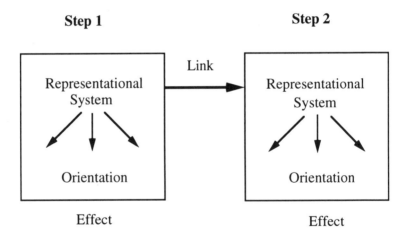

Basic Distinctions of the R.O.L.E. Model

In a spell checking program, as an analogy, the computer may be oriented to check a whole document or only selected portions of a document. Correct spellings may be represented by either a list of correct spellings or rules governing correct spellings. The way in which these various elements are defined and then linked together will determine the efficiency and accuracy of the program.

In the making of a meal, an analogy may be made between a specific recipe and the R.O.L.E. model elements. A recipe describes which ingredients are to be used, whether they should be fresh, marinated, preheated, etc., what they should be mixed or 'linked' with, and what kinds of effects should be produced at each step in the recipe. As another example, the opening passage of Genesis, implies that the way God represents his goals - i.e., "God *said*, 'Let there be...'" - is different than the representational system he uses to evaluate what he has created - i.e., "And God *saw* that it was good". In terms of the R.O.L.E. model it could be said that in God's 'micro strategy' for creation, words are linked to actions, the results of which are then visually inspected to determine whether they are complete.

Thus, the goal of the R.O.L.E. modeling process is to identify the essential elements of thinking and behavior used to produce a particular response or outcome. This involves identifying the critical steps of the mental strategy and the role each step plays in the overall neurological "program." This role is determined by the four factors which are indicated by the letters which make up the name of the **R.O.L.E.** Model.

1. <u>R</u>**epresentational Systems** have to do with which of the five senses are most dominant for the particular mental step in the strategy: **V**isual (sight), **A**uditory (sound), **K**inesthetic (feeling), **O**lfactory (smell), **G**ustatory (taste)[4]. As we have established, each representational system is designed

---

[4] In the NLP model, the various representational systems are often annotated as simply V, A, K, O or G for Visual, Auditory, Kinesthetic, Olfactory and Gustatory. Language and pure sound is distinguished by the subscripts A_d for words versus A_t for music and other non-verbal sound. The "d" stands for "digital" (separate discreet chunks) and the "t" indicates "tonal."

to perceive certain basic qualities of the experiences it senses. These include characteristics such as *color, brightness, tone, loudness, temperature, pressure,* etc. As we have mentioned earlier, these qualities are called "sub-modalities" in NLP since they are subcomponents of each of the representational systems.

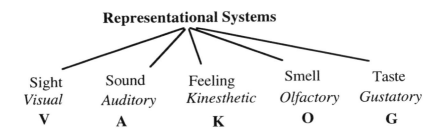

For example, if we were to consider the micro cognitive elements of the thinking strategy of a particular genius such as Leonardo or Einstein, the question would be, "When they think about a particular topic, which representational system do they use?" Through which of the senses did Einstein formulate his theory of relativity? Did it just come to him in words or as a completed mathematical formula? Were images or feelings involved? How did Leonardo conceive his machines? If he visualized them, were they in color? What role did the perspective or movement of the image play in his creative process? These are the types of question to be answered with respect to the "R" of the R.O.L.E. model: Which senses are involved, which sensory qualities were emphasized and to what degree were they relevant and necessary?

2. **Orientation** has to do with whether a particular sensory representation is focused (**e**)xternally toward the outside world or (**i**)nternally toward either (**r**)emembered or

(c)onstructed experiences.[5] For instance, one may "see" something in the outside world, in memory or in one's imagination.

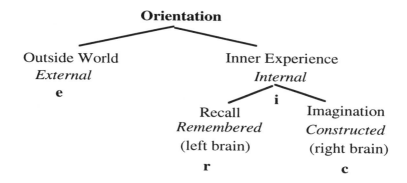

The habitual orientation of a representational system will influence a person's cognitive performance and that person's areas of strength. An individual who primarily orients his or her senses internally might be strong in theoretical processes. A person who is more externally oriented will most likely be a good observer. For instance, inventor Thomas Edison's comment that "Invention is 1% inspiration and 99% perspiration," implies an emphasis on the external orientation of his strategy in the form of observation and experimentation. Theoretical physicist Albert Einstein, on the other hand, tended to be more internally oriented and emphasized 'thought experiments' claiming, "Imagination is more important than knowledge." Mozart was able to orient his auditory representational system in all areas with equal ease, demonstrating exceptional abilities to perform (A^e), recall (A^r) and compose (A^c) music.

---

[5] In NLP shorthand, orientation is noted as a superscript to the letter indicating the particular sensory modality being used. For instance, V^r would indicate remembered visual imagery, K^e would indicate internal tactile 'kinesthetic' sensations, A_d^i would indicate internal dialog or 'self talk', etc.

3. **Links** have to do with how a particular step or sensory representation is linked to other representations in a person's micro strategy. For example, an appreciation of art tends to involve a linking of external images or sounds to internal emotional responses; i.e. people speak of being "moved" by a painting or a piece of music. Similarly, the "expression" of emotions through painting, music, poetry, dance and sculpture indicate a link in the direction starting with feelings and connecting to other representational systems.

There are two basic ways that representations can be linked together: sequentially and simultaneously.[6] Sequential links act as *anchors* or triggers such that one representation follows another in a linear chain of events. These links are established through Aristotle's 'law of association'. They relate to the order of the cognitive steps in a person's micro strategy. For example, a person may have a habitual sequence of representational systems in his or her decision making strategy such that external visual input is connected to emotional responses. His or her internal feelings trigger mental questions. The questions, in turn, bring about visual fantasizing about future choices or problems, and so on.

---

[6] In NLP notation 'sequential' links between representational systems are indicated by an arrow between one cognitive step and another, while simultaneous links are represented by a slash. Thus, $A_d -> V^r$ would indicate that after hearing some words an individual begins to form a constructed mental picture. The two cognitive processes are discrete and separate from each other in time. The notation A_t/V^r would indicate a cognitive process involving the immediate association of qualities of non-verbal sound with 'sub-modalities' of remembered imagery (for instance, music influencing the color or quality of movement of a visual memory).

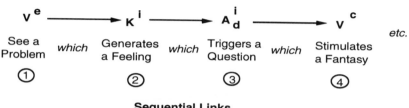

Sequential Links

Simultaneous links occur in what are called *synesthesias* (meaning 'a synthesis of the senses'). Synesthesia links have to do with the overlap between sensory representations through what Aristotle called the 'common sensibles'. As Bower's experiments demonstrated, visual and auditory qualities may be linked via shared 'formal qualities'. Similarly, certain qualities of feelings may be linked to certain qualities of imagery - for example, visualizing the shape of a sound or hearing a color.

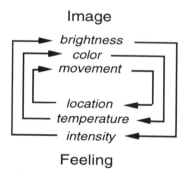

Synesthesia Links

Both of these types of links are essential to thinking, learning, creativity and the general organization of our experiences. A key issue in defining a particular micro strategy is "What type of links between the senses are being utilized?" If there is a sequential pattern, what is the necessary order of the associations between the senses? If there are simultaneous links, which qualities of one sense are linked to which qualities of the other sense?

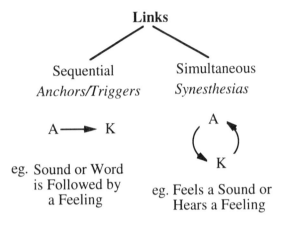

Clearly, the linkages between the senses are an important aspect of the cognitive processes underlying genius. The source of Disney's animated masterpiece *Fantasia* is the linking or 'synesthesia' between music and constructed visual imagery. Da Vinci's notebooks involve the continual movement between pictures and words. And, as he personally claimed, Aristotle's process of induction involved the linking of multiple sensory perceptions in the 'common sense'.

4. **Effect** has to do with the result or purpose of each particular step in the thought process. Effects relate to the role of a particular cognitive micro process with respect to the macro strategy or T.O.T.E. in which that micro strategy is functioning. For instance, the function of the step could be to a) generate or input a sensory representation, b) test or evaluate a particular state with respect to some criterion or c) operate to change some part of an experience or behavior. That is, depending on its orientation and type of link, a feeling could be a) information about what is happening in one's environment (that an object is hot or cold, for example),

b) part of a judgment or evaluation about one's environment (such as feeling that one likes or dislikes something) or c) an attempt to change or adjust one's behavior (like an athlete recalling a feeling of excitement in order to 'get up' for a contest).

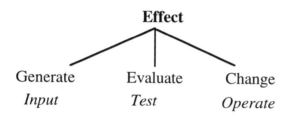

Effect

Generate   Evaluate   Change

Input   *Test*   *Operate*

The effect a particular representation produces in a micro strategy is a significant element of genius. In NLP there is a distinction made between an individual's most highly *developed*, most *highly valued* and most *conscious* representational system. This distinction reflects the typical effect of a particular representational system. If an individual, like Einstein for example, used visual images, feelings and words in his micro strategy, we will want to sort out the effect of each representational system in the strategy. Were images used to gather information, make conclusions or to conceptualize possible imaginary scenarios? Was the function of feelings to provide information or draw conclusions? Was the role of language to input ideas, apply rules or run calculations?

A person's most highly 'developed' system is the sense with which that person is able to make the greatest number of distinctions. A person's most highly 'valued' representational system is the one that person tends to use to evaluate the meaning of an experience and make decisions. A person's most 'conscious' system is the one in which that person has the most intentional ability to change and utilize. If someone has specialized strongly in the visual modality then the most highly developed, highly valued and conscious representational system may all be visual. Some people may have developed one of their senses to a high degree, but not value it as much as another one of their senses. For example, some people may highly value their feelings, but not be very aware of feelings or able to control them. Some people have a highly developed ability to visualize, but are not conscious of making visual images. A key issue in modeling the strategies of geniuses involves determining the degree to which the various senses are developed, valued and consciously utilized.

Language as a Tool of Thinking and Modeling

One way to determine the influence of a particular representational system in an individual's micro strategy is to examine how it is reflected in a person's language patterns. Language is clearly an important indicator of a person's internal cognitive processes. In his book *On Interpretation* Aristotle maintains:

> *"Spoken words are the symbols of mental experience and written words are the symbols of spoken words. Just as all men have not the same writing, so all men have not the same speech sounds, but the mental experiences, which these directly symbolize, are the same for all, as also are those things of which our experiences are the images."*

Aristotle's claim that words "symbolize" our "mental experience" echoes the NLP notion that written and spoken words are 'surface structures' which are transformations of mental 'deep structures'. As a result, words can both reflect and shape mental experiences. This makes them a powerful tool for thought. Because, as Aristotle points out, the "mental experiences" symbolized by the words are similar for different people, words are also a useful tool for modeling. By looking for the deep structure beyond the specific words used by an individual, we can identify the process level of the mental operations encoded within that person's language patterns. Similar mental processes may then be communicated and developed in other people through language and other 'surface structures'.

This requires that we consider the formal properties of language as much as its content; since a strategy is more about the form of a person's thinking process than the content. In examining the formal properties of language

Aristotle distinguished between the relative role of nouns and verbs.

> *"By a noun we mean a sound significant by convention, which has no reference to time, and of which no part is significant apart from the rest...Thus in the word 'pirate-boat' the word 'boat' has no meaning except as part of the whole word. The limitation 'by convention' was introduced because nothing is by nature a noun or name - it is only so when it becomes a symbol; inarticulate sounds, such as those which brutes produce, are significant, yet none of these constitutes a noun."*

> *"A verb is that which, in addition to its proper meaning, carries with it the notion of time. No part of it has any independent meaning, and it is a sign of something said of something else...'Health' is a noun, but 'is healthy' is a verb; for besides its proper meaning it indicates the present existence of the state in question."*

According to Aristotle, words are sounds that become symbols of mental experiences through the process of association. Nouns are sounds that become associated with our perceptions of 'things' (the "incidental objects of sense"). Verbs are sounds associated with our perceptions of the attributes of, or relationships between things (submodalities and "common sensibles") as they unfold with respect to time. Nouns are more related to the content of our experiences, while verbs symbolize characteristics and processes.

In the model of NLP, certain key verbs, or 'predicates', provide a strong indication of how a person is thinking. Words such as "see," "clearly," "show," "image," for instance, are indicative of visual processes. Words like "says," "sounds," "heard," "rings a bell," "tell," etc. indicate auditory or verbal experiences. Language patterns such as "feel," "rough," "be in touch with," "painful," "cold," etc. imply kinesthetic processes, and so on.

Modeling the Micro Structure of Aristotle's Thinking Strategy

By filtering for these types of words in a person's language, we can uncover important information about that individual's mental processes and strategies. For example, consider the following statement by Aristotle:

*"(1) No one can learn or understand anything in the absence of sense, and (2) when the mind is actively aware of anything it is necessarily aware of it along with an **image**...To the thinking soul **images** serve as if they were contents of perception...just as if it were **seeing**, it calculates and deliberates what is to come by reference to what is present; and when it makes a **pronouncement**, as in the case of sensation it **pronounces** the object to be **pleasant** or **painful**, in this case it **avoids** or **pursues**."*

In the NLP view, Aristotle's description of the general functioning of "the mind" is probably a projection of his own general mental strategy. Judging by his choice of words, it would seem that this strategy has a particular sequence which begins with the association of external sensory input to internal visual representations (V^i). The mind then "calculates and deliberates" by "seeing" or constructing mental "images" (V^c) of "what is to come by reference to what is present" (most likely through internal patterns of association). These images are evaluated via a verbal process. The mind makes a "pronouncement" (A_d^i) from which physical actions are initiated. The "pronouncement" is most likely derived through the process of applying some kind of syllogism.

Aristotle's language patterns imply that, for him, the visual representational system is both conscious and highly developed. The abilities to "calculate" and "deliberate what is to come by reference to what is present" just as if one "were seeing" presupposes that one is consciously aware of one's internal imagery, is able to perceive distinctions and relationships between images and can manipulate those images to a certain degree. Aristotle's statement that the mind makes a "pronouncement" about an experience would imply that the output of the verbal representational system is most highly valued. That is, while mental images provide the input and operations for the mental strategy, language evaluates these visual contents and provides the basis for behavioral action. Of course, Aristotle's description that the object is determined to be "pleasant or painful" implies some kind of internal feeling response (K^i), but his language does not make it clear whether or not the pain or pleasure are directly experienced.

In another statement, however, Aristotle indicates that the experience of internal feelings does indeed play an important role in this overall strategy in the form that he called "appetites" and "desires." Appetites and desires were feelings formed relative to some goal or end - which was provided for them by the contents of ongoing perception, memory or imagination.

> "[M]ind is never found producing movement without appetite...but appetite can originate movement contrary to calculation...[I]t is the object of appetite which originates movement, this object may be either the real or the apparent good...

> "[A]ppetites run counter to one another, which happens when a principle of reason and desire are contrary and is possible only in beings with a sense of time (for while mind bids us hold back because of what is future, desire is influenced by what is just at hand: a pleasant object which is just at hand presents itself as both pleasant and good, without condition in either

case, because want of foresight into what is farther away in time)."

The implication is that "appetites" are internal feeling states which operate on what Freud called the 'pleasure principle' - the pursuance of pleasure and avoidance of pain. These feeling reactions may be brought about by either ongoing experiences or through mental calculations. Ongoing experiences can create a feeling of "pleasantness" or "unpleasantness" - presumably via the ratios between the "pairs of contraries" (or 'sub-modalities') which make up their sensory qualities. The "goodness" of an object, on the other hand, seems to come as the result of 'calculations' (projections of future consequences).

Aristotle maintains that conflicts between feelings are created by the perception of time because principles of "reason" and "desire" can potentially operate in different time frames. "Reason" tends to be more associated with the perception of the future and "desire" with the present. We also tend to associate "reason" and the process of "reasoning" with verbal analysis. Aristotle implies that the experience of "what is future" can produce a perception of something as "good," but what is "just at hand" can be "both pleasant and good." Problems arise when one is torn between "what is future" and what is "just at hand" or "because of a want of foresight into what is farther away in time."

Synthesizing Aristotle's comments together as a reflection of his own internal mental processes and considering them in the light of his other comments about the 'psyche' and his own analytical process, we can begin to form a picture representing the cognitive micro structure of his thinking strategy:

1. Sensory experience serves as both the input *("no one can learn or understand anything in the absence of sense")* and ultimate confirmation of internal mental processes

(credit must be given to observation rather than to theories, and to theories only insofar as they are confirmed by the observed facts.").

2. As input, sensory experience has two influences:

   a) the ratios of the 'submodalities' associated with the sensory experience produce an immediate sensation *("the sense itself is a 'mean' between any two opposite qualities which determine the field of that sense")* which may be perceived as either pleasurable or painful;

   b) the sensory experience becomes associated with an internal "image" or representation related to the external input *("out of sense-perception comes to be what we call memory, and out of frequently repeated memories of the same thing develops experience; for a number of memories constitutes a single experience")* - such as an "incidental object of sense". This "image" or map can produce a sense of "desirability" through ratios of internal submodality qualities.

3. Calculations and deliberations are made through a train of cause and effect associations connecting the present experience to projections of perceived future consequences *(just as if [the mind] were seeing, it calculates and deliberates what is to come by reference to what is present).*

4. Some kind of verbal evaluation is made about the future consequences (most likely in the "if-then" format of the syllogism) which "pronounces" something "good" and approachable or as something to be avoided *("it pronounces the object to be pleasant or painful, in this case it avoids or pursues").*

5. The three influences from the present (immediate sensation), past (the "image" derived from memories)

and the future (calculations of consequences) converge on the internal feelings associated with "Appetite." If the three evaluations (pleasure, desire & goodness) overlap, the choice of external behavioral action is obvious; if not, a conflict ensues in which presumably the stronger of the three prevails.

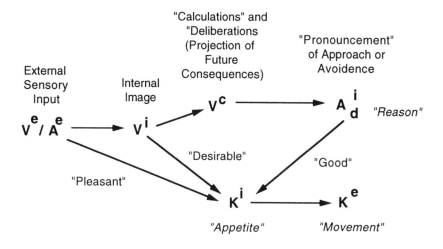

Cognitive Micro Structure of Aristotle's General Thinking Strategy

While it seems clear that Aristotle's strategies were responsible for producing some of the greatest advances in human thought (both in his own time and in later ages), modern society and education have tended to focus more on the discoveries resulting from these strategies than on the mental processes through which those discoveries were made. In the next section we will explore some of the ways we can apply Aristotle's micro, macro and meta strategies to make our own discoveries.

Applications of Aristotle's Strategies

The objective of the NLP modeling process is not to end up with the one 'right' or 'true' description of a particular person's thinking process, but rather to make an instrumental map that allows us to apply the strategies that we have modeled in some useful way. An 'instrumental map' is one that allows us to act more effectively - the 'accuracy' or 'reality' of the map is less important than its 'usefulness'. A metaphorical map (such as the 'thought experiments of Albert Einstein), for instance, may have as much instrumental value as a 'realistic' map.

"Instrumental perfection" (Thompson, 1967) is achieved when a particular system of action corresponds tightly with the cognitive system used to describe it. The basic criterion for "instrumental perfection" is the degree of "closure" between the cognitive and behavioral systems - i.e., the congruence between the distinctions and relationships in the cognitive system and the behavioral operations and interactions for which they stand. The degree of "closure" is determined by the extent to which the variables in the cognitive map or logical system allow us to identify and mobilize empirical operations and resources that lead to effective and appropriate actions in the behavioral system.

Thus, the instrumental application of the micro, macro and meta strategies that we have modeled from a particular individual involves putting them into structures that allow us to use them for some practical purpose. This purpose may be similar to or different from that of the model which initially used them.

One way to think about practically applying the information modeled from an individual's mental strategies is that it may be implemented with respect to different parts of the T.O.T.E. That is, we may identify and apply a person's *goals* only; using other operations to achieve those goals and other evidence procedures to assess progress towards the goals. Or, we may model the *operations* of an individual and apply those operations to achieve different goals than those for which they were originally intended. We may also choose to identify and use only the *evidences* or *evidence procedures* used by the model, applying them to different goals and with different operations than those for which they were originally developed.

Thus, we may use all or only parts of the information we have modeled from a particular genius. In Aristotle's case, for example, we can apply the strategies we have modeled by:

a) Exploring topics and areas that he did not himself consider or that were unavailable in his lifetime (such as using them as guidelines for our own study of genius),

b) Combining elements of his strategies with other methods and approaches in order to enhance and enrich them, or

c) Using them as the inspiration for building a completely new approach to thinking about something.

The following applications demonstrate how we can use the information we have gathered from our modeling of Aristotle's strategies in several different ways.

The S.C.O.R.E. Model:
Implementing Aristotle's Strategies for
Defining 'Problem Space'

One simple but powerful way to apply Aristotle's strategies for identifying 'problem space' is to matrix them with the S.C.O.R.E. model in NLP. The S.C.O.R.E. model (Dilts & Epstein, 1987, 1991) is essentially a problem solving model that identifies the primary components necessary for effectively organizing information about the problem space related to a particular goal or process of change. The letters stand for *Symptoms, Causes, Outcome, Resources,* and *Effects.* These elements represent the minimum amount of information that needs to be gathered to effectively address that problem space.

1. **Symptoms** are typically the most noticeable and conscious aspects of the presenting problem or present state. Defining symptoms involves identifying 'constraining causes' - i.e., the ongoing relationships, presuppositions and boundary conditions (or lack of boundaries) within a system which maintain the present or 'symptomatic' state.

2. **Causes** are the underlying elements responsible for creating and maintaining the symptoms. They are usually less obvious than the symptoms they produce. Defining causes involves identifying the 'antecedent' or 'precipitating causes' for those symptoms - i.e., past events, actions or decisions that influence the present or 'symptomatic' state through a linear chain of 'action and reaction'.

3. **Outcomes** are the particular goals or desired states that would take the place of the symptoms. Defining

outcomes involves identifying 'formal causes' - i.e., determining the fundamental form of the outcome and how specifically will one know when one has reached it. Defining outcomes is an important part of establishing the problem space in that it is the gap between the present and desired states that determines the scope of the problem.

4. **Resources** are the underlying elements responsible for removing the causes of the symptoms and for manifesting and maintaining the desired outcomes. In a sense, defining resources involves finding the 'middles' relating to reaching the desired outcomes and transforming the causes of the symptoms.

5. **Effects** are the longer term results of achieving a particular outcome. Positive effects are typically the reason or motivation for wanting the outcome to begin with (projected negative effects can create resistance or ecological problems). Specific outcomes are generally stepping stones to get to a longer term effect. Defining effects involves identifying 'final causes' - i.e., future objectives, goals or ends which guide or influence the system giving current actions meaning, relevance or purpose.

As an example, let's say a person is experiencing anxiety in certain public speaking contexts. Exploring the *symptom* would involve identifying the behavioral and environmental conditions and constraints that accompany the anxiety. For instance, is there a particular size of group, type of group or topic that produces the anxiety? Does it relate to constraints such as time limits or restricted space? Is the person constrained by his or her posture, breathing pattern or pattern of movement? Is the person constrained by his or her 'psyche'? What sort of internal feelings, mental imagery and self talk accompany the anxiety?

Exploring the *causes* of the symptom would involve focusing on the antecedent causes of the anxiety. Has the person always experienced anxiety in these contexts? When did the anxiety first start? Is the anxiety related to particular associations or 'anchors' such as certain beliefs or memories (i.e., past humiliations or failures)? How are those beliefs or memories represented? As feelings? images? words? smells? What are the ratios of submodality qualities associated with those beliefs or memories that make them seem unpleasant or painful? If there are images, are they moving or still? Colorful or black and white? Dim or bright? If there are words, are they loud or quiet? High pitched or low pitched? Rhythmic or monotoned? If there are feelings, are they warm or cool? Hard or soft? Heavy or light? Which 'common sensibles' are most relevant? Where are the images, sounds, feelings, smells, etc. located? In front of the person? Behind the person? Above? Below? Is there movement? Is the person experiencing the memories 'in time' or 'through time'?

Exploring the *outcome* would involve clearly and solidly establishing the fundamental form of the desired state that would take the place of the anxiety in the problematic public speaking contexts. How does the person want to respond instead of experiencing anxiety? How would the person know he or she was *not* anxious? How would the person act differently in terms of his or her posture, breathing pattern or pattern of movement? How would the person's internal feelings, mental imagery and self talk change? As I mentioned earlier, the form of the outcome will establish the scope and level of the problem. That is, if the person's outcome is to simply be more comfortable when speaking, then the scope of the problem will probably stay focused on the level of capabilities and behaviors. If the person's outcome is to be a trainer or politician, the problem space will also likely involve issues related to beliefs and identify.

Exploring the desired *effects* would involve identifying the longer term purposes and positive results of effective public speaking. What are the positive effects, benefits and 'payoffs' of competent public speaking? What other capabilities, activities and projects does effective public speaking open up? What core values and beliefs does it fulfill? How will the person be able to be more of who he or she truly is through effective public speaking? Who else, that the person is close to, would be positively affected by the person's public speaking ability? What feelings of satisfaction, confidence and contribution will the longer term results of effective public speaking include? Can the person represent those positive beliefs, values and projections as feelings? Images? Words? Which submodality qualities would make those effects seem even more desirable?

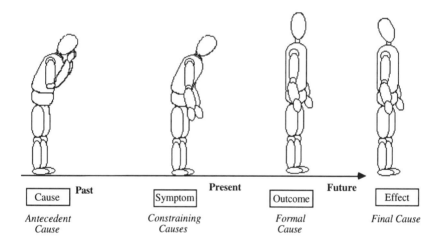

Placing The S.C.O.R.E. Elements of a Problem Space on a Time Line

One way to organize information relating to the S.C.O.R.E. model is to put it on a time line such that the antecedent cause is farthest back on the time line to a location representing the time frame in which the symptom started. The present state or symptom can be placed in a location representing the present or ongoing time frame. The desired outcome would be positioned slightly beyond the present to a location representing the time frame in the future in which the outcome is to be achieved. And the effect would be placed somewhere just beyond the outcome. This may be done mentally, on paper or, as the diagram suggests, by using physical locations. One advantage of using physical locations is that they help to more easily and clearly sort out the different causes and keep them separate. It also makes it possible to tangibly and experientially explore the physiological pattern (such as posture, breathing, movement, etc.) associated with each element.

Placing the elements on a time line also makes it easier to see potential conflicts and issues related to time and the perception of what is "just at hand" and what is "future." For instance, in the example of anxiety related to public speaking that we have been exploring, there is a kind of dilemma between that which is "just at hand" and is perceived as "unpleasant" or "painful" (speaking in front of a group), and something in the "future" that is considered desirable or "good" (the positive effects of public speaking). Often in such cases, something in the environment triggers an internal "image" related to several unpleasant experiences in the past *("for a number of memories constitutes a single experience").* Given that the mind "calculates and deliberates what is to come by reference to what is present" anxiety is produced due to the projection of the recurrence of the past problems.

If there is no representation of the desired outcome or effects, the person would probably avoid public speaking. If there is a representation of a desired future outcome and/or effect a conflict ensues between what is perceived as unpleasant in the present and what is "pronounced" desirable and good in the future. The resolution comes when the appropriate resources are found that adequately address the problem space by reducing or transforming the sense of unpleasantness related to the present and enriching or intensifying the desirability of the future 'good'.

Exploring resources would involve identifying areas of 'solution space'. Solution space is a function of mobilizable capabilities and operations which have not yet been applied to the problem situation that would a) reduce or transform the constraining and antecedent causes or their degree of influence, and b) support reaching the outcome and desired effects.

Resources relating to the achievement of the outcome and effects may be discovered or developed using Aristotle's strategy of 'induction'. In what situations that could be anxiety producing, besides public speaking, is the person able to achieve his or her desired outcome? In what other situations has the person been able to transform anxiety into confidence? What do those situations have in common? What do these resourceful situations share in terms of the person's posture, breathing pattern or pattern of movement? What themes in terms of the person's beliefs, internal feelings, mental imagery and self talk are held in common?

Resources relating to constraining and antecedent causes may be discovered by applying Aristotle's principles of 'conversion' to seek counter examples. For example, once we think we have identified the antecedent and constraining causes associated with the symptom we can identify potential resources by identifying the counter examples and exceptions to the rules that point to which other attributes and operations influence those cause-effect relationships. If the anxiety is associated with a particular size of group, for instance, we can ask whether there has ever been a time when the person spoke in front of a group this size and was *not* anxious? What was the difference? If this was a group of friends/children/animals would the person still feel anxious? What makes the difference? What changes of posture, breathing pattern or pattern of movement would make it difficult for the person to maintain the feeling of anxiety even in front of that size of group? What changes in mental imagery or self talk (color, distance, volume, location, etc.) would reduce the anxiety?

Finding resources through counter examples has a double advantage in that the counter example will have an influence both on the level of behavior or capability and on the level of belief. That is, as an 'exception to the rule' a counter example provides us with alternative operations and pathways within the system we are managing; but a counter example also challenges the universality or 'rigidity' of certain limiting beliefs. For instance, the statement, "Groups that size always make me anxious," is a belief as much as it is a statement about an actual constraining cause. Thus, finding counter examples not only relieves constraints but opens up the possibility for new and more empowering beliefs.[7]

As another example, suppose we have discovered that the person's anxiety is associated with the memory of a past humiliating experience while speaking in front of a group. We can explore areas of potential resources and solution space by asking what knowledge and capabilities the person now has that he or she did not have at that time, that would have made the situation different? How would that past situation have been different if the person had possessed this knowledge or those capabilities at that time? If the person had been as clear about his or her outcome and desired effect as he or she is now, would it have made a difference? How would the person's perception of the memory change if it was experienced 'through time' or 'in time'? What changes of posture, breathing pattern or movement would have positively influenced the outcome of that past experience? What changes in mental imagery or self talk (color, distance, volume, location, etc.) alter the emotional affect of the memory?

---

[7] Counterexamples are a powerful therapeutic tool that can even influence physical health. For instance, the NLP Allergy technique (Dilts, 1988 and Dilts, Hallbom & Smith, 1990) applies this structure to help people achieve relief from allergic reactions.

Activating or bringing resources into the problem space may be achieved through 1) some 'real time' process such as simulation or role playing, 2) imagination or 3) the process of association or 'anchoring' (e.g. a resource may be associated with a particular object, symbol or even a touch, that may be used to help activate that resource in the problematic situation).[8]

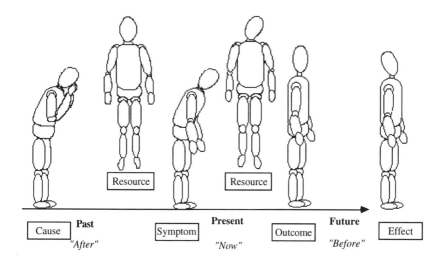

Bringing Resources Into a Problem Space

Although we have been using a personal example as an illustration, this process can obviously be applied to other 'problem spaces' such as group or organizational issues where symptoms may be issues such as a drop in motivation or productivity. In such an example antecedent causes may range from role conflicts to communication problems. Establishing outcomes would involve setting specific objectives

[8] NLP has many techniques for activating and transferring resources. In addition to 'anchoring' there are processes such as 'future pacing', the 'new behavior generator', the 'swish pattern' and many others described in the numerous books on NLP.

relating to motivation or productivity. Effects and final causes would include longer term benefits (such as better profitability) and the pursuit of the group or organizational vision and mission. Resources could include changes in technology or procedures and the implementation of training programs or other instruments of organizational learning, etc.

In summary, the process involves the following basic steps:

1. Identify the symptom and the 'constraining causes' related to maintaining the present state.
   What is the 'symptom' in this problem?
   What constraints, relationships, presuppositions and boundary conditions (or lack of boundaries) are associated with the symptom?

2. Identify the 'antecedent causes' related to the history and development of the symptom.
   What is the 'cause' of the symptom in this problem?
   Which past events, actions or decisions were involved in creating the symptom?

3. Identify the outcome and the fundamental formal characteristics of the outcome that will be your evidence that the outcome is being reached.
   What is the desired 'outcome' or goal that would take the place of the symptom?
   What fundamental assumptions and perceptions define this outcome? What will you see, hear or feel that will let you know you have attained your desired state?

4. Identify the desired effects or 'final causes' of reaching the outcome
   What will be the longer term 'effects' of reaching that outcome?
   What will reaching the outcome do for you? What longer term future objectives, goals or ends give the outcome meaning, relevance or purpose?

5. Identify resources that will help to reach the desired outcome and effect by using the process of induction to explore the structure of other successful situations.
   What resources would help achieve the outcome?
   In what other situations or contexts are you able to easily attain your desired outcome and / or effect? What is common to those situations?

6. Identify resources that will help to transform antecedent or constraining causes or alter their influence by applying the principles of 'convertibility' in order to find counter examples.
   What resources would help influence or transform or alleviate the past cause or present constraints?
   In what situations or context does / would the cause or constraints not produce the symptom? What is the difference?

7. Activate or transfer the appropriate resources within the context in which the symptom has been occurring.

Implementing Aristotle's Strategy for Exploring and Organizing a Problem Space

I mentioned earlier that Aristotle's ability to record and express his ideas and discoveries was as important as his ability to make them. This next application combines Aristotle's strategies with an NLP strategy for creative writing and composition (Dilts, 1983) as a method to explore, organize and express one's thoughts about a particular problem space.

The NLP composition strategy leads a person to elaborate and enrich a beginning sentence into a paragraph by using key words or 'prompts' to draw out related ideas through the process of association. For example, one method for finding what Aristotle called "the middle" involves the use of words known as 'connectives'. Connectives are words or phrases that link one idea to another; such as:

because	*before*	*after*
while	*whenever*	*so that*
in the same way that	*if*	*although*

We relate ideas together through these 'connective' words. For instance, if we were to say "Aristotle was a genius," and follow it with the word "because" we would be lead to identify some 'middle term' related to our conclusion. As an example, we might say, "Aristotle was a genius *because* he was able to bring clarity and simplicity to complex issues." This 'middle term' now becomes a first term, and we repeat the process by saying, "He was able to bring clarity and simplicity to complex issues *because* he developed effective strategies for organizing his experience of the world." The process is then repeated again; "He developed effective strategies for organizing his experience of the world *because* he was able to balance both his own childlike curiosity and his ability to think logically."

This process is continued either a) an arbitrary number of times (such as four or five repetitions) or b) until it becomes difficult to make any other associations. Then, we can collect together our group of associations into a paragraph by simply leaving out the connective word "because" and capitalizing the first word of each phrase. In the above example we would then find a paragraph reading:

> *"Aristotle was a genius. He was able to bring clarity and simplicity to complex issues. He developed effective strategies for organizing his experience of the world. He was able to balance both his own childlike curiosity and his ability to think logically."*

Different connectives will tend to lead us to think in terms of the different types of causes. Words like "while" and "whenever", for instance will lead us to think in terms of 'constraining causes'. Words like "before" and "after" will probably lead us to think in terms of 'precipitating causes'. A phrase like "so that" would lead us to think in terms of 'final causes'; whereas a word like "if" or phrase like "in the same way that" will prompt us to think in terms of 'formal causes'. A word like "although" prompts us to find potential constraints and counterexamples and helps us to check the strength of our premises.

For example, if we took the same beginning statement used above, "Aristotle was a genius" but applied the connective phrase "so that" we will end up with a completely different train of associations. We might say, "Aristotle was a genius *so that* The wisdom of the Greek civilization was expressed and preserved for future generations *so that* We can continue to revive and apply that wisdom to today's problems and issues *so that* The generations that follow us will have a better world *so that...*", etc. Applying the connective "if" would lead us in another direction: "Aristotle was a genius *if* We consider the amount of influence someone has on later generations as an indicator of genius *if* We value long term contributions more than short term successes *if* We are able to seriously 'calculate and deliberate what is to come by reference to what is present' *if...*", etc.

It is also possible to sequence connectives in order to draw out more complex patterns of associations. For instance, we could start by saying, "Aristotle was a genius *in the same way that* Leonardo was a genius." Then we could shift to another type of connective, such as "because" in order to draw out our ideas about that relationship.

We can also direct our associations to perceptions involving different sensory representational systems and different time frames by adding some additional prompts after the connective. For example, adding the words "because I see that" will lead us to focus on our own visual perspective. Adding the words "because he said that" will direct us to another perspective and representational modality.

The table below shows a listing of possible connectives, perspectives and representational system words that can be combined using this type of strategy to explore a problem space.

Connective	Perspective	Representational System and Time Frame	
because	I	see(s) - saw - will see	*that*
before	We	look(s) - looked - will look	*like*
after	You	show(s) - showed - will show	
while	They	hear(s) - heard - will hear	
whenever	He	sound(s) - sounded - will sound	
if	She	say(s) - said - will say	
although	It	feel(s) - felt - will feel	
so that		touch(es) - touched - will touch	
in the same way that		move(s) - moved - will move	

The following steps summarize one way to apply some of the information we have gathered about Aristotle's strategy for analysis using the method I have just described.

1. Choose a topic, subject or phenomenon to analyze or 'unravel' and identify several examples to refer to.
   e.g. Topic: *Genius*
   Examples: *Aristotle, Leonardo, Einstein*

2. Consider what is common to all of the examples you have chosen.

3. Make four beginning sentences by answering Aristotle's four fundamental questions:

What is its nature?

   X is/are _____.

What are its attributes?

   X has/have (many) _____.

What causes or makes it?

   _____ causes/makes X.

What does it cause or make?

   X causes/makes _____.

For example:
"Genius is the ability to discover, create or represent fundamental ideas and relationships."
"Geniuses have the ability to perceive many dimensions and levels of a problem space."
"Special but learnable cognitive strategies cause genius."
"Genius makes it possible to find new ideas and translate them into reality."

4. Check your premises by applying Aristotle's rules of conversion, finding areas where there are potential counter examples and exceptions to the rule.

  e.g. *Is it possible to discover, create or represent fundamental ideas and relationships and not be a genius?*
  Is it possible to have the ability to perceive many dimensions and levels of a problem space and not be a genius?
  Is it possible to be a genius without special but learnable cognitive strategies?
  Would it be possible to find new ideas and translate them into reality if there were no geniuses?

5. Explore the 'causes' and 'middles' related to your premises by using prompt words such as "because" and writing down the association that comes up for you. Continue to use the prompt after each answer in the manner described earlier in order to draw out your ideas related to the topic.

  a) To explore constraining causes you can use the words *"while"* or *"whenever."*
  b) To explore precipitating causes you may want to use the words *"before"* or *"after."*
  c) To explore formal causes you can try the words *"in the same way that"* or *"if."*
  d) To explore final causes you can substitute the phrase *"so that."*
  e) To explore potential counterexamples and constraints in order to check the strength of your cause-effect premises you can substitute the word *"although."*

  You can add sensory oriented terms such as *"because I see"* or *"after he felt,"* etc. in order to explore different sensory channels and perspectives.

6. Read the sentences/ideas you have written one after the other leaving out the connective words. If what you have written does not adequately represent all of your ideas, you may repeat the process again with a different set of prompts. If you are satisfied with the flow of ideas then you may now refine or add to them to make them into a paragraph and write them down.

7. When you have finished exploring all four beginning sentences, you may want to identify another set of three examples that have the same quality. Determine what is common to these examples. Find the characteristics that are similar between the two sets of common elements from the different sets of examples.

Finding A System of Causes
In A Problem Space

Another way to apply this method as a means of exploring potential causes and problem space would be to pick a problem or symptom and then systematically go through each of the connectives to find any relevant associations, assumptions or beliefs. For example, if we were to choose to explore the problem space of the symptom of anxiety related to public speaking we could have the person start with a statement of the problem or symptom such as "I get anxious when I speak in front of a large group." Holding this problem statement constant, we lead the person through each connective to explore the total 'space' of causes related to that symptom:

e.g.

I get anxious when I speak in front of a large group
because _____

I get anxious when I speak in front of a large group
before _____

I get anxious when I speak in front of a large group
after _____

I get anxious when I speak in front of a large group
while _____

I get anxious when I speak in front of a large group
whenever _____

I get anxious when I speak in front of a large group
so that _____

I get anxious when I speak in front of a large group
if _____

I get anxious when I speak in front of a large group
although _____

I get anxious when I speak in front of a large group
in the same way that _____

Different perspectives, representational systems and time frames could be added in order to make an even more thorough exploration of the problem space. That is, applying the table provided earlier, the person could cycle through various prompts such as, "I get anxious when I speak in front of a large group *after I hear that...*" or "I get anxious when I speak in front of a large group *because they look like...*" or "I get anxious when I speak in front of a large group *in the same way I felt that...*" , etc.

This process can then be repeated with the statement of the outcome to identify potential desired effects and final causes. Thus, if the person's outcome statement is, "I want to feel comfortable and confident when I speak in front of a large group," we would have the person hold this statement constant and repeat the cluster of connectives:

e.g.

I want to feel comfortable and confident when I speak in front of a large group

> *because* _____
>
> *before* _____
>
> *after* _____
>
> *while* _____
>
> *whenever* _____
>
> *so that* _____
>
> *if* _____
>
> *although* _____
>
> *in the same way that* _____

Resources may be identified by altering the outcome statement slightly and repeating the process. Instead of saying, "I want to feel comfortable and confident when I speak in front of a large group," the person can say:

I can/will be comfortable and confident when I speak in front of a large group

because _____

before _____

after _____

while _____

whenever _____

so that _____

if _____

although _____

in the same way that _____

Again, the table provided earlier may be used to explore different perspectives, representational systems and time frames in order to make an even more thorough exploration of the desired state and potential 'solution space'.

Through the use of such verbal 'prompts', the sophstication and power of Aristotle's strategy can be harnessed and applied to everyday issues and problems. The method is so simple that even a child can do it. In fact, I have been involved in developing applications of this strategy that help children as well as adults to develop problem solving and creative writing skills.[9] The applications involve putting the prompting words on the faces of a specially designed block. The block may then be rotated, revealing the key words in a particular sequence. The method has been used with success to teach children and adults who have difficulty writing, as well as to release and enhance the skills of average writers.

---

[9] Available from Text Blox Inc. of Santa Cruz, California. See Afterword for further information.

Summary

In this chapter we have applied NLP processes for micro, macro and meta modeling to studying and utilizing Aristotle's strategies for getting to 'first principles'. We have explored how Aristotle used such meta strategies as asking basic questions and the process of 'inductive reasoning' to explore the basic structure of various 'problem spaces' and then to express that structure in the form of verbal 'syllogisms'.

On the level of his macro strategies, we have explored how Aristotle sought to determine the influence of formal causes, antecedent causes, constraining causes and final causes in the mechanisms of both biological and inorganic phenomena. We also examined his views on the role of time perception and different types of perception of time, and some of Aristotle's methods for evaluating the depth and 'universality' of his own conclusions, assumptions and premises.

At a micro level, we reviewed Aristotle's model of the mind (or 'psyche') and the role of the five senses in the thinking process. We examined Aristotle's perspectives about the mechanism and significance of memory, imagination and the fundamental process of association. We also explored Aristotle's ideas about the influence of specific characteristics and qualities of sensory experience and the important role of 'common sensibles' in thinking. By utilizing certain language patterns as a tool for modeling underlying cognitive patterns we outlined the micro structure of Aristotle's thinking strategy.

Synthesizing the information from these various explorations into an 'instrumental map', we have gone over some techniques and methods for applying Aristotle's strategies by combining them with certain NLP principles and processes. I have presented one method for defining a 'problem space' and am seeking new solution spaces utilizing the S.C.O.R.E. model, and another involving the use of key words and special verbal 'prompts' for discovering, organizing and expressing new areas of a problem space and potential resources and solutions.

In addition to what we have learned about Aristotle we have also introduced most of the basic NLP distinctions and models including the S.O.A.R., T.O.T.E., R.O.L.E. and S.C.O.R.E. models. The S.O.A.R. model provides us with the basic 'meta' distinctions of 'problem space', 'states' and 'operators'. The T.O.T.E. model provides the basic distinctions related to the fundamental feedback loops that make up our 'macro' strategies in terms of our 'goals', 'evidence's and choices of 'operations'. The R.O.L.E. model provides the essential distinctions for modeling the cognitive micro structure of a person's strategies including representational systems and their orientation links to other mental processes and their effects within the strategy. The S.C.O.R.E. model provides the fundamental elements involved in defining a problem space and reaching appropriate resources and adequate solution space.

In the following chapters, we will continue to revisit and apply Aristotle's methods to our study of the strategies of the other geniuses we will be examining. Using Aristotle's methods, perhaps we can arrive at some universal premises and first principles that will enlighten us even more richly about the practical nature of the strategies of genius.

Bibliography for Chapter 1

Aristotle, *Britannica Great Books,* Encyclopedia Britannica Inc., Chicago Ill., 1979.

The Encyclopedia Britannica, Encyclopedia Britannica Inc., Chicago Ill., 1979.

The Great Psychologists: Aristotle to Freud; Watson, R., J.B. Lippincott Co., New York, NY, 1963.

Toward a Unifying Theory of Cognition, M. Waldrop, *Science,* Vol. 241, July 1988.

SOAR: An Architecture for General Intelligence; Laird, J. E., Rosenbloom, P., and Newell, A., *Artificial Intelligence*, 33:1-64, 1987.

Chunking in SOAR; The Anatomy of a General Learning Mechanism; Laird, J. E., Rosenbloom, P., and Newell, A., *Machine Learning*, 1:11-46, 1986.

Plans and the Structure of Behavior, Miller, G., Galanter, E., and Pribram, K., Henry Holt & Co., Inc., 1960.

Principles of Psychology, William James, *Britannica Great Books,* Encyclopedia Britannica Inc., Chicago Ill., 1979.

The Structure of Magic Vol. I & II, Grinder, J. and Bandler, R.; Science and Behavior Books, Palo Alto, California, 1975, 1976.

Neuro-Linguistic Programming: The Study of the Structure of Subjective Experience, Volume I ; Dilts, R., Grinder, J., Bandler, R., DeLozier, J.; Meta Publications, Capitola, California, 1980.

Frogs into Princes, Bandler, R. and Grinder, J.; Real People Press, Moab, Utah, 1979.

Using Your Brain, Bandler, Richard; Real People Press, Moab, Utah,1984.

The Syntax of Behavior, Grinder, J. & Dilts, R., Metamorphous Press, Portland, OR, 1987.

Change Your Mind, Andreas, S., Andreas, C., Real People Press, Moab, Utah,1987.

Time Line Therapy, James, T., Woodsmall, W., Meta Publications, Capitola, CA, 1987.

Imagined Worlds: Stories of Scientific Discovery; Andersen, P., and Cadbury, D., Ariel Books, London, 1985.

Tools for Dreamers: Strategies for Creativity and the Structure of Invention, Dilts, R. B., Epstein, T., Dilts, R. W., Meta Publications, Capitola, Ca.,1991.

Applications of Neuro-Linguistic Programming, Dilts, R., Meta Publications, Capitola, Ca., 1983.

Organizations in Action, Thompson, J., McGraw Hill Inc., New York, NY, 1967.

Beliefs: Pathways to Health & Well Being, Dilts, Hallbom, Smith, Metamorphous Press, Portland, OR, 1990.

Sir Arthur Conan Doyle's
Sherlock Holmes

Chapter 2

Sherlock Holmes

Uncovering the Mysteries of Genius

Overview of Chapter 2

- Sherlock Holmes: An Example of Applying Strategies of Genius
- Holmes' Meta Strategy and 'The Great Chain of Life'
- Holmes' Micro Strategies for Observation, Inference and Deduction
- Holmes' Macro Strategy for Finding 'Antecedent Causes'
- Levels of Cues and Inferences
- Implementing Holmes' Strategy

    Observation and Deduction

    Calibration Exercise

    Detecting Deceit

    Observing Micro Behavioral Cues Associated with Cognitive Strategies: The B.A.G.E.L. Model
- Conclusion
- Bibliography and References for Chapter 2
- Footnotes to Chapter 2

SHERLOCK HOLMES
An Example of Applying
Strategies of Genius

Identifying the thinking process of a particular individual is a lot like detective work. This is especially the case with people who are not physically present or no longer living. Most of what we have to work with is in the form of clues left by those individuals in their writings and in the products or expressions of their thinking. We must work backwards from these clues to deduce the structure of the mental process which produced them.

It is fitting on a number of levels that Sir Arthur Conan Doyle's Sherlock Holmes be included in this series. First of all, as a fictitious character, Holmes represents a good example of the purpose of identifying strategies of genius to begin with: to model an exceptional thinking process and apply it to contexts other than one in which it was initially developed. Conan Doyle (1859-1930) modeled the methods and mannerisms of the great detective from one of his medical school professors, Dr. Joseph Bell of Edinburgh. Conan Doyle so admired his teacher's abilities to detect and diagnose medical problems that he fantasized about how the processes of this 'medical detective' could be applied to actual detective work. The result was Sherlock Holmes.

Sherlock Holmes' popularity and appeal comes from the way he thought. What makes Holmes special is his strategy for approaching a problem - his ability to observe, think and, perhaps most importantly, to be aware enough of his own process such that he can describe and explain it to someone else. Conan Doyle succeeded in being able to robustly capture the thinking process of his teacher and apply it to the interesting and exceptional contexts that made up Holmes' adventures.

Thus, while Holmes' character and adventures are fictitious, his thought process is authentic. The fact that he is imaginary only highlights the point that a particular strategy may be applied across many content areas, actual or simulated. It is important to keep in mind that this study of the cognitive strategies of genius is not about objective reality but about enriching subjective experience. This exploration of genius is about the structure of our inner models of the world, not the objective nature of the world. In fact, most acts of genius involve pushing or extending the perceived boundaries of our existing models of reality.

On another level, Holmes' particular area of genius is a metaphor for the task of uncovering the mysteries of the thought processes of genius. Using the cognitive modeling tools of Neuro-Linguistic Programming, we are attempting to be a kind of Sherlock Holmes of the mind. In that respect, his way of approaching a problem can provide some insights into the principles and skills that may be useful in accomplishing that task. At the same time, we are also attempting to be a Watson and chronicle that which we have discovered and experienced.

Holmes' Meta Strategy and 'The Great Chain of Life'

In the very first Holmes book, *A Study in Scarlet*, Conan Doyle gives us a hint about the 'meta strategy' through which Holmes viewed the problem space in which he worked. Watson is visiting Holmes for the first time and reports:

I picked up a magazine from the table and attempted to while away the time with it, while my companion munched silently at his toast. One of the articles had a pencil mark at the heading, and I naturally began to run my eye through it.

Its somewhat ambitious title was "The Book of Life," and it attempted to show how much an observant man might learn by an accurate and systematic examination of all that came in his way. It struck me as being a remarkable mixture of shrewdness and absurdity. The reasoning was close and intense, but the deductions appeared to me to be far fetched and exaggerated. The writer claimed by a momentary expression, a twitch of a muscle or a glance of an eye, to fathom a man's innermost thoughts. Deceit, according to him, was an impossibility in the case of one trained to observation and analysis. His conclusions were as infallible as so many propositions of Euclid. So startling would his results appear to the uninitiated that until they learned the processes by which he had arrived at them they might well consider him a necromancer.

'From a drop of water,' said the writer, 'a logician could infer the possibility of an Atlantic or a Niagara without having seen or heard of one or the other.

'So all life is a great chain, the nature of which is known whenever we are shown a single link of it. Like

all other arts, the Science of Deduction and Analysis is one which can only be acquired by long and patient study, nor is life long enough to allow any mortal to attain the highest possible perfection in it.'[1]

The article, Watson discovers, was written by Holmes. The title *The Book of Life* suggests that, like all geniuses, Holmes cast his endeavors inside the framework of an ambitious and ceaseless mission to uncover more of the deeper principles expressed in the phenomena of life. Holmes views 'life' as an interconnected system, a "great chain, the nature of which is known whenever we are shown a single link of it." Each part of the system carries information about all of the parts of the system - somewhat like a hologram, in which the whole image is spread to each piece of the hologram. This belief seems to be an important part of Holmes' strategy for investigation. Holmes' form of 'analysis and deduction' are an expression of the belief that a part of any system is an expression of the whole. As he maintained:

"The ideal reasoner would, when he had once been shown a single fact in all its bearings, deduce from it not only all the chain of events which led up to it but also all the results which would follow from it."[2]

Holmes' claim that a "momentary expression, a twitch of a muscle or a glance of an eye" can give us insight into a person's "innermost thoughts" is particularly relevant to our study. The implication is that even in seemingly trivial behaviors there are clues to what and how a person is thinking. Holmes claims that this ability is a learnable skill that may be acquired by study but that to someone unfamiliar with these skills it would appear that the person who has developed them would be a magician or "necromancer." In his article, Holmes provides some advice about how to go about acquiring this skill.

'Before turning to those moral and mental aspects of the matter which present the greatest difficulties, let the inquirer begin by mastering more elementary problems. Let him, on meeting a fellow-mortal, learn at a glance to distinguish the history of the man, and the trade or profession to which he belongs. Puerile as such an exercise may seem, it sharpens the faculties of observation, and teaches one where to look and what to look for. By a man's finger-nails, by his trouser-knees, by the callosities of his forefinger and thumb, by his expression, by his shirt-cuffs - by each of these things a man's calling is plainly revealed. That all united should fail to enlighten the competent inquirer in any case is almost inconceivable.'[3]

Holmes gives us a first insight into some key elements of his strategy when he describes his exercise in observation. The macro structure of his strategy involves the process of gathering a number of minor elements together to form a gestalt. By looking at a series of details, such as finger-nails, trouser-knees, callosities of the forefinger and thumb, expression, shirt-cuffs, etc., Holmes is able to infer what they would indicate "all united." While most people either ignore details or get caught up in them, Holmes is able to step back and see what they indicate as a totality. He is able to infer the characteristic of the whole forest by looking at the individual trees.

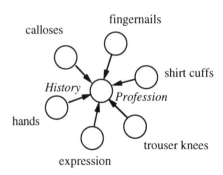

System of Cues 'Uniting' to Form a Conclusion

In fact, Holmes claimed that *"It has long been an axiom of mine that the little things are infinitely the most important,"* [4] and that his method was *"founded upon the observation of trifles,"* [5] concluding that *"To a great mind, nothing is little."*[6]

It is significant that Holmes suggests the observation of "fellow-mortals" as the starting place to develop the skills to comprehend the 'great chain' of life. While Holmes' genius is usually related to solving crimes and mysteries, it is important to remember that this ability derives from skill acquired by "mastering more elementary problems" - the observation of people. As Holmes explains to Watson:

> *"Observation with me is second nature. You appeared to be surprised when I told you, on our first meeting that you had come from Afghanistan."*
>
> *"You were told, no doubt."*
>
> *"Nothing of the sort. I knew you came from Afghanistan. From long habit the train of thought ran so swiftly through my mind that I arrived at the conclusion without being conscious of the intermediate steps. There were such steps, however. The train of reasoning ran, 'Here is a gentleman of a medical type, but with the air of a military man. Clearly an army doctor, then. He has just come from the tropics, for his face is dark, and that is not the natural tint of his skin, for his wrists are fair. He has undergone hardship and sickness, as his haggard face says clearly. His left arm has been injured. He holds it in a stiff and unnatural manner. Where in the tropics could an English army doctor have seen much hardship and got his arm wounded? Clearly in Afghanistan.' The whole train of thought did not occupy a second."* [7]

Here, Holmes gives a more specific description of some of the micro aspects of his strategy and offers us another insight into the nature of his genius - his ability to be aware of and reconstruct the "intermediate steps" of his "train of reasoning." Holmes' comment that, "From long habit the train of thought ran so swiftly through my mind that I arrived at the conclusion without being conscious of the intermediate steps," highlights one of the biggest problems in identifying the strategies of geniuses - the key mental processes have become so habitual and subtle that they take place outside of conscious awareness.

In other words, *the more one develops the ability to actually do something well, the less one is aware of **how specifically** one is doing it.* When they are in the act of accomplishing a task, people focus on *what* they are doing and not the subtle mental processes by which they are doing it. Thus, most effective behavior is characterized by 'unconscious competence'. While this reduces the amount of conscious effort one has to put into achieving a goal, it makes it difficult to describe to others how to develop the same degree of competence. Furthermore, people often downplay critical steps in their own thinking process as being 'trivial' or 'obvious' without realizing that those seemingly unimportant images, words or feelings that they are taking for granted are exactly what someone else might need to know how to perform the mental strategy.

Holmes' ability to be aware of his own thought process is called *meta-cognition;* which should be distinguished from 'self consciousness'. Unlike self consciousness, meta-cognition does not come from a seemingly separate 'self' who judges and interferes with the process under observation. Meta-cognition involves only the awareness of the steps of one's thought process. As Holmes demonstrates, meta-cognition will often only reach consciousness *after* the thought process is completed.

The value of meta-cognition is that, by making you aware of how you are thinking, it allows you to constantly validate or correct your inner thinking strategies. In fact, Holmes claimed that his genius was *"but systematized common sense."*[8] To use a computer analogy for a moment, most of the time a computer user does not see nor care about the programs that are making the computer function. But if you want to improve the functioning of the computer, "fix a bug" in its functioning or translate the program for a different type of computer, you need to be able to view and trace the set of instructions that make up the program.

What we learn from Holmes' description is that his process does indeed involve a "train of reasoning" as well as observation. Holmes does not simply observe a bunch of details and draw a conclusion. Rather, he makes inferences from relationships brought out through combinations of observations. That is, he does not simply look at somebody's skin color and deduce that they have been in the tropics. He looks at the relationship between the tint of his face and the tint of his wrists and infers that it is not the natural skin color, then he makes the conclusion that the person has been in the tropics. The conclusion is not in fact drawn from the observations themselves but from the cluster of inferences arrived at by linking certain observations together. A group of inferences is first drawn from observations of behavioral and environmental details and a conclusion is then drawn from the inferences.

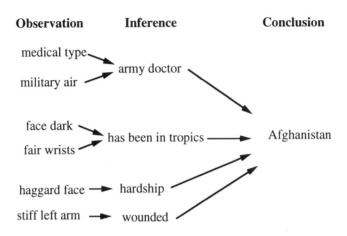

Drawing Inferences From a Cluster of Observations

The process of drawing an inference from the perception of a cluster of details is what Holmes considered "observation," not simply the act of perceiving the details. As he said to Watson, *"You see but you do not observe."*[9]   In *A Study In Scarlet* Holmes demonstrates and describes some of the micro aspects of his strategy again when he correctly deduces the background of a man who has come to see him as a client and whom he has never before met.

How in the world did you deduce that [he was a retired sergeant of Marines]?

Even across the street I could see a great blue anchor tattooed on the back of the fellow's hand.   That smacked of the sea.   He had a military carriage, however, and regulation side whiskers.   There we have the marine.   He was a man of some amount of self-importance and a certain air of command.   You must have observed the way in which he held his head and swung his cane. A steady, respectable, middle-aged man, too, on the face of him - all facts which lead me to believe that he had been a sergeant.[10]

In this example we again find Holmes linking together observations to make inferences and linking together inferences to make a conclusion. This process represents an example of what might be called *"convergent thinking"* - that is, inferences are linked and synthesized together, moving from the general to the specific, to form a single result.

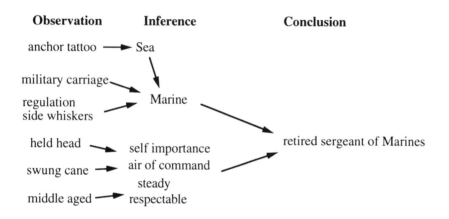

Forming a Conclusion from Observation and Inference

Holmes' Micro Strategies for Observation, Inference and Deduction

Clearly, Holmes' ability requires more than simply looking at details. As he himself points out, it is more than seeing. He 'deduces' his conclusions by relating observations and inferences to one another. In both this example with the marine sergeant and in his first encounter with Watson, Holmes first looks for clues from which he can infer the general characteristics of a person (i.e., the elderly fellow was a marine, and Watson was an army doctor) which he then combines with other observations and more specific inferences to draw his conclusion (i.e., the elderly gentleman had an air of self importance and command, and Watson had been in the tropics and had been wounded).

To do this, Holmes combines two processes: 1) noticing and giving meaning to externally perceived details and 2) synthesizing a cluster of meanings into a conclusion. He claimed that there should be *no combination of events for which the wit of man cannot conceive an explanation.*[11]

In *The Sign of Four*, Holmes clearly distinguishes and describes the relationship between his two micro strategies of *observation* and *deduction*.

But you spoke just now of observation and deduction. Surely the one to some extent implies the other."

"Why, hardly," he answered, leaning back luxuriously in his armchair and sending up thick blue wreaths from his pipe. *"For example, observation shows me that you have been to the Wigmore Street Post-Office this morning, but deduction lets me know that when there you dispatched a telegram."*

"Right!" said I. "Right on both points! But I confess that I don't see how you arrived at it. It was a sudden impulse upon my part, and I have mentioned it to no one."

"It is simplicity itself," he remarked, chuckling at my surprise - "so absurdly simple that an explanation is superfluous; and yet it may serve to define the limits of observation and deduction. Observation tells me that you have a little reddish mold adhering to your instep. Just opposite the Wigmore Street Office they have taken up the pavement and thrown up some earth which lies in such a way that it is difficult to avoid treading in it in entering. The earth is of this peculiar reddish tint which is found, as far as I know, nowhere else in the neighbourhood. So much is observation. The rest is deduction."

"How, then did you deduce the telegram?"

"Why, of course, I knew that you had not written a letter, since I sat opposite to you all morning. I see also in your open desk there that you have a sheet of stamps and a thick bundle of postcards. What could you go into the post-office for, then, but to send a wire? Eliminate all other factors, and the one which remains must be the truth."[12]

In the terms of NLP, Holmes' micro strategy for *observation* involves linking a feature, visually input from his ongoing external environment, to inner memories. This is done by matching features of what he is seeing in his external environment to features of remembered situations and events. In the example above the feature is the color of the mud.

Observation

Feature Matching

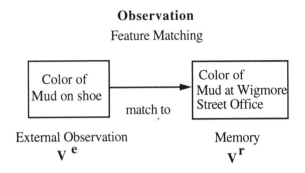

External Observation   Memory
V^e V^r

Holmes' Micro Strategy for Observation

In the model of NLP, this is a significant aspect of Holmes' strategy. In NLP a distinction is made between the *form* and the *content* of our experience. Shoes and mud are examples of content - the objects of our perception. Color is a formal quality that can apply across many contents. Color is the formal feature through which Holmes is able to associate and link his ongoing sensory experience with other experiences in his memory.

To observe, Holmes clearly relies on the visual representational system. Color is one of a number of features of vision that we have previously identified as 'submodalities'. Each of our sensory representational systems registers objects and events in terms of such features. In addition to color, our sense of sight, for instance, registers size, shape, brightness, location, movements, etc. The auditory representational system senses sounds in terms of features such as volume, tone, tempo and pitch. The kinesthetic system represents feelings in terms of intensity, temperature, pressure, texture and so on.

Unlike the average person, when Holmes is observing he pays more attention to the more formal qualities of what he is observing than to the content of his observation (the "incidental objects of sense"). While submodalities could be considered 'details' in a way, they are actually not just a smaller piece of an experience but rather a more abstract and formal feature of the object under observation. By extracting key features and using them as his basis for a memory search, Holmes is open to a wider variety of associations than someone who simply sees "mud."

Holmes description of his micro strategy for *deduction* indicates that it is primarily a 'process of elimination'. While Holmes' strategy for observation involves connecting a particular perception to other contexts and events through matching features, his strategy for deduction is oriented towards paring down the potential possibilities his observation has suggested in order to reach a single conclusion.

Deduction

Process of Elimination

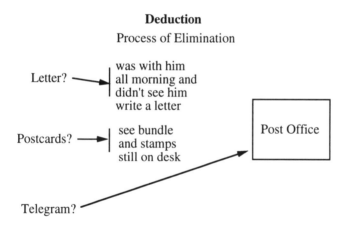

Holmes' Micro Strategy for Deduction

This deduction is accomplished by *imagining* or *inferring* other effects on the environment that a particular behavioral path would have to be made and then checking for the confirmation or absence of these effects in the environment. In order to have mailed a letter, Watson would have had to have written a letter. If Watson had gone to mail a postcard then he would have taken the stack of postcards on his desk.

As Holmes points out to Watson:

> *"If you can say definitely, for example, that some murder had been done by a man who was smoking an Indian lunkah, it obviously narrows your field of search. To the trained eye there is as much difference between the black ash of a Trichinopoly and white fluff of bird's-eye as there is between a cabbage and a potato."*
>
> *"You have an extraordinary genius for minutiae,"* I remarked.
>
> *"I appreciate their importance."*[13]

Holmes' process of deduction seems to rely heavily on the visual representational system. He uses visual memories or external observations that appear to be prompted or connected by verbal statements or questions. He certainly does not mention feelings or emotions as being a part of his strategy. In fact he stated, *"I use my head, not my heart,"*[14] and claimed that *"The emotional qualities are antagonistic to clear reasoning."* [15]

Watson's descriptions of Holmes *"staring at the ceiling with dreamy, lack-lustre eyes"*[16] while he was deep in thought also reflect the behavioral cues associated with visualization in NLP. The eyes oriented upward and defocused is considered to be the classic visual 'accessing cue' according to NLP. Such a posture would be indicative of deep internal visual processing.

Holmes' Macro Strategy for Finding 'Antecedent Causes'

Putting together the information we have gathered about Holmes' micro strategies for observation and inference, we can form a general idea of his basic macro strategy. It would appear that Holmes had a very highly developed strategy for finding what Aristotle called 'antecedent' or "precipitating' causes - past events, actions or decisions that influence the present state of a thing or event through a linear chain of 'action and reaction'.

The essential steps in Holmes' macro strategy for identifying antecedent causes seem to be:

1. Use observation to determine the effect of events on the environmental context.

2. Use inference to determine the possible behaviors that could have led to those environmental effects.

3. Use deduction to reduce the possible paths of behavior to a single probability.

As Holmes put it,

"It is an old maxim of mine, that when you have eliminated the impossible, whatever remains, however improbable, must be the truth."[17]

In the language of NLP, Holmes isolates certain key features of the *present state* of an event (i.e., color of mud on Watson's shoe) and uses them to make inferences about a possible *previous state* (i.e., Watson was at Wigmore Street Post Office because the color of mud is the same). Then he imagines possible combinations of *behavioral operations* which could have caused that previous state to occur (i.e., mailing a letter, mailing postcards, sending a telegram). He then uses other observations to confirm or reject the various possible behavioral paths (i.e., Watson did not write a letter that morning, a stack of postcards was still on his desk).

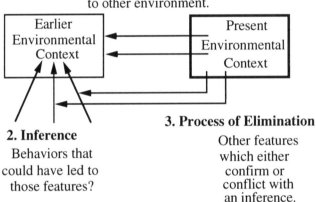

1. Observation

Features connecting
present environment
to other environment.

Earlier
Environmental
Context

Present
Environmental
Context

3. Process of Elimination

2. Inference

Behaviors that
could have led to
those features?

Other features
which either
confirm or
conflict with
an inference.

Diagram of Holmes' Basic Strategy for Deduction

There is one very important part of Holmes strategy, however, that he never mentions - how he determines what could be called the *problem space* within which to work. A problem space is defined by the parts of a system one considers to be relevant to the problem. What you consider the space of a problem to be will determine what kind of states you look for and how you define them. In order to draw an inference about a previous state, you must make *assumptions* about the problem space in which you are operating. One's definition of and assumptions about a problem space will influence and will be influenced by a number of key elements of problem solving:

1. *Interpretation of the meaning of an input or event.*

Interpretations in the form of inferences or conclusions involve connecting and fitting a particular input or event into other frameworks. For instance, in order for Holmes to conclude that Watson had been in Afghanistan after he had inferred that Watson was an army doctor with a tan and a wound, he had to have some knowledge of contemporary world events - in particular, recent British military campaigns. Holmes would not have drawn the same conclusion in today's world if he met a tan and wounded British Doctor. Likewise, in order for Holmes to perceive Watson as being a "medical type" with a "military air" or to recognize "regulation side whiskers" on the retired marine sergeant he had to attach his observations to certain assumptions. Many of Holmes inferences are based upon assumptions about cultural habits and attitudes and knowledge about context. The difficulty with this is that assumptions may be valid only within a narrow social or historical scope. This can make interpreting the meaning of clues and events subject to a lot of potential variation. As Holmes himself pointed out, *"Circumstantial evidence is a very tricky thing. It may seem to point very straight to one thing, but if you shift your own point of view a little, you may find it pointing in an equally uncompromising manner to something entirely different."*[18]

2. *Completeness/thoroughness of coverage of the problem space.*

Since everyone must make assumptions in order to give something meaning, we might ask, 'How does one minimize problems brought about by inappropriate assumptions or mistaken interpretations?' Holmes appears to apply the correct assumptions more often than his colleagues. How does he do it? One answer relates to how thoroughly one covers the total possible problem space. In his comment about circumstantial evidence, Holmes implies that there are multiple perspectives which can be taken. Perspective is one key element of problem space. Time frames are another.

Perceiving events from different time frames can change the implications that they have. Perhaps one reason that Holmes outperforms his peers and competitors is that he is simply more complete in his coverage of the possible perspectives and time frames that could be part of a particular problem space. In Holmes' words, *"One tries test after test until one or other of them has a convincing amount of support."*[19]

3. Order in which problem features / elements are attended to.

The sequence in which one makes observations and inferences can also influence the conclusion one draws - especially when inferences are being drawn from one another. Some inferences are not possible to make unless others have already been made. Holmes' use of the description "train of thought" implies a kind of sequence in which there is a logical dependency between each of the elements. As Holmes pointed out, *"When a fact appears to be opposed to a long train of deductions, it invariably proves to be capable of bearing some other interpretation."* Sequence is implicit in the concept of a 'strategy'. We have already identified a macro level sequence to Holmes process involving first observation, followed by inference and then finally deduction. On a more micro level, Holmes appears to initially pay attention to clues that would give him contextual information and then detail the actions or events that have taken place within that context.

4. Priority given to problem elements / features.

While Holmes appreciates the importance of "minutiae" he does not value all of them equally. In addition to sequence, the priority or emphasis given to various clues or elements determines their influence in shaping an inference or conclusion. As Holmes points out, *"It is of the highest importance in the art of detection to be able to recognize, out of a number of facts, which are incidental and which are vital.*[20] Clearly, Holmes emphasizes the importance of different clues depending on his perception of their relevance to what he is investigating. For instance, certain clues give more indications about the character of a person, others give more information about the recent behaviors of a person, others are more priorital in determining what environment someone has recently been in.

5. *Additional knowledge about the problem from sources outside the problem space.*

The assumptions used to give meaning to clues and features are often derived from information that comes from knowledge brought to bear on a particular problem from frameworks or sources not directly related to the problem space. Holmes used not only knowledge about cultural patterns and world events but also relatively obscure and sometimes esoteric knowledge to make inferences and draw conclusions. He maintained, *"Breadth of view is one of the essentials of our profession. The interplay of ideas and the oblique uses of knowledge are often of extraordinary interest."*[21]

6. *Degree of Involvement of Fantasy and Imagination*

Another source of knowledge that originates outside of a particular problem space is *imagination*. Holmes often utilized his imagination to make inferences, claiming that his methods were based on a *"mixture of imagination and reality"*[22] and that he employed *"the scientific use of the imagination."*[23] For instance, in the case of *Silver Blaze* Holmes is able to locate a lost race horse by imagining what a horse might do if it were alone on the English moors and then looking for confirmation of his imaginary scenario in the environment. He tells Watson, *"See the value of imagination...We imagined what might have happened, acted upon the supposition, and find ourselves justified."*[24] Holmes' use of his imagination seems to be a complementary process to deduction. While problem solving based on deduction employs observations to eliminate possible pathways, problem solving based on imagination employs observations to confirm a supposed scenario.

In general, Holmes' macro strategy is to connect particular observations to a number of frameworks both inside and outside of the scope of the problem space he is addressing.

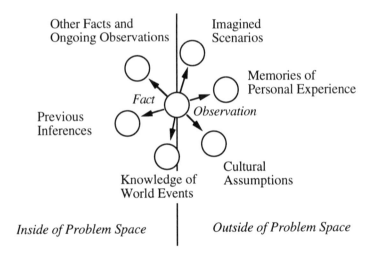

Holmes' Macro Strategy for Exploring a Problem Space

This creates an enriched problem space which gives priority and meaning to observations and inferences. Holmes then synthesizes this information together into a single conclusion which is confirmed by other observations or a group of suppositions that is reduced to a single possibility through a process of elimination. Holmes emphasized the importance of this last step when he pointed out that so often *"Insensibly one begins to twist facts to suit theories, instead of theories to suit facts."*[25]

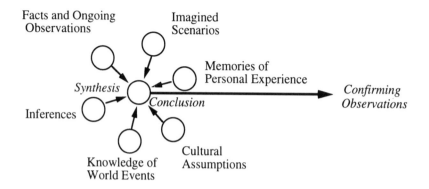

Facts and Ongoing Observations

Imagined Scenarios

Memories of Personal Experience

Synthesis

Conclusion

Confirming Observations

Inferences

Knowledge of World Events

Cultural Assumptions

Synthesizing Information About a Problem Space to Reach a Conclusion

A good example of this strategy comes from the *Sign of Four* in which Holmes is able to draw a number of conclusions about Watson's brother from examining his watch.

> *"I have heard you say it is difficult for a man to have any object in daily use without leaving the impress of his individuality upon it in such a way that a trained observer might read it. Now, I have here a watch which has recently come into my possession. Would you have the kindness to let me have an opinion upon the character or habits of the late owner?"*

> *...He balanced the watch in his hand, gazed hard at the dial, opened the back, and examined the works, first with his naked eyes and then with a powerful convex lens. I could hardly keep from smiling at his crestfallen face when he finally snapped the case to and handed it back.*

> *"There are hardly any data," he remarked. "The watch has been recently cleaned, which robs me of my most suggestive facts."*

"You are right." I answered. "It was cleaned before being sent to me."

"Though unsatisfactory, my research has not been entirely barren," he observed, staring at the ceiling with dreamy, lack-lustre eyes. "Subject to your correction, I should judge that the watch belonged to your elder brother, who inherited it from your father."

"That you gather, no doubt, from the H. W. upon the back?"

"Quite so. The W. suggests your own name. The date of the watch is nearly fifty years back, and the initials are as old as the watch: so it was made for the last generation. Jewelry usually descends to the eldest son, and he is most likely to have the same name as your father. Your father has, if I remember right, been dead many years. It has, therefore, been in the hands of your eldest brother."

"Right, so far," said I. "Anything else?"

"He was a man of untidy habits - very untidy and careless. He was left with good prospects, but threw away his chances, lived for some time in poverty with occasional short intervals of prosperity, and finally, taking to drink, he died. That is all I gather."

I sprang from my chair and limped impatiently about the room with considerable bitterness in my heart.

"This is unworthy of you, Holmes," I said. "I could not have believed that you would have descended to this. You have made inquiries into the history of my unhappy brother, and now you pretend to deduce this knowledge in some fanciful way. You cannot expect me to believe that you have read all this from his old watch! It is unkind and, to speak plainly, has a touch of charlatanism in it."

"My dear doctor," said he kindly, "pray accept my apologies. Viewing the matter as an abstract problem, I had forgotten how personal and painful a thing it might be to you. I assure you, however, that I never even knew you had a brother until you handed me this watch."

"Then how in the name of all that is wonderful did you get these facts? They are absolutely correct in every particular."

"Ah, that is good luck. I could only say what was the balance of probability. I did not at all expect to be so accurate."

"But it was not mere guesswork?"

"No, no: I never guess. It is a shocking habit - destructive to the logical faculty. What seems strange to you is only because you do not follow my train of thought or observe the small facts upon which large inferences may depend. For example, I began by stating that your brother was careless. When you observe the lower part of that watch-case you notice that it is not only dinted in two places but it is cut and marked all over from the habit of keeping other hard objects, such as coins or keys, in the same pocket. Surely it is no great feat to assume that a man who treats a fifty-guinea watch so cavalierly must be a careless man. Neither is it a very far-fetched inference that a man who inherits one article of such value is pretty well provided for in other respects."

I nodded to show that I followed his reasoning.

"It is very customary for pawnbrokers in England, when they take a watch, to scratch the numbers of the ticket with a pin-point upon the inside of the case. It is more handy than a label as there is no risk of the *number being lost or transposed. There are no less than four such numbers visible to my lens on the inside of this case. Inference - that your brother was often at low water. Secondary inference - that he had occasional bursts of prosperity, or he could not have redeemed the pledge. Finally, I ask you to look at the inner plate, which contains the keyhole. Look at the thousands of scratches all round the hole - marks where the key has slipped. What sober man's key could have scored those grooves? But you will never see a drunkard's watch without them. He winds it at night, and he leaves these traces of his unsteady hand. Where is the mystery in all this?"[26]*

In this example, Holmes demonstrates how he synthesizes associations from a number of different frameworks to build a characterization of Watson's unfortunate brother. Holmes pieces together contextual information with cultural assumptions and his own personal memories to provide a rich space in which to give meaning to the seemingly trivial details he has observed on the watch.

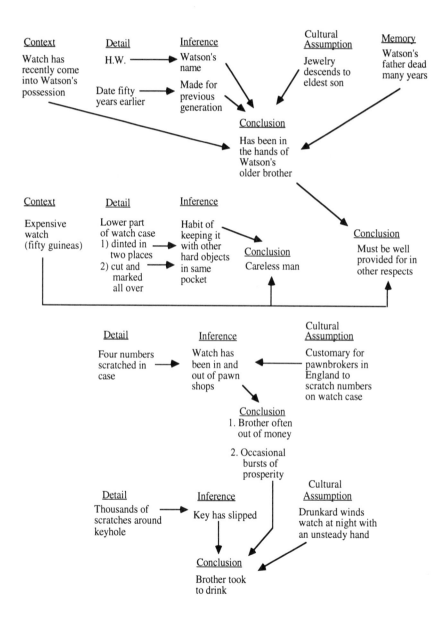

Synthesis of Contextual Information and Cultural Assumptions to Form Conclusions

Levels of Cues and Inferences

Holmes strategy for inferring behavioral and personality characteristics from an object in the possession of Watson's brother provides some interesting parallels to the goal of determining the thinking strategies of geniuses from the clues they have left behind. In modeling an individual, there are a number of different aspects, or levels, of the various systems and subsystems in which that person operated that we may explore. We can look at the historical and geographical *environment* in which he or she lived - i.e., *when* and *where* of the person's activity. We can examine his specific *behaviors* and actions - i.e., *what* the person physically did in that environment. We may also look at the intellectual and cognitive strategies and *capabilities* by which the person selected and guided his actions in his environment - i.e., *how* he or she generated these behaviors in that context.

We could further explore the beliefs and values that motivated and shaped the thinking strategies and capabilities that the person developed to accomplish behavioral goals in his or her environment - i.e., *why* the person did things the way he or she did them in those times and places. We could look deeper to investigate a person's perception of the self or identity he or she was manifesting through that set of beliefs, capabilities and actions in that environment - i.e., the *who* behind the why, how, what, where and when.

Holmes seems to have been a master at tracing and applying the interconnections between these levels. Clusters of clues left in the environment tell us about the behaviors that have caused them. Clusters of behaviors are clues about the cognitive processes and capabilities that produce and guide those behaviors. Cognitive strategies and maps are clues about the beliefs and values that shape and motivate them. Clusters of beliefs and values provide clues to the identity and personality at their core.

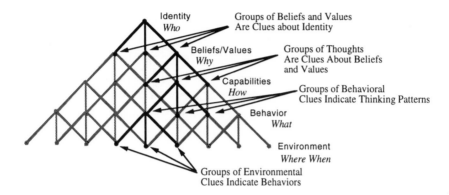

Identity
Who

Groups of Beliefs and Values
Are Clues about Identity

Beliefs/Values
Why

Groups of Thoughts
Are Clues About Beliefs
and Values

Capabilities
How

Groups of Behavioral
Clues Indicate Thinking Patterns

Behavior
What

Environment
Where When

Groups of Environmental
Clues Indicate Behaviors

Relationship Between Different Levels of Cues

For example, in the case of Watson's watch, Holmes puts together cluster of minute environmental clues left on the watch together with contextual and cultural assumptions to infer what behaviors caused these clues. He then synthesizes these behavioral causes together with some other cultural assumptions to converge on a conclusion about the deeper conditions that brought about those behaviors.

Environment	Behavior	Capabilities	Beliefs & Values
Clues	Causes	Conditions	Motives
Where When	*What*	*How*	*Why*
Lower part of the watch case 1) dinted in two places and 2) cut and marked all over	Habit of keeping it with other hard objects in same pocket	Carelessness	
Four numbers scratched in case	Watch in and out of pawn shops	Often out of money Occasional Prosperity	
Thousands of scratches by keyhole	Key has slipped	Took to drink	

Examples of Levels of Cues and Inferences

Holmes stops at the level of the 'how', however. He is not able to deduce the beliefs or sense of self that might have created the psychological conditions behind Watson's brother's behavior. And his degree of understanding of the psychological processes behind the behaviors is only very sketchy. Of course, Holmes was not a psychologist. As a detective he had to focus on the concrete behavioral aspects of his cases. Most of the examples we are given in the Holmes stories are about discovering the behaviors that have left their traces in the environment rather than uncovering cognitive strategies.

Yet, Holmes did also claim that a "momentary expression, a twitch of a muscle or a glance of an eye" can give us insight into a person's "innermost thoughts." In *The Adventure of the Cardboard Box*, Holmes provides a powerful example of applying his methods to uncover a "train of thought" in Watson. Instead of inferring behavioral actions ('antecedent causes') from environmental clues, he infers cognitive processes ('final causes') from clusters of behavioral clues.

Finding that Holmes was too absorbed for conversation I had tossed aside the barren paper, and leaning back in my chair I fell into a brown study. Suddenly my companion's voice broke in upon my thoughts:

"You are right, Watson," said he. "It does seem a most preposterous way of settling a dispute."

"Most preposterous!" I exclaimed, and then suddenly realizing how he had echoed the inmost thought of my soul, I sat up in my chair and stared at him in blank amazement.

"What is this, Holmes?" I cried. "This is beyond anything which I could have imagined."

He laughed heartily at my perplexity.

"You remember," said he, "that some little time ago when I read you the passage of one of Poe's sketches in

which a close reasoner follows the unspoken thoughts of his companion, you were inclined to treat the matter as a mere tour-de-force of the author. On my remarking that I was constantly in the habit of doing the same thing you expressed incredulity."

"Oh, no!"

"Perhaps not with your tongue, my dear Watson, but certainly with your eyebrows. So when I saw you throw down your paper and enter upon a train of thought, I was very happy to have the opportunity of reading it off, and eventually of breaking into it, as a proof that I had been in rapport with you."

But I was still far from satisfied. "In the example which you read to me," said I, "the reasoner drew his conclusions from the reactions of the man whom he observed. If I remember right, he stumbled over a heap of stones, looked up at the stars, and so on. But I have been seated quietly in my chair, and what clues can I have given you?"

"You do yourself an injustice. The features are given to man as the means by which he shall express his emotions, and yours are faithful servants."

"Do you mean to say that you read my train of thoughts from my features?"

"Your features and especially your eyes. Perhaps you yourself recall how your reverie commenced?"

"No, I cannot."

"Then I will tell you. After throwing down your paper, which was the action which drew my attention to you, you sat for half a minute with a vacant expression. Then your eyes fixed themselves upon your newly framed picture of General Gordon, and I saw by the alteration in your face that train of thought had been

started. But it did not lead very far. Your eyes flashed across to the unframed portrait of Henry Ward Beecher which stands upon the top of your books. Then you glanced up at the wall, and of course your meaning was obvious. You were thinking that if the portrait were framed it would just cover that bare space and correspond with Gordon's picture over there."

"You have followed me wonderfully!" I exclaimed.

"So far I could hardly have gone astray. But now your thoughts went back to Beecher, and you looked hard across as if you were studying the character in his features. Then your eyes ceased to pucker, but you continued to look across, and your face was thoughtful. You were recalling the incidents of Beecher's career. I was well aware that you could not do this without thinking of the mission which he undertook on behalf of the North at the time of the Civil War, for I remember your expressing your passionate indignation at the way in which he was received by the more turbulent of our people. You felt so strongly about it that I knew you could not think of Beecher without thinking of that also. When a moment later I saw your eyes wander away from the picture, I suspected that your mind had now turned to the Civil War, and when I observed that your lips set, your eyes sparkled, and your hands clenched I was positive that you were indeed thinking of the gallantry which was shown by both sides in that desperate struggle. But then, again, your face grew sadder; you shook your head. You were dwelling upon the sadness and horror and useless waste of life. Your hand stole towards your own old wound and a smile quivered on your lips, which showed me that the ridiculous side of this method of settling international questions had forced itself upon your mind. At this point I agreed with you that it was

preposterous and was glad to find that all my deductions had been correct."[27]

Here we find Holmes applying his methods of observation and deduction to decipher subtle behavioral clues in order to uncover the deeper cognitive processes that generated those behaviors. Again Holmes combines clusters of observations with assumptions, context and memory to find a deeper significance in seemingly trivial actions; each step in his sequence of inferences providing the context for his next inference. But rather than having to start with clues left in the environment and to derive the behavior that caused them, Holmes is able to focus on clusters of behavioral clues and infer the mental processes that caused them. He has been able to shift the focus of his strategy up to another level.

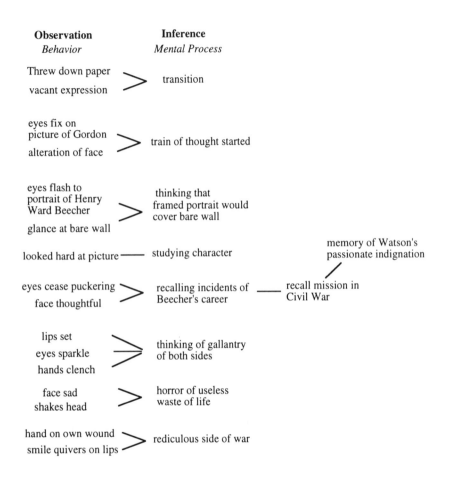

Reading a 'Train of Thought' Through Physical Cues

Implementing Holmes' Strategy

The primary fruit of modeling is that we are able to apply what we have learned to develop the processes that we have uncovered from our model in ourselves and others. Let's see how we might develop and implement some of the skills and strategies of Sherlock Holmes in the context of our own lives.

Holmes' strategy basically involves the synthesizing of a cluster of environmental and behavioral clues to form a conclusion out of the whole. This process involves a number of key elements and sub-skills including:

Observation - Matching the features of environmental clues left in one context to characteristics of other contexts.

Assumption - Presupposed knowledge or beliefs about the larger framework or "problem space" in which some clue is occurring. Assumptions determining the meaning or significance of a clue.

Inference - Imagining what kinds of actions could have produced the environmental clues you are examining inside of the problem space you are assuming.

Deduction - Eliminating or confirming possible actions by finding other confirming or disconfirming clues for each possibility.

Meta Cognition - Being introspectively aware of your own thought process, and keeping track of the "trains of thought" that lead to your conclusions.

Observation and Deduction

To begin to think like Holmes, it would make sense to start with his own suggestion to observe someone and attempt to "learn at a glance to distinguish the history of the man, and the trade or profession to which he belongs." Holmes suggests clues such as "finger-nails," "trouser-knees," "callosities of the forefinger and thumb," "expression," "shirt-cuffs," etc., claiming that "by each of these things a man's calling is plainly revealed."

As an exercise, imagine that you are Sherlock Holmes and that you believe "life is a great chain, the nature of which is known whenever we are shown a single link of it." When you meet someone new that you do not know, whether it is at your office, a party, a conference, or some other type of gathering, see if you can tell anything about his or her personal history or profession before you are told. You might even practice by going out to a street corner, an airport or another public place and observing people. Put your observations and inferences together, and draw a conclusion about the profession or background of a person. Then check the accuracy of your guess with the person or someone else who knows him or her.

Keep in mind that Holmes typically brought together clusters of clues to make his inferences. He also started with general characteristics first and then moved to specifics. So look for several cues that might add up to something.

You might first use clues to infer behavior habits and personal history and then combine your inferences with other clues to draw your conclusion about the person's profession. For instance, you may make the inference that a person who is wearing bifocal glasses might need to often switch back and forth between reading and looking at people. Then you might combine that inference with other clues to try to narrow down your guess even more. Once you have made an inference, think of what other cues should accompany it and look for those details which may confirm or eliminate a particular possibility. For example, in what kinds of professions would a person *not* be able to wear bifocals.

In fact, if you find it too difficult to specifically determine a person's profession, start by eliminating professions. That is, you might be able to quickly determine that someone is definitely *not* a police officer, military person or musician. This could be quicker and almost as valuable as the positive identification of a person's profession.

If you can't make out the person's profession, just infer whatever you can about his or her background or history. Is the person married? Right or left handed? What is the person's nationality? Where has the person been recently?

Remember that context, cultural assumptions, personal memory, imagination, etc. play a major role in determining the meaning of various clues. Before trying this exercise, it may be useful to make a list of assumptions and assess the context in which you are observing. Given the type of context you are in, for example, what kind of professional backgrounds are you most likely to find there? There are also probably a number of cultural patterns that may not only help you to interpret your observations but tell you where to focus initially. For instance, in many Western societies, a person who wears a gold ring on the ring finger of their left hand is married; right handed people generally wear their watches on their left wrist and left handed people wear their watches on their right wrist; and so on. There may even be more specific cultural patterns. For instance, there might be different habits of dress for sales executives from Britain versus the United States, Italy or Germany.

Widen your 'problem space' as much as you can. Think of what kinds of clues would tell you whether a person is a doctor, lawyer, accountant, businessperson, construction worker, sales person, musician, off duty police officer, military person on leave, etc. Holmes implies some general categories in his recommendations of possible cues:

"Finger-nails" and the "callosities of the forefinger and thumb" and "expression" would fall into the class of physical and behavioral characteristics associated with a particular profession. Are there any distinguishing behavioral characteristics culturally associated with the different professions listed above? Within your cultural context, for example, would a doctor walk differently than an electronic technician? Particular kinds of posture, tone of voice and vocabulary might be characteristic of certain professions. What sort of reading material would people of different professions carry? Which part of a newspaper would you expect to find them reading? What role does age play in various professions?

"Shirt-cuffs" and "trouser-knees" fall into the category of patterns and characteristics of dress, and the effect of a person's profession on his or her clothing. First, what are the types of clothing people in these different trades or professions would wear, or not wear, in addition to whatever uniforms might be part of the profession? What sort of people might wear jeans or designer clothes? What kinds of watches, glasses, hair styles, ties or tie bars, rings, belt buckles, shoes, pins, 'make up' or jewelry might give you clues? A traveling sales executive might carry a samples case, for instance. Secondly, how might the typical activities a person engages in within their profession affect their clothing? A person who works at a desk all day and leans on his or her elbow might have more wear in that part of his or her jacket.

Also look for details which seem contrary to the context or typical cultural patterns. As Holmes pointed out, *"Singularity is almost invariably a clue."* [28] For example, an adult who is not wearing a wedding ring but is carrying a baby may be a single parent or may be another relative or caregiver.

Regardless of the accuracy of your guesses, develop *metacognition* of your own thought process by keeping track of the train of thought by which you made your conclusion. Use the following table as a guide.

Observations		Assumptions		Inferences	Conclusion
Environmental Details	Behavioral Details	Contextual	Cultural		

After you have finished making your observations and deductions, go back over which environmental and behavioral clues you noticed and combined in order to make your inferences. Notice in what order you combined them and to what degree of priority you gave to the various clues. Also note what contextual and cultural assumptions you made in order to interpret the meaning of these clues. See if you can be aware of any memories or fantasized scenarios you brought into your thought process to create, confirm or eliminate possibilities.

If you draw a conclusion that is only partially correct, backtrack over your thought process and find which inferences were legitimate and which ones were off. If you see a clue that you think should be distinctive, like a certain style of clothing or hair, but you are not able to draw an inference from it, write it down so that you can find out what it means later on.

As an extension of this exercise, ask an acquaintance to give you an object that he or she has been given or inherited that belonged to someone else for a long time and see what you can find out about the previous owner through your observations.

Calibration Exercise

NLP provides specific ways to develop some of Holmes' observational skills, especially in relationship to people. One basic NLP process is known as "calibration." It is a way to use a *"momentary expression, a twitch of a muscle or a glance of an eye"* to gain insight into a person's "innermost thoughts." It involves linking behavioral cues to internal cognitive and emotional responses.   Find a partner and try the following exercise together.

1. Ask your partner to think of some concept that your partner feels she or he knows and understands.
2. Observe your partner's physiology closely as if you were Sherlock Holmes for a moment. Watch your partner's eye movements, facial expressions, breathing rate, etc.
3. Then ask your partner to think of something that is confusing and unclear.
4. Once again, watch your partner's eyes and features carefully. Notice what is different between the patterns of features.
5. Now ask your partner to pick either concept and think of it again. Observe your partner's features. You should see traces of one of the clusters of features associated with either understanding or confusion.
6. Make a guess and then check with your partner to find out if you were correct.
7. Have your partner think of other concepts that she or he understands or finds confusing and see if you can guess which category they fall into. Confirm your guess by checking with your partner.
8. As a test of your skill, explain some concept to your partner and determine whether your partner has understood it or is unclear or confused by observing his or features.

Again, use this as an opportunity to develop meta cognition. Keep track of what cues and train of thought led you to your decisions.

Detecting Deceit

According to Holmes deceit was "an impossibility in the case of one trained in observation and analysis." The following exercise combines observational skill with analytical skill and a little imagination. Try it with a partner.

1. Ask your partner to hide a coin in either hand and purposely try to fool you as to which hand it is in.
2. You get to ask five questions of your partner in order to try to determine which hand the coin is in. Your partner must answer all of the questions, but does not have to answer truthfully.
3. After your five questions you must make a guess as to which hand you think the coin is in. Your partner will then open both hands and show you the answer.

Imagine you are Sherlock Holmes and could use your observation and 'calibration' skills to see through your partner's ruse as if you were a human 'lie detector'. The best way to do this is by observing for subtle unconscious cues associated with "yes" and "no" responses. It is generally a good idea to set up your calibration *before* your partner realizes that is what you are doing. For example, when you are explaining the exercise, ask, "Do you understand the instructions?" or "Should we discuss anything else before we begin?" Since your partner will not be trying to fool you at this point, you should see the cues associated with a congruent "yes" or "no" response.

Pay particular attention to cues that your partner will probably not be aware of or cannot consciously manipulate. For instance, if you are an acute observer you might see very subtle responses like skin color changes, pupil dilation, or slight breathing shifts, etc. One helpful principle to apply is what I call the "1/2 second rule" - which is that any response that comes within a half second of your question has probably not been mediated by your partner's conscious awareness. So focus your attention on the first 1/2 second of the response. Keep in mind that people will be able to infer what you are going to ask before you even complete your question. For instance, if you ask "Are you holding the coin in your right hand?" By the time you have said the word "right," your partner will most likely know unconsciously that your next word will be hand. Consciously, however, your partner will probably wait until the sentence is completed before attempting to mask his or her answer. So you can start observing his or her reactions even before you have finished your sentence.

Remember, Holmes was continually widening the space in which he was operating beyond the accepted immediate context. In addition to observing for the congruence of your partner's reactions to your questions, look at your partner's hands to see if you can tell which hand is subtly squeezing more tightly. You can enrich the problem space still further and increase your chances of getting a congruent answer by bringing associations from outside of the ongoing context. Like Holmes, you can make of use cultural assumptions such as asking, "Is the coin in the hand you hold your fork with?" You may also make use of any memories you can recall, such as, "Is the coin in the hand you opened the door with?" or "Are you holding the coin in the hand that I was holding it in when I gave it to you?" Since your partner will have to direct some of his or her attention to thinking of the experiences you are referring to, it will extend your chances of getting an initial unconscious response that has not been filtered by conscious attention.

You might also try asking Meta Questions - questions *about* the response the person has given you. For instance, after your partner has answered you, ask, "Did you just tell me the truth?" or "Should I believe what you just answered?" Similarly, don't just observe your partner's initial non verbal response to your question, watch your partner's reaction to his or her own answer. Often people will react to their own answers in a situation that involves as much self consciousness as this exercise. This secondary response might confirm or conflict with the initial answer.

Observing Micro Behavioral Cues Associated with Cognitive Strategies: The B.A.G.E.L. Model

Another application of Holmes' strategies involves combining them with what is known as the B.A.G.E.L. model in NLP. In *The Adventure of the Cardboard Box*, Holmes was able to *"follow the unspoken thoughts of his companion"* by inferring a sequence of mental processes after observing the clusters of micro behavioral clues that accompanied them. The ability to observe behavioral cues that reveal internal cognitive processes is a core skill in NLP and an essential component in our own study of the strategies of genius.

Holmes commented to Watson that a person can "read" your "train of thoughts" from your physical features *"and especially your eyes."* The B.A.G.E.L. model identifies a number of types of behavioral cues, involving one's physical features and one's eyes, that are associated with cognitive processes - in particular, those involving the five senses. B.A.G.E.L. stands for the first letter in a group of English words identifying key categories of behavioral patterns.

The letter "B" is related to Body posture. Body posture is an important influence and reflection of a person's internal processes. For example, most people would probably find it very difficult to be creative with their head down and their shoulders hunched forward. If you put yourself into that physiology you will find it's going to be difficult to feel inspired. NLP has discovered that when people are visualizing they tend to be in an erect posture. When people are listening, they tend to lean back a bit with their arms folded or head tilted. When people are having feelings, they tend to lean forward and breath more deeply. These cues won't necessarily tell you if the feeling is positive or negative; only that an individual is accessing feelings. So somebody might be feeling very relaxed and have the same general posture as somebody who's feeling depressed.

The letter "A" refers to types of non-verbal Auditory cues. For example, voice tone and tempo can be a very powerful cue. When people are visualizing, they will tend to speak in a slightly higher and faster tone of voice. When people are into feelings, their voices are often lower and slower in tempo. These types of vocal patterns can effect people's states. For example, if someone says in a low slow voice, "Now I want you to watch this complex movement very carefully," you would probably feel more like going to sleep than observing. On the other hand if, someone says, "Okay everybody, really get relaxed and comfortable!" in a very rapid and high pitched voice, you might experience a different kind of incongruity. Voice tone and tempo can serve as a cue to trigger cognitive processes. Attention to the sense of hearing is often triggered by melodic voice changes and fluctuations of tone, tempo and rhythm.

The letter "G" refers to Gestures. People are often gesturing to the sense organ that is most active for them in a moment. People will touch or point to their eyes when they are attempting to visualize something or when they get an insight. People gesture toward their ears when they are talking about something they heard or are trying to hear. Likewise people will touch their mouth when they are thinking verbally (like Rodin's The Thinker). When people touch their chest or stomach it generally indicates feeling.

The letter "E" relates to Eye movements. Eye movement patterns are one of the most interesting micro behavioral cues, and the one most associated with NLP. It has been said that "The eyes are the windows of the soul" In NLP, the eyes are considered a window to the mind. Where a person's eyes are looking can be an important cue. Eyes up tends to accompany visualization. As I mentioned before Watson's descriptions of Holmes *"staring at the ceiling with dreamy, lack-lustre eyes"* describes the classic 'accessing cue' for internal visualizating in the model of NLP. Horizontal movement of the eyes tends to go along with listening. Eyes down accompany feeling. An eye position to the left hand side is often indicative of memory, while a movement to the right hand side indicates imagination. These cues, summarized in the diagram below, are gone over in more depth in many of the standard books on NLP.

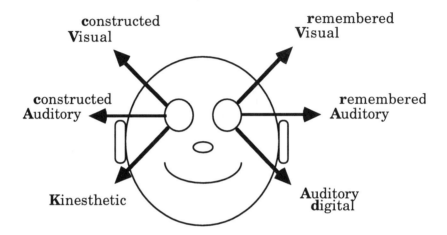

**Basic Relationships Between Eye Positions and
Cognitive Processes
(For a Right Handed Person)**

The letter "L" refers to language patterns. As we discussed in the previous chapter on Aristotle, people often give clues or cues about their thinking process through language. For example, somebody might say, "I just *feel* that something is wrong." This statement indicates a different sensory modality (kinesthetic) than somebody who says, "I'm getting a lot of *static* about this idea," (auditory) "Something *tells* me to be careful," (verbal) or "It's very *clear* to me" (visual). Each statement indicates the cognitive involvement of a different sensory modality.

Learning to observe these types of cues can be of immense practical value. In fact, many NLP techniques rely on the observation of these cues in order to be effective. They can provide you with important information about how another person is thinking - even when that person is not aware of it himself. In addition to being an aid in the process of modeling, they are an important and powerful communication tool that may be used by therapists, managers, teachers, lawyers, salespeople, etc., to better understand (or read) people with whom they are interacting.

As a way to develop this skill, repeat the exercise described earlier in which you 'calibrated' the non-verbal cues of a partner relating to states of confusion and understanding. Ask a partner to again recall examples of concepts or ideas he or she understands or is confused about and follow his or her "unspoken thoughts" by observing the micro behavioral cues identified by the B.A.G.E.L distinctions using the table provided below. Notice what you can tell about the representational modalities your partner is activating with respect to the different concepts of subjects.

	State 1 "Confusion"	State 2 "Understanding"
Posture		
Eye Position		
Breathing		
Micro Movements		

Table For Comparing Non-Verbal Cues Associated With Different Mental States

You can then talk to your partner about the different concepts or subjects and listen to the kinds of language patterns he or she uses when referring to those different topics or concepts. If your partner uses words like "It is *hazy*," or "I am *unclear*," he or she is probably attempting to visualize them. If, on the other hand, your partner says, "I just can't get a *handle* on it," or "I am unable to *grasp* it," he or she is employing the kinesthetic representational system as a way to try to understand; and so on.

Another way to develop this level of observational acuity is to observe people's memory strategies or decision making strategies. For instance, if you give someone directions, tell a person a telephone number or provide an individual with a piece of information to remember, observe that person's micro behavioral cues as he or she engages in the process of committing the information to memory.

In what way does his or her body posture shift or adjust? Does the person sit up straight? lean back? lean forward? If you are giving directions, for instance, a kinesthetically oriented person may literally orient his or her body in different directions and gesture with his or her hands as that person is listening to you.

Does the person make any unconscious noises like "Hmmm.." or move his or her mouth as if sub-vocalizing. A verbally oriented person may repeat the directions or information several times.

What gestures does the person make, if any? Does he or she touch any part of his or her face? head? body?

Pay special attention to the person's eyes and eye movements. As that person is thinking or recalling, which direction do his or her eyes move? Up? Laterally? Down? What does that tell you about how that person is thinking? If the person looks up and to the right, for instance, he or she may be constructing a visual map of what you are saying. If the person touches his or her face and looks down and to the left, he or she is probably internally verbalizing or repeating what you have been talking about.

What kind of language patterns does the person exhibit as he or she discusses or clarifies the information he or she is to remember? Does the person ask you to repeat the information? write it down? show it to him or her in a book or map?

Like Holmes did with Watson, you may even want to attempt to 'enter' the thoughts of the other person as a proof that you are in 'rapport' with them. For instance, if the person is looking up and appears to be struggling, you can say, "You're right, I have not been clear enough." Or, if the person looks laterally off to the left or right, you can ask, "Will it help if I repeat it more slowly?" If the person looks down and to the right and frowns, you can say something like, "If you're feeling a little overwhelmed I can walk you through it again."

You can practice in a similar way by observing people's unconscious decision making strategies. If you are at a meal with a group of people, for example, observe their micro behavioral cues as they decide what to choose from the menu. Some will attempt to visualize the meal. Others will check their kinesthetic system to determine what "feels right." Others will want to discuss the menu items before choosing. While these details may initially seem like trivial details or 'minutiae' they can provide important insights into people. The unconscious cognitive process by which a person decides what to eat from a menu may reflect other important aspects of that person's decision making strategies and character.

These are types of skills that NLP has actually helped teachers and psychologists to develop in order to provide practical help to people experiencing real challenges and difficulties - such as children with learning problems. As an example, if you observe good spellers, they will almost invariably look up and to the left (visual memory) when they are recalling the spelling of a word. People who have difficulties spelling, such as people who are 'dyslexic', on the other hand, experience great difficulties in forming images of words and almost never look up to the left when they are spelling. By observing and coaching children to help them develop the appropriate cognitive strategy and supporting behavioral cues, a person can help them to make dramatic improvements in many basic learning skills.

The books *Tools for Dreamers*, *Skills For the Future* and *NLP Volume I* provide a number of exercises and methods to help develop your ability to elicit and observe these kinds of cognitive strategies.

Obviously, in our further explorations of genius, the behavioral cues of the B.A.G.E.L. combined with the observational strategies of Holmes will be an important source of information about the strategies used by the individuals we are examining.

Conclusion

Even though he was a fictitious character, Sherlock Holmes was the embodiment of a thinking process that is both authentic and remarkable. By studying the strategies and patterns associated with this thought process we can identify and develop useful skills that have potentially important and powerful applications in 'real life.'

Bibliography and References for Chapter 2

The Complete Sherlock Holmes, Sir Arthur Conan Doyle, Doubleday & Company, Inc., Garden City, New York, 1979.

The Encyclopedia Sherlockiana, Jack Tracy, Avon Books, New York, NY, 1979.

Encyclopedia Britannica, Encyclopedia Britannica Inc., Chicago Ill., 1979.

Tools for Dreamers: Strategies for Creativity and the Structure of Invention, Dilts, R. B., Epstein, T., Dilts, R. W., Meta Publications, Capitola, Ca., 1991.

Neuro-Linguistic Programming: The Study of the Structure of Subjective Experience, Volume I ; Dilts, R., Grinder, J., Bandler, R., DeLozier, J.; Meta Publications, Capitola, California, 1980.

Plans and the Structure of Behavior, Miller, G., Galanter, E., and Pribram, K., Henry Holt & Co., Inc., 1960.

SOAR: An Architecture for General Intelligence; Laird, J. E., Rosenbloom, P., and Newell, A., *Artificial Intelligence*, 33:1-64, 1987.

Skills for the Future, Dilts, R. with Bonissone, G. ; Meta Publications, Capitola, California, 1993.

Footnotes to Chapter 2

1. *A Study in Scarlet*
2. *The Five Orange Pits*
3. *A Study in Scarlet*
4. *A Case of Identity*
5. *The Boscombe Valley Mystery*
6. *A Study in Scarlet*
7. *A Study in Scarlet*
8. *The Blanched Soldier*
9. *A Scandal in Bohemia*
10. *A Study in Scarlet*
11. *The Valley of Fear*
12. *The Sign of Four*
13. *The Sign of Four*
14. *The Illustrious Client*
15. *The Sign of Four*
16. *The Adventure of the Cardboard Box*
17. *The Beryl Coronet*
18. *The Boscombe Valley Mystery*
19. *The Blanched Soldier*
20. *The Naval Treaty*
21. *The Valley of Fear*
22. *The Problem of Thor Bridge*
23. *The Hound of the Baskervilles*
24. *Silver Blaze*
25. *A Scandal in Bohemia*
26. *The Sign of Four*
27. *The Adventure of the Cardboard Box*
28. *The Boscombe Valley Mystery*

Walt Disney

Chapter 3

Walt Disney

The Dreamer, The Realist
And The Critic

Overview of Chapter 3

Walt Disney and the Three Phases of Creativity

Walt Disney's ability to connect his innovative creativity with successful business strategy and popular appeal allowed him to establish an empire in the field of entertainment that has survived decades after his death. Disney (1901 - 1966) embodies the ability to make a successful organization based on creativity. He represents the process of turning fantasies into concrete and tangible expressions. In a way, Disney's chosen medium of expression, the animated film, characterizes the fundamental process of all creative genius; the ability to take something that exists only in the imagination and forge it into a physical existence that directly influences the experience of others in a positive way. This was something Disney was able to do prolifically and in a number of different mediums.

In his lifetime, apart from Disneyland and the initial stages of Walt Disney World, he produced, directly or as executive producer, and stored in the company's library 497 short subjects, 21 animated features, 56 live-action motion pictures, 7 "True-Life Adventure" features, 330 hours of the Mickey Mouse Club, 78 half-hour Zorro shows, and 330 hours of other TV shows.

The simple yet worldwide appeal of Disney's characters, animated films, live action features and amusement parks demonstrate a unique ability to grasp, synthesize and simplify very basic, yet quite sophisticated principles. Disney was also responsible for a number of important technical and organizational innovations in the fields of animation and film-making in general.

The tools and distinctions of NLP make it possible to create explicit maps of the successful thinking strategies of people with special talents like Walt Disney. NLP explores the way people sequence and use fundamental mental abilities such as sight, hearing and feeling in order to organize and perform in the world around them. One of the major elements of Disney's unique genius was his ability to explore something from a number of different **perceptual positions**. An important insight into this key part of Disney's strategy comes from the comment made by one of his animators that, *"...there were actually three different Walts: the **dreamer**, the **realist**, and the **spoiler**. You never knew which one was coming into your meeting."*[1]

This is not only an insight into Disney but also into the structure of creativity. Creativity as a total process involves the coordination of these three subprocesses: dreamer, realist and critic. A dreamer without a realist cannot turn ideas into tangible expressions. A critic and a dreamer without a realist just become stuck in a perpetual conflict. A dreamer and a realist might create things, but they might not achieve a high degree of quality without a critic. The critic helps to evaluate and refine the products of creativity. There is a humorous example of a boss who prided himself on his innovative thinking abilities but lacked some of the Realist and Critic perspective. The people who worked in the company used to say, "He has an idea a minute... and some of them are good."

The point is that creativity itself involves the synthesis of different processes or phases. The Dreamer is necessary for creativity in order to form new ideas and goals. The Realist is necessary for creativity as a means to transform ideas into concrete expressions. The Critic is necessary for creativity as a filter and as a stimulus for refinement.

Certainly, each one of these phases represents a whole thinking strategy of its own—strategies that more often tend to conflict with each other rather than support each other. Of course, the specifics of how Disney used and coordinated his imagination (the *Dreamer*), methodically translated those fantasies into a tangible form (the *Realist*) and applied his critical judgment (the *Critic/Spoiler*) are something that we need to explore in more depth.

Micro Analysis of Disney the *Dreamer*

In the words of Disney the 'Dreamer', *"My business has been a thrilling adventure, an unending voyage of discovery and exploration in the realms of color, sound and motion."* [2] As a Dreamer, Disney took an intense and passionate interest in the process of creativity.

The descriptions of Disney's physiology at the time he was thinking creatively present a classic portrait of the micro behaviors or 'accessing cues' associated with deep visual fantasizing. For example, one of his associates reports:

> *"When Walt was deep in thought he would lower one brow, squint his eyes, let his jaw drop, and stare fixedly at some point in space, often holding the attitude for several moments... No words could break the spell..."* [3]

This description could easily be of a hypnotic subject having a positive hallucination. The trance-like quality attributed to Disney's behavior while 'dreaming' in the description above indicates just how fully he committed his entire neurology and attention to the creative process. This same kind of 'hypnotic' quality, reminiscent of Watson's descriptions of Sherlock Holmes *"staring at the ceiling with dreamy, lack-lustre eyes,"* has been observed in many other creative geniuses throughout history.

The following caricature of Disney's "most typical expression", from Thomas and Johnson (1983), adds further confirmation to the observation cited above. Examining the picture as if we were Sherlock Holmes trying to read Disney's "innermost thoughts," we see that the picture shows Disney looking up and to the right. According to the model of NLP this indicates that he is fantasizing, or constructing internal visual images (V^c). As a 'rule of thumb', eye position generally indicates the 'lead' system or input system implying that visual fantasy is Disney's primary focus. Disney is also depicted leaning forward on his elbows in what would be considered a feeling oriented (or 'kinesthetic') posture (K^i). The fact that the picture also illustrates him as touching his left hand to his face is significant as well. In NLP this gesture is known as the 'telephone position' and accompanies internal verbalization (A_d), indicating that Disney is using at least three sensory representational systems simultaneously.

Animator's Caricature of Disney's "Most Typical Expression"

This brings up an important key in modeling Disney's impressive creativity: the linking process known as *synesthesia*—literally *'a synthesizing of the senses.'* A synesthesia occurs when someone overlaps two or more of the senses together, as when one feels what one sees, or sees images of sounds that one hears, etc. This process of linking the senses was a common one in Disney's creative thought process and was most likely at the basis of many of his creative inspirations. In describing the film *Fantasia*, for instance, Disney wrote:

> *"We take music and visualize the stories and pictures which that music suggests to our imaginations. It is like seeing a concert."*[4]
>
> *"When I heard the music it made pictures in my head... here are the pictures."*[5]

From an NLP standpoint, Disney is describing a strategy sequence in which:

1. The external auditory input (A^e) of music directly causes
2. constructed internal imagery (V^c) through the process of synesthesia.

   Disney would then
3. transform these fantasies into external images (V^e) via the process of animation.

Disney reveals the involvement of another representational system when he claims:

> *"There are things in that music* (Bach's Toccata and Fugue in D Minor) *that the general public will not understand until they <u>see</u> things on the screen representing that music. Then they will <u>feel</u> the depth in the music."*[6]

Here, Disney is indicating that to 'see' something is to 'understand' it, again confirming that his primary representational strategy is visually oriented. He is also indicating that seeing something allows one to 'feel' its depth. This would tend to indicate that Disney also had strong links between seeing and feeling.

According to Aristotle, Disney's abilities to overlap the senses were a result of 'common sensibles' - perceptual qualities that were shared by all of the senses. Common sensibles allow information to be transferred between the different sensory representational systems. They include features such as *movement, intensity, location, number,* etc. which can be perceived by more than one sensory modality.

The structure and impact of one's imagination and creativity is often determined by the establishment of links between the senses. For example, the history of visual art can be viewed at a very general level as the history of expressing internal feeling states through a synesthesia with the various visual characteristics or 'submodalities' (i.e., color, shape, focus, etc.). In the renaissance, depth was the critical submodality; for Rembrandt it was direction and brightness of light, for the impressionists such as Van Gogh it was color and texture, for modern artists distortion of shapes, etc. While Disney claimed, "We could do many things with color no other medium could do,' the key element in his creative process was movement.

By choosing movement, Disney was working with a common sensible as well as a visual submodality. This allowed him to reach even greater depth of expression. We need only compare the results of his studio with others to see how his use of movement as a 'common sensible' made such a big difference. Consider the following comment he made to his animators:

"I would suggest that you concentrate more on caricature, with action; not merely the drawing of a

character to look like something, but giving your character the movements and actions of the person you are trying to put over. Remember, every action should be based on what that character represents." [7]

Here, Disney is clearly stating that the purpose in animation is not to copy something we can already see externally, but rather to express something internal through the quality of movement. What put Disney at the top of his field, made his animated pictures timeless classics and made him an international success was his ability to extract the essence of something through its movement and translate it into visual imagery - as opposed to just making his animated pictures *"look like something."*

Perhaps Disney's focus on the quality of movement was also a metaphor for his own creative personality - the "Dreamer" in himself. As he claimed:

"[I]t is stress and challenge and necessity that make an artist grow and outdo himself." [8]

"I can never stand still. I must explore and experiment. I am never satisfied with my work. I resent the limitations of my own imagination." [9]

And, even though he certainly achieved great financial success, Disney's dreams were not motivated by this type of outward monetary reinforcement. As he maintained:

"You know, the only way I've found to make these pictures is with animators - you can't seem to do it with accountants or bookkeepers." [10]

Money - or rather the lack of it to carry out my ideas - may worry me, but it does not excite me. Ideas excite me." [11]

In summary, Disney's major representational system as a Dreamer was his vision. But it was not necessarily directed only toward specific pictures of things. He used the quality of movement as a 'common sensible' to overlap other senses onto imagery and to see underlying forms and patterns. As he maintained in response to a question about the future:

> *"What I see way off is too nebulous to describe. But it looks big and glittering.*
>
> *"That's what I like about this business, the certainty that there is always something bigger and more exciting just around the bend; and the uncertainty of everything else."*[12]

Disney the Dreamer was visionary, saw the big picture and believed in what was possible. Consider the prophetic statement he made about the future of his art and industry in a 1941 article:

> *"For the near future, I can practically promise a third-dimensional effect in our moving characters. The full inspiration and vitality in our animators' pencil drawings will be brought to the screen in a few years through the elimination of the inking process. Then, too, our medium is peculiarly adaptable to television, and I understand that is already possible to televise in color. Quite an exciting prospect, I should say! And, since* Fantasia, *we have good reason to hope that great composers will write directly for our medium just as they now write for ballet and opera.*
>
> *"This is the promise of the next few years. Beyond that is the future which we cannot see, today. We, the last of the pioneers and the first of the moderns, will not live to see this future realized. We are happy in the job of building its foundations."*[13]

Micro Analysis of Disney the *Realist*

As important as his ability to dream, was Disney's expertise at forging those dreams into reality. The fact that Disney involved all of his senses during his creative process no doubt made the products of his creativity quite robust and compelling. As one of his associates commented, *"Snow White existed in Disney's head as a very real thing and...he was determined it should reach the screen just as he conceived it."*

Like Leonardo da Vinci, Disney seemed to have an intense commitment to visually understand the deepest nature of whatever he was exploring, claiming, *"Animation can explain whatever the mind of man can conceive."* And, as with Leonardo, Disney seems to have been as committed to being a 'realist' as he was to being a 'dreamer:'

> *"Our work must have a foundation of fact in order to have sincerity."*[14]

> *"I definitely feel that we cannot do the fantastic things based on the real, unless we first know the real."*[15]

> *"When we consider a new project, we really study it... not just the surface idea, but everything about it."*[16]

Clearly, Disney, like Leonardo, felt that to be truly inventive one needed to have a feedback loop between the 'dreamer' and the 'realist.'

> *"In animation it's* what *to draw, not just the ability to draw. It isn't just drawing the darn thing, it's thinking about it and giving it personality. I was into technique before I should have been. I needed more life. You've got to learn to draw.*

"In the studio we have had an art school; we put all the arts together...I had four instructors, in composition, life, anatomy, and locomotion — the study of action and reaction. It was needed for this medium. The trouble is [the animators] all wanted to draw beautiful pictures. I went for locomotion, not static. It's like putting your hand across your eyes: the fingers elongate. And when something stops — a woman stops — the skirt goes on. When a mouse stops, his tail goes around. I used to put in my entire time with the artists until they got better."[17]

Making something tangible and real involves tools and technical developments. Disney always kept up to date on the technical progress of his time, claiming:

"Our business has grown with technical achievements. Should this technical progress ever come to a full stop, prepare the funeral oration for our medium. That is how dependent we artists have become on the new tools and refinements which technicians give us...There is no knowing how far steady growth will take the medium, if only the technicians continue to give us new and better tools."[18]

Disney's primary strategy, and his major strength, as a realist was the ability to chunk and sequence his dreams into pieces of a manageable size. In fact, Disney was the innovator of the process of *story-boarding* (a process now used by all major film developers). In the story room (the 'Dreamer' room) Disney had set aside a wall where anyone could tack up an idea or suggestion. One day, after he had just had the wall repainted, he came in and a group of animators had tacked pictures all over newly painted wall. After recovering from his initial shock, Disney noticed that he could easily follow the flow of the story just by looking at the sequence of pictures. So he put up cork board all over the walls of the room and established 'storyboarding' as his primary form of idea development.

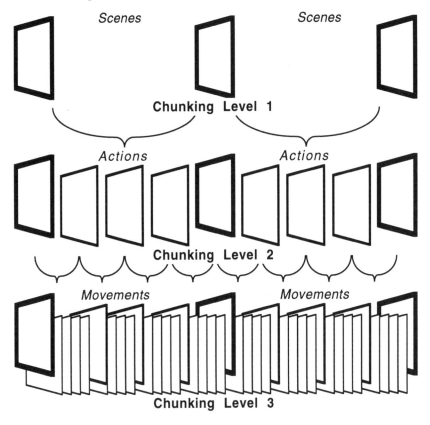

Figure 2 Story-Boarding/Animation Process

A story-board is like a visual table of contents—it is a set of still drawings that represent the sequence of critical events to take place in the storyline of a film. Storyboarding is essentially an extension of the process of animation to a larger scale. Animation takes place through a process that involves starting with the drawing of still pictures representing the critical events of a particular movement. These drawings are typically done by the chief animator. Once the critical chunks have been defined, the individual drawings connecting these pictorial "milestones" are filled in by the secondary animation team. Disney simply extended this process of chunking and sequencing to a larger level— becoming a kind of "meta" animator.

The "story-boarding" process, which is a very powerful way of organizing and planning, can be applied to any level of the film-making procedure. It may be applied at chunk sizes ranging from the smallest details of actually animating a particular movement of a particular character (at 32 individual pictures per second), to a particular action or event in a scene, to a scene itself, or to the sequencing of the entire film.

I have done some animating myself, and it is quite a unique way to experience the world - breaking each second down into 32 separate images. One's awareness and appreciation of movement increases dramatically. When watching a butterfly or bird flap its wings and fly through the air, one gets a sense for what Leonardo must have experienced as he strove to unlock the secrets of flight by observing the flight of birds.

From the point of view of strategy, the story-boarding process of chunking and sequencing the critical pieces required to achieve a particular result is not limited to film making but can be used for any kind of planning. It can be used to chart and organize a business project, a training seminar, a book, a counseling session, a computer program and so on.

Disney, of course, is primarily famous for his creation and portrayal of characters and stories. This is something quite different from technical competence and involves a different type of strategy. As Disney pointed out:

"We had our technic well in hand. We had learned how to make our characters act convincingly. We had learned a lot about staging and camera angles. We knew something about timing and tempo. But a good

*story idea, in our business, is an imponderable thing.
It seems to be largely made up of luck and inspiration.
It must be exceedingly simple to be told in seven or
eight hundred feet. It must, above all, have that elusive
quality called* charm. *It must be unsophisticated,
universal in its appeal and a lot of other things you
can't nail down in words but can only feel intuitively."*[19]

The special quality and appeal of Disney animation comes
from a strategy by which characters were developed, and
illustrates a second important aspect of Disney's creativity
strategy. Disney was able to associate *into* his characters,
take on their persona and view the world from their perspective. In the language of NLP, this would be called the ability
to take *'second position'* (DeLozier and Grinder, 1987). *'First
position'* involves seeing, hearing and feeling a particular
event from one's own perspective. 'Second position' involves
seeing, hearing and feeling an event from someone else's
perceptual position, including their values, beliefs and emotions. For example, imagine you are standing on a street
corner watching a person ride by on a bicycle. If you remain
in your own 'first position' as an observer viewing the
character riding the bicycle, you would be seeing it through
your own eyes as a bystander. Being in 'second position'
would involve looking from the perspective of the rider, being
on the bicycle seat, looking down at your hands on the
handlebars, etc. A *'third position'* perspective would one in
which you would actually be seeing yourself as a bystander
watching the bicycle rider from a more distant disassociated
vantage point (as a camera might record the situation).
    Disney seemed to have had a unique ability to assume
'second position'. As one of his animators recalls:

*"Mickey's voice was always done by Walt, and he felt
the lines and the situation so completely that he could
not keep from acting out the gestures and even the
body attitudes as he said the dialogue."*[20]

By associating himself into his characters' perceptual positions, Disney experienced his imaginary characters' motives and behavior more intimately. It probably also enhanced his creativity by allowing him to spontaneously discover how the character might act in a particular situation, rather than having to figure it out analytically.

In fact, both Disney's processes of going to second position and synesthesia stimulate a more spontaneous form of creativity in which new ideas are generated one upon the other (as in the example of Genesis discussed at the beginning of this book). In the words of one of Disney's animators:

> *"He did not dream a big, overall dream; he made it up as he went along. Each thing he did suggested something else, something new, something that had never been tried, something an audience might want to see."*[21]

In addition to being a major part of his creativity strategy, this process of physically associating into characters also seems to have played an important role in Disney's abilities as a 'realist.' If you can act something out or role-play it you have begun to make it tangible and real and it is easier for others to concretely experience the dream.

In summary, Disney the Realist was more feeling and action oriented than vision oriented. The Realist is future focused but operates in a more short term perspective than the Dreamer, acting 'as if' the long term vision is reachable and using successive approximations to 'chunk down' the dream into reality. As Disney put it:

> *"[Animation is] a medium whose potential limits are still far off in the future...As for the past, the only important conclusions that I can draw from it are that the public will pay for quality, and the unseen future will take care of itself if one just keeps growing up a little every day...*

"[Our success] was built by hard work and enthusiasm, integrity of purpose, a devotion to our medium, confidence in its future, and, above all, by a steady day-by-day growth in which we all simply studied our trade and learned."[22]

It is the combination of dreamer and realist that allows one to truly impact the world. Disney believed he was doing something more than simply making cartoons. During work on his ambitious and innovative animated feature *Fantasia* (a film that is still as popular today as it was when it was released over fifty years ago), Disney stated to the animators:

"This is not 'the cartoon medium.' We have worlds to conquer here."[23]

In fact, the great English political satirist and fellow cartoonist, David Low, paid Disney a remarkable compliment when he said:

"I do not know whether he draws a line himself. I hear that at his studios he employs hundreds of artists to do the work. But I assume that his is the direction, the constant aiming after improvement in the new expression, the tackling of its problems in an ascending scale and seemingly with aspirations over and above mere commercial success. It is the direction of a real artist. It makes Disney, not as a draftsman but as an artist who uses his brains, the most significant figure in graphic art since Leonardo."[24]

Micro Analysis of Disney the *Critic*

Because of Disney's intense commitment to his work, his critical judgment about it was also intense. In fact, Disney's critical evaluations were so formidable that his animators nicknamed the screening room in which their work was first viewed the "sweatbox:"

> *"The animators saw Walt at the story meetings where he acted out everything as it should be, and then again in the 'sweatbox,' when they showed him the scenes as they had animated it."*[25]

While Disney the dreamer was excited and stimulated by ideas, Disney the critic had different criteria.

> *"He expected everyone to work as hard as he did, and to be as interested and excited about what we were doing. He never spared feelings, because his interest was in the product and not in who had the best idea or who made a poor suggestion or expected applause. We were all in it together and the fellow who went off on his own, developing an idea that Walt had not approved, was asking for trouble, and received it."*[26]

The 'spoiler' critically evaluated the fruit of the realist's labor. The focus of the Critic shifted from the spontaneous creativity of the Dreamer and the organization and exploration of the Realist to the qualities of the end result. In the 'sweatbox' new ideas and innovative explorations were not highly valued, as they were to the Dreamer and the Realist, but rather the "product."

In fact, Disney's was the first studio to spend the time and money to film the initial black and white drawings of his animators and evaluate them *before* they went into final production. As Disney commented:

> *"I think it is astounding that we were the first group of animators, so far as I can learn, who ever had the chance to study their own work and correct its errors before it reached the screen...every foot of rough animation was projected on the screen for analysis, and every foot was drawn and redrawn until we could say, "This is the best we can do." We had become perfectionists, and as nothing is ever perfect in this business, we were continually dissatisfied."*[27]

Apparently, Disney learned the importance of being a critic through experience - most notably the initial financial failure of his dream project *Fantasia*. According to his brother Roy:

> *"After Snow White, [Walt] wanted to make two animated features a year. We couldn't sustain it. We grew like a mushroom and operated uneconomically. The war, plus the overloading, and a failure to study the market, put us down. Every creative fellow is so concentrated, he doesn't like to think through the market, Walt was that kind of guy until he learned his lesson. Afterward he got very conscious of market studies. He learned fast."*[28]

As Disney himself put it:

> *" I'm happier when what we do pleases a lot of people. The public is our customer. The respect we've built up with the public is something we've established and embedded in the organization. You build a story. Any writer who wants to crawl off in a hole somewhere is stupid. He has no sounding board, no new ideas. I*

*don't crawl off in any hole. I talk, bounce it, I change
my mind."*[29]

There is an interesting anecdote about Disney that illustrates some key elements of the cognitive strategy of his
'critic.' Just prior to the opening of the ride, *Pirates of the
Caribbean*, at Disneyland, Disney was making a last minute
inspection of the scenes along the ride. He was dissatisfied
with the one depicting New Orleans. He felt something
important was missing that would make the ride more
authentic but could not put his finger on what it was. Much
effort had gone into every detail of the scene and his
designers were exasperated. It seemed that the 'spoiler' was
out and about.

Finally, Disney gathered around him as many people as he
could locate, including the maintenance and food service
employees. He asked everyone to effectively go to 'second
position'—that is, imagine they were one of the characters in
the scene, participating in what was taking place. Disney
then systematically took everyone through each of the sensory representational systems. He asked, "Does it look right?"
He had spent a lot of time and money on authentic costumes
and foliage and had modeled his buildings from New Orleans'
French Quarter down to the wrought iron decorations. "Does
it sound right?" he queried. He had installed the most
modern audio technology with multiple sound tracks, each
timed and positioned perfectly to provide the sounds of
music, voices, boats and even animals. He then asked, "Does
it feel right?" He had controlled and adjusted the temperature and humidity to exactly match that of a sultry New
Orleans night. He next asked, "Does it smell right?" He had
created an elaborate setup by which he could infuse and
intermingle smells of spicy Cajun food with the smells of
gunpowder, moss and brine. Everything checked out, but he
still felt something was missing. "What is it?" he asked.
Finally, a young man who had been sweeping one of the

floors said, "Well Mr. Disney, I grew up in the South, and what strikes me is that on a summer night like this there ought to be lightning bugs." Disney's face lit up. "That's it!" he exclaimed. The young man was given a handsome bonus and Disney actually imported live lightning bugs, at a considerable cost, until he could work out a scheme to imitate them.

The fact that the young man was given a bonus makes an important point about being a 'Critic'. Critics are not only negative and destructive. The purpose of a Critic is to insure that something meets certain criteria. A Critic can respond quite positively when criteria are met. In fact, the positive reaction of a Critic frequently offers greater motivation than when it comes from a Realist or Dreamer. We expect a Dreamer to be encouraging, but when a Critic says that our ideas are good we know there must be something to them.

Often, in fact, it is the critic that is responsible for stimulating new ideas as is evidenced by Disney's account of the origin for the idea for Disneyland:

> "I had the idea of Disneyland before the war. I was casing all these amusement parks. My wife said, if you're going to go to another amusement park, I won't go with you...The places were never clean...I couldn't get my wife to go with me any more. There was nothing for the parents to do but eat with the squirrels."[30]

Since it was ideas that excited and stimulated him, Disney the Critic continually pushed those around him to be more creative as well, charging that *"Everyone has to contribute, or they become laborers."*[31]   According to his co-workers:

> "Walt felt that every idea had been thought of, every gag and even every story - the key was how you used the material to express your own work. So he was never concerned about where ideas came from."[32]

In fact, Disney was one of the first to institute and administrate an incentive system purely for creativity - as opposed to external productivity.

> "Disney had introduced a bonus system whereby anyone suggesting a gag that was used in a picture received five dollars and anyone providing an idea that formed the basis for an entire cartoon received a hundred dollars."[33]

Considering that these are depression era dollars this represents a considerable incentive. Incidentally, this bonus system was not limited to his writers and animators. It was extended to everyone at his studio, including the gardening and maintenance people. Since his business was creativity, Disney wanted to make creativity a business.

In fact, what is truly remarkable is that Disney had successfully instituted the principles of 'total quality' and the 'learning organization' almost 50 years before they became popular. The movement towards total quality and the learning organization have emerged as accelerating advances in management, technology and business methods have made it clear that the ability to learn, on both an individual and organizational level, is an ongoing necessity if organizations are to survive and succeed. Companies and other social systems have begun to realize that effective learning must be an incremental, goal-oriented process that requires organization and constant effort to maintain. An effective learning organization is one that supports the process of learning in all areas - one that encourages *learning to learn*. This requires a basic valuing and understanding of the learning process. An effective learning organization needs to support not only learners and teachers but anyone who is involved in learning contexts within an organization.

According to Peter Senge (1990), there are five 'disciplines' which need to be practiced by everyone in an organization in order for it to truly become a 'learning organization':

1. Awareness and examination of mental maps and assumptions.
2. Attaining and encouraging personal mastery.
3. Developing vision and creating the future.
4. Encouraging team learning.
5. Developing the ability for systemic thinking.

It seems that Disney intuitively sought to develop and support all of these disciplines through his strategy of balancing Dreamer, Realist and Critic. In Disney's words:

> *"We poured the money back into the business in a long-range expansion program pointing at feature-length production and the protection of our new prestige through constantly increasing quality.*

> *"*Pinocchio *might have lacked* Snow White's *heart appeal, but technically and artistically it was superior. It indicated that we had grown considerably as craftsmen as well as having grown big in plant and numbers, a growth that is only important in proportion to the quality it adds to our product in the long run.*

> *"In fact, our studio had become more like a school than a business. We were growing as craftsmen, through study, self-criticism, and experiment. In this way the inherent possibilities in our medium were dug into and brought to light. Each year we could handle a wider range of story material, attempt things we would not have dreamed of tackling the year before. I claim that this is not genius or even remarkable. It is*

the way men build a sound business of any kind -
sweat, intelligence, and love of the job."[34]

Summary of Disney's Creativity Strategy

Perhaps the most comprehensive description of how Disney's 'Dreamer,' 'Realist' and 'Critic' operated in conjunction with each other is encapsulated in Disney's statement that:

> *"The story man must **see clearly** in his own mind how every piece of business in a story will be put. He should **feel** every expression, every reaction. He should get **far enough away** from his story to take a **second look** at it... to **see** whether there is any dead phase... to **see** whether the personalities are going to be interesting and appealing to the audience. He should also try to **see** that the things that his characters are doing are of an interesting nature."*[35]

The first part of the description focuses on the interaction between the dreamer and the realist. It is clear that the "second look" is the domain of the 'spoiler' or critic.

Certainly, the statement defines three distinct perspectives.

1. The 'Dreamer'—Vision, first position, whole story:
   "The story man must see clearly in his own mind how every piece of business in a story will be put."

2. The 'Realist'—feeling and action, second position, associated, moving:
   "He should feel every expression, every reaction."

3. The 'Spoiler'—third position, distant:
   "He should get far enough away from his story to take a second look at it.

   a. Whole story:

   "To see whether there is any dead phase."

   b. Individual characters:

"To see whether the personalities are going to be interesting and appealing to the audience."

c. Specific behaviors of characters:

"He should also try to see the things that his characters are doing are of an interesting nature."

Disney's "Second look" provides what is called a *double description* of the event. This 'double description' gives us important information that may be left out of any one perspective. Just as the differences in point of view between our two eyes gives us a double description of the world around us that allows us to perceive depth, Disney's double description of his own creations served to give them an added element of depth.

Of particular interest in NLP is that the "second look" involves a specific reference to being 'far enough away.' If it was too close it could be overly influenced by the other perceptual positions. Similarly, it could also overly influence them. If the critic is too close to the dreamer, it may inhibit those dreams.

In summary, Disney's process of creative dreaming primarily took place through visual imagination but also involved the overlapping and synthesizing of the senses. The Dreamer focuses on the 'big picture' with the attitude that anything is possible.

Disney's process of 'realizing' his dreams took place through Disney's physical association into the characters of the dream and through the 'storyboarding' process of chunking the dream into pieces. The Realist acts "as if" the dream is possible and focuses on the formulation of a series of successive approximations of actions required to actually reach the dream.

Disney's process of critical evaluation involved the separating of himself from the project and taking a more distant 'second look' from the point of view of his audience or customers. The Critic seeks to avoid problems and ensure quality by logically applying different levels of criteria and checking how the idea or plan holds up under various "what if" scenarios.

Meta Program Patterns

On a macro level the types of cognitive processes associated with Disney's Dreamer, Realist and Critic are related to what are known as 'meta program' patterns in NLP. Meta program patterns are descriptions of the different ways in which a 'problem space', or elements of a problem space, may be approached.

As with the other NLP distinctions, a person can apply the same meta program pattern regardless of content and context. Also, they are not "all or nothing" distinctions and may occur together in varying proportions.

For instance, in approaching a problem one can emphasize moving *toward* something or *away from* something, or some ratio of both. Thus, a problem may be approached in varying degrees of 'proactivity' and 'reactivity.'

Chunk-size relates to the level of specificity or generality with which a person or group is analyzing a problem or problem space. Situations may be analyzed in terms varying degrees of detail (micro chunks of information) and generalities (macro chunks of information).

Problem situations may be examined with reference to long term, medium term or short term time frames; and within the context of the past, present or future. The *timeframe* within which a problem or outcome is considered can greatly influence the way in which it is interpreted and approached. There might be both long term and short term solutions.

Some people tend to look at history for solutions more so than the future. A good example is the difference between former Soviet leader Michail Gorbachev and the people who attempted to overthrow him before the break up of the Soviet Union. One was trying to prepare for the future, the others were trying to preserve the past.

Problems and outcomes may be considered in relation to the achievement of the *task*, or in relation to issues involving *relationship*, such as 'power' and 'affiliation.' The question of balance of focus with respect to task and relationship is obviously a key one with respect to problem solving for managers. In the achievement of the task, either goals, procedures or choices may be emphasized. Issues involving relationship may be approached with an emphasis on the point of view of oneself, others or the context ('the company,' 'the market,' etc.) to varying degrees.

A problem may be examined by comparing similarities (*matching*) or differences (*mismatching*) of problem elements. At the level of a group this relates to whether they are trying to reach consensus or encourage diversity.

Strategies for approaching problems may emphasize various combinations of vision, action, logic or emotion. Micro cognitive patterns on an individual level may be expressed in terms of a general *thinking style* on the macro level or group level. Vision, action, logic and emotion are more general expressions of visualization, movement, verbalization and feeling.

Different problem solving styles and approaches are characterized by different clusters and sequences of meta program patterns in various ratios. One person's approach might involve an 80% focus on relationship and 20% focus on task, and 70% emphasis on long-term versus 30% short-term considerations. Someone else may emphasize the task as 90% of the focus and think mostly in terms of short term considerations.

The different clusters of meta program patterns clearly cover different areas of problem space. In this respect, there are no 'right' or 'wrong' meta programs. Rather, their effectiveness in connection with problem solving relates to the ability to apply them to cover the space necessary to adequately deal with a problem.

On the level of macro strategy, the different phases of Disney's strategy may be characterized by particular clusters of meta program patterns in addition to their micro level cognitive structure.

In general, the Dreamer phase tends to be oriented towards the longer term future. It involves thinking in terms of the bigger picture and the larger chunks in order to generate new alternatives and choices. Its primary level of focus is on generating the content or the 'what' of the plan or idea. In Aristotle's terms, the Dreamer addresses 'final causes'.

The Realist phase is more action oriented in moving towards the future, operating with respect to a shorter term time frame than the Dreamer. The Realist is often more focused on procedures or operations. Its primary level of focus is on 'how' to implement the plan or idea. The Realist addresses the 'formal' and 'precipitating' causes.

The Critic phase involves the logical analysis of the path in order to find out what could go wrong and what should be avoided. The Critic phase needs to consider both long and short-term issues, searching for potential sources of problems in both the past and the future. Its primary level of focus is on the 'why' of the plan. The Critic must address the 'constraining' causes.

The table below summarizes the key meta program patterns associated with Disney's creative strategy.

	Dreamer	Realist	Critic
	What	*How*	*Why*
Representational Preference	Vision	Action	Logic
Approach	Toward	Toward	Away
Time Frame	Long Term	Short Term	Long/ Short Term
Time Orientation	Future	Present	Past/Future
Reference	Internal - Self	External - Environment	External - Others
Mode of Comparison	Match	Match	Mismatch

Physiology And Disney's Creative Cycle

As with other cognitive processes, physiology is an important influence on creativity and the ability to plan effectively. There are micro and macro level behavioral cues that accompany the Dreamer, Realist and Critic states that can help to more effectively enter the 'state of mind' necessary to create a powerful plan or idea.

For instance, think of what it is like when you are 'dreaming' or in the early stages of planning or creating when there are many options and choices. What kinds of behavioral cues do you think are the most significant for your 'dreaming' process? What is your posture like? Do you move around? How do you orient your head and eyes?

Think of what it is like when you are 'realizing' an idea or 'dream'. What kinds of behavioral cues do you think are the most significant for your 'realizing' process?

Think of what it is like when you are thinking 'critically' and evaluating your plan. What kinds of behavioral cues do you think are the most significant for your 'critical' thinking process?

Which of the three types of thinking styles - Dreamer, Realist or Critic - seems to be the most natural for you?

Based on the descriptions of Disney's behavior and the modeling of a number of different people who are effective in reaching these states, the following generalizations may be drawn about key patterns of physiology associated with each of the thinking styles making up Disney's creative cycle:

Dreamer: Head and eyes up. Posture symmetrical and relaxed.

Realist: Head and eyes straight ahead or slightly forward. Posture symmetrical and slightly forward.

Critic: Eyes down. Head down and tilted. Posture angular.

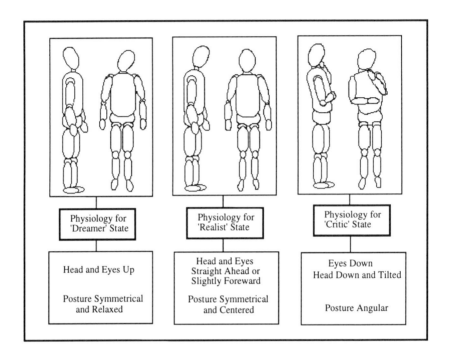

Physiology for 'Dreamer' State	Physiology for 'Realist' State	Physiology for 'Critic' State
Head and Eyes Up	Head and Eyes Straight Ahead or Slightly Foreward	Eyes Down Head Down and Tilted
Posture Symmetrical and Relaxed	Posture Symmetrical and Centered	Posture Angular

**Patterns of Physical Cues Associated With
Dreamer, Realist and Critic**

Applications of Disney's Creativity Strategy

The tools and distinctions of NLP can be used to model the specific cognitive patterns used by exceptional people such as Walt Disney in such a way that they may be transferred to others. One of the goals of NLP is to make an explicit and operational map of the inner strategies of successful people like Walt Disney. Using NLP we can synthesize our information about Disney's creative thinking strategies into techniques that may be used by anybody desiring to employ some of the creative processes that contributed to Disney's genius.

Everybody already has the Dreamer, Realist, Critic inside them. Unfortunately, what usually happens is that the Dreamer and the Critic get into a fight. If you take a typical business meeting, you can have a Dreamer, a Realist and a Critic in this meeting. Rather than functioning in some organized strategy, the Dreamer says something, the Critic argues against it, then the Dreamer has a polarity reaction to the Critic. The Dreamer and critic go in conflicting directions until, finally, the Realist says, "We're out of time." And you get this mass of chaos as opposed to a process in which these strategies support each other.

One of the biggest problems is that the Critic doesn't just criticize the dream. The Critic criticizes the *Dreamer*. It is different to say, "That *idea* is stupid," than to say, "*You* are stupid for having that idea." Part of why Disney could function so effectively is that he didn't criticize his team or himself, he criticized the plan to accomplish the dream. I think that what keeps the Critic and the Dreamer from being stuck in a polarity response is the Realist.

It is important to structure the relationship between these stages of creativity so it creates a harmonious process. The key is to acknowledge that there will be multiple perspectives of the same thing—double or triple descriptions. You need to see a plan from the critic's point of view as well as from the Realist's point of view and the dreamer's point of view.

Example of Installing Disney's Creative Cycle

In this Section we are going to explore the process of installation. Once you have identified an effective strategy the next question is, *"How do you install it so it functions naturally on its own?"*

Dreamer

First, we know from Disney that we have a 'vision space' for the Dreamer. We know some of the micro-aspects of the Dreamer. He is trying to visualize the gestalt. And, from basic NLP principles, we know that vision is going to be associated with a particular physiology—remember the caricature that the animator drew of Walt Disney; he was looking up to the right.

Realist

Then we want to establish the Realist. And as we know, the micro-strategy of the Realist involves:

1. Identifying with the characters in the dream.
   and
2. Chunking the dream into a set of steps or 'storyboard'.

Critic

Lastly there is the Critic. The Critic is going to need to be distant enough from the dream and the plan to get a good 'second look' at the dream. Not only will distance help the Critic can see the whole picture, but if the Critic was too close he might interfere.

The following set of steps describes a technique for enhancing personal creativity that uses the key elements of Disney's creative strategy:

1. Establish a neutral location or 'Meta Position' and select three physical locations and label them:

   (1) Dreamer

   (2) Realist

   (3) Critic

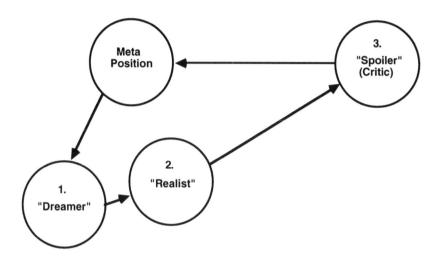

Figure 3 Disney's Creative Cycle

2. Anchor the appropriate strategy to each physical location. Use Meta Position to make sure the physiological state associated with each state stays 'pure.'

   a. Think of a time you were able to creatively dream up or fantasize new ideas without any inhibitions; step into location (1) and relive that experience.

   b. Identify a time you were able to think very realistically and devise a specific plan to put an idea effectively into action; step into position (2) and relive that experience.

   c. Think of a time you were able to constructively

criticize a plan—that is, to offer positive and constructive criticism as well as to find problems. Make sure the location is far enough away from the others that it doesn't interfere. Step into location (3) and relive that experience.

3. Pick an outcome you want to achieve and step into the dreamer location. Visualize yourself accomplishing this goal as if you were a character in a movie. Allow yourself to think about it in a free and uninhibited manner.

4. Step into the realist location, associate into the "dream" and feel yourself in the positions of all of the relevant characters. Then, see the process as if it were a 'storyboard' (a sequence of images).

5. Step into the critic position and find out if anything is missing or needed. Then, turn the criticisms into 'how' questions for the dreamer.
   a. Remember, the critic is to criticize the plan, not the realist or the dreamer.
   b. It is often helpful to have the critic initially acknowledge which elements of the plan are satisfactory before asking questions.

6. Step back into the dreamer position to creatively come up with solutions, alternatives and additions to address the questions posed by the critic. If the critic's questions seem too harsh or it is difficult to think of the questions without accessing the critic state, go through Meta Position before returning to the dreamer location. You may even wish to rephrase the critic's questions from Meta Position.

7. After you have repeated this cycle several times, consciously think of something else that you really enjoy and are good at but continue to walk through the dreamer, realist and critic locations. This will promote lateral thinking and unconscious gestation.

8. Continue to cycle through **steps 4, 5** and **6** until your plan congruently fits each position.

Transcript of Demonstration

R.D.: We know some of the steps of Disney's strategy. We also want to draw out of you some of your own natural strategies. Installation is both pacing and leading. Who would like to volunteer as the demonstration subject?

(Person X comes up)

Here is the first step. Find a location for your dreamer.

Put aside any content for now. We want to set up the states without content. We want to first focus on only the process. So, here I would like you to think of the time when you were really able to dream freely, when your mind could cover an incredible amount of space, and it didn't matter if it was real. In fact, what was really great about it, was that it was a kind of escape to a fantasy world, away from the real world. It was your own world that you could make up.

Then step into this location—experience that state.

(X steps into the location, body erect but relaxed, eyes straight ahead)

And maybe to enhance it even a little more, put your head and eyes up just a little bit. So your vision can reach a little farther.

When you really feel that you have been able to get to it you can step back out.

(X smiles and hesitates before he steps back from location)

R.D.: (To audience) Sometimes people don't want to leave that space!

(To X) Somewhere about here, a little bit behind that dreamer location, I would like you to think of a time you were planning, you were making something concrete as much as you could. You are a realist when you are thinking, "What has to be done to make this happen?" "What steps will reach that goal"?

It is important that you use this micro-strategy to identify the realist because some people confuse the realist with the critic. And believe me critics are not realistic. They can be just as out there as a dreamer. "This *could* go wrong, that *could* go wrong."

When you are the realist you are future pacing yourself through the steps to the dream and creating an action plan for the steps.

(To X) Get into that state of mind and step into the realist location.

(X steps into the realist space, body tilted slightly forward, eyes pointing ahead but slightly down)

And when you have a good sense of it there you can step back out.

(To audience) Since I do computer programing, I know this state very well. You start planning this thing and getting into it. The next thing you know is that it is five o'clock in the morning!

(To X) Now, over here I want to find a location some distance from both your dreamer and your realist. Here is where we are going to put your critic. And to me the physical distance is important. Disney said, "I have to get far enough away and take a second look... so that I am looking at it as my audience would." You want to think about judging something as if it is not your own idea.

The critic is generally highly auditory and rules oriented. If you are really good at criticizing other people's ideas, then, you can use that for yourself.

You might also want to think about it from the point of view of your own worst critic. If you are working on a particular project, let's say designing a training program, I would suggest that you put yourself into the perspective of the person who is most likely to be resistant. Find your worst critic because, if that person can't find any problem with it, then it is going to be a fairly solid plan.

That is what I would like you to do; have a cold and piercing examination of something at the time when you were really critical. I don't mean just negative. And then step into the critic location.

(X steps into critic location, leaning to side, head is cocked, hand on his chin)

Alright, now step away from that space and come back here to meta position.

Now we have our three locations. By the way, you can always use additional strategies to enhance the locations. For instance, if you are in the dreamer position you can use a metaphor, an image of somebody else who was successful and model them, you can even pretend that you are Walt Disney himself.

"How would Walt Disney respond to this problem?"

"How would Leonardo da Vinci approach it?"

You might also choose to just dream about the first step of something instead of the whole thing. But I suggest you keep a broad view. Usually the problem that we have in pursuing an idea isn't because we don't think about it precisely enough, it is because we don't have a broad enough vision.

(To X) Now I want you to think of the content of that idea or problem you were working on. Is it possible to say the general area? Is it personal?

X: It is a lot about my metaphor of how things happen.

R.D.: In other words, it is a sort of inner personal issue. So what is your goal?

X: To find another process that I would fancy more which would include more tolerance.

R.D.: OK. Here is the starting point. First start here in the dreamer location and dream up a miraculous world where there would be all these things that were so seductive to you that they could draw you into them. As if you waved a magic wand and you could have a world that you would like.

(To audience) Now I see something that might be significant already. This physiology wasn't there the first time *(X has his hand on his chin)*. I saw this physiology when you were in the critic spot.

(Laughter)

This is where NLP can be very useful. Step back out and acknowledge the critic, but let him know he will have his say later. Now step in and just be the dreamer for a moment.

(X steps in with dreamer physiology this time)

So, here there is just this space. See the whole thing, what does it look like?

You have that sort of seductive tolerance.

Maybe you can have a metaphor or even a fantasy, some kind of vision.

This is not about how to solve a problem, this is about how to have a vision. So you don't have to check if the vision is going to work, just have it.

OK, have you got something?

(X nods)

Good. Take this vision, step into the realist location and ask yourself, "OK. What would happen if that was the case?" What are the steps it would take to manifest this vision? Who are the characters that are involved? For instance, if there are parts of you, how would these parts interact with each other? Would it be like Mickey Mouse and Goofy? Maybe it would be more like Indiana Jones? *(Some laughter in the room)* But it doesn't have to be a metaphor.

You don't have to get the whole movie. This is like the first cut. You just go, "How am I going to make this work?"

(X's hand begins to move toward his chin. Robert grabs the hand) You will have your chance critic!

(Laughter from the participants)

At least let him get some good stuff you can tear in to.

(X returns to realist physiology)

You can get a few of the steps that might be necessary to carry out that dream....

Good. *Now* we can let the critic out. Come way over here to the critic location.

(X steps into critic location in critic's physiology)

So what do you think of those steps? What is missing? Is it going to work or is it simple still?

You don't have to find the solution, all you have to do is find what is wrong?

This is the person who does problem finding, not problem solving. The problem finding is as an important part as problem solving.

X: I don't know for instance how I can know that I have reached the first step.

R.D: OK. So, this is one question that this critic has.

X: And it can't work if I can't check anything.

R.D.: Great. These are very important issues relating to evidence procedure. Now, take those concerns and walk up over there to the dreamer location and the dreamer is going to dream up a way that you are going to know how it got to the first step. The dreamer might say, "Oh, yes, the first step, I know how!" "What a neat challenge!"

You can make a metaphor. It could be crazy. It's just a dream.

(X's physiology changes. He breaks into a broad smile)

X: Mm... *(Laughter in the crowd.)*

R.D.: Einstein used to try to visualize what it would look like to ride a light beam. This is a little crazy, isn't it? Of course, it upset our concept of the universe.

Now, take that enriched vision and step over here to the realist location.

(X moves to realist location. His physiology shifts to that of the realist state)

How are you going to implement that? Say to yourself, "Alright, I've got to do this, I've got to do that!" "What are the steps?" "How am I going to know it?" "Maybe come up with some clever way of figuring that out!"

Put yourself into it. You are at the first step and you know that you are at the first step. What pieces are there?

Do you have something?

X: Ah-hum...

R.D.: Alright. Now over to the critic again.

(X moves into critic location and physiology)

Well, what do you think?

(X hesitates, then starts to smile.)

(Bursts of laughter from audience)

It is getting hard to be staying so critical, eh?

Let us go to the next part for a moment. Without thinking about anything in particular consciously, I want you to walk to the dreamer location, pause for a moment, then walk to the realist location, and then return again to the critic spot. And do that three times without anything in particular in mind.

X: Am I supposed to see the vision?

R.D.: You can or you may let your mind wander to something else for a moment.

(X. walks through the locations according to R.D.'s instructions)

(To audience) Have you ever seen people pacing up and down when they are trying to solve a problem? We do that kind of thing all the time.

(X finishes the three loops)

R.D.: (To X) Now, come to meta-position and consciously think for a moment about the vision. Right now. Has it changed at all since you last checked in on it?

X: Yes, it did. Each step has a complementary function. Other options came out. It has become more congruent and stronger.

(To Audience) In other words, all he was supposedly doing was walking, but the strategy continued to run because it was anchored to the locations.

He is starting to put the pieces together in a more balanced way. The states are anchored to physical spaces and they don't care about what your conscious mind is thinking at that moment. These states are going to have an effect on what is happening even if you were thinking about what you had for dinner last night.

Again, you keep taking three perspectives. You will align them to a common vision. When you are aligning all the functions literally and physically in the same direction, you get yourself out of the way. When I step out of the realist location, all that is left there to criticize is the plan, not me. I am not in that plan. There is no person there, it is the steps of the plan.

Then you have set up an aligned strategy that is going to create a positively reinforcing feedback loop. It uses all of your neurology in coordination.

These physiological states are literally accessing a few billion brain cells at a time. You could visualize the activity as lights which go through the body, so that you hear this brilliant, bright light coming down and it is very focused. You kind of watch the nervous system, twinkling as all different parts light up and you get that system working on something. As Mozart said, "It eventually becomes a pleasant lively dream that magically produces something concrete."

(To X) May Walt Disney be with you!

(To audience) By the way, notice the importance of setting the first couple of loops through the locations. If I get the critic physiology in the dreamer's location, I contaminate this space. This is probably going to happen 90% of the time when people try to solve a problem. They start off immediately by contaminating the space— whether it is a single person or a group of people.

If you can sequence it and chunk it then you are going to have something that works smoothly. So your first couple of loops are really important. After that it becomes desirable for the physiology to start to integrate together because eventually you might find that all of those three functions form one larger macro-strategy that happens at the same time—remember the caricature of Disney. But it is important to the installation to start very cleanly.

I always find it amazing that people don't have any places for creativity in their homes, or in their companies. I find sometimes when I am working on a problem, if I really want to dream it, it is as if my dreamer lives out in the woods near my house. So I go out into this forest full of gnomes and fairies.

Then my office is sort of my realist place. I get there and I work away on my computers. Then I have to leave it and go down to my kitchen or living room and I've got to think about that idea that I had from the critic position. Is it really going to work?

Sometimes the more you can initially separate these when you first start solving the problem and get the circuit going, the more trouble and confusion it saves you later on.

Are there any questions?

Q 1: Is it important that it begins with vision in the dreamer and auditory in the critic?

R.D.: This has to do with the degree to which it is your own *versus* Disney's strategy that you want to install. My answer is:

Having a choice is always better than not having it. If you start up with something that's auditory you might want to add vision just to see how it would enhance the process. So I would keep the choice at least.

Q 2: Can we use it for something we want to achieve in the future?

R.D.: Yes. What you work on doesn't have to be a problem you are trying to solve. I suggest you all just start with some vision you have. If the circuit works you may surprise yourself.

After the Exercise

Q 1: It was very powerful. Can you do it with more than one person at a time?

R.D.: You can take a whole group through it. You can cover a much broader space that way.

I use this process in my own computer company. We have actually different rooms where we can go to think different ways: one to brainstorm, another to plan and another to evaluate. When we brainstorm we most often sit in a circle. But when we start planning we all sit next to each other and look at the plan on a board. And when we are evaluating we sit around a table with the plan in the center and ask: "Is this really going to work?" So you can also set up the environment to support a multi-person circuit as well.

Q 2: Where is the decision point then?

R.D.: It is at the critical evaluation.

Q 3: Could we consider that at the evaluation time there is one person in charge of the decision process?

R.D.: In some companies where you have a hierarchical structure, yes. But what they call "buy in" management is based on group consensus rather than on hierarchy. It all depends on the kind of evidence procedure you are using.

Q 4: I was surprised that it changed my whole relationship with time. I have a project due three years from now that I am going to start tomorrow night, and after this, there is no limit in time because now I dreamed that I could always dream and realize what I dream!

R.D.: Sometimes people start with a dream that literally is very distant in their minds, maybe in terms of years from now. And after going through the Disney strategy it is right here and not in the distance anymore.

Q 5: In the critic state, I was often quite negative and sad; but now, knowing that I can go afterwards to the dream state, I feel much better.

R.D: The whole dynamic of the circuit shifts if the critic knows that I will go to him for advice, and that he can seek help from the other functions as well. Then it is not like being so lost or alone.

Sometimes the magic that happens here is that it really starts to become constructive criticism. The critic begins to give positive feedback as opposed to negative. And when your own worst critic says, "Go for it!" you know nothing can stop you.

Q 6: I noticed that the critic part actually gave a feeling of security.

Q 7: We felt after finishing the three part round that we needed to bring in a fourth part—which was the "will" part that the subject felt like putting in front of the dreamer's part.

R.D.: At some stage you want to take the dream and connect it to your mission. I think this is what you are talking about with the "will." So once I attached the vision, the dream, to the mission then it becomes a commitment. This is a nice next step.

I want to say one thing about potential problems with this process.

The thing that we have to realize with any strategy is that the chain is no stronger than the weakest link. In other words, if some part of the strategy is weak it can throw the whole thing out of balance. Sometimes a person says, "I can't visualize, I can't do the dreamer's step." And clearly the ability to be creative is going to be relative to your ability to develop and utilize your senses. Some people are much more comfortable as the critic, they spend 90% of their lives in that position. This is where developing flexibility with micro-strategies is so crucial.

The locational sorting of the different processes helps to organize and coordinate them and avoid interferences or 'contamination' between the states.

Turning a criticism into a question helps to avoid the 'negative' effects of the critic and stimulate the Dreamer.

Once a creative cycle is robustly 'installed' it can be enriched by processes which stimulate lateral thinking and unconscious gestation.

Team Learning Process: 'Storyboarding' Multiple Perspectives of Idea and Problem Spaces

The creative cycle of a group or team often involves the movement between large chunks (the big picture or 'vision') and small chunks (the establishment of micro objectives to reach the larger goal). A key part of managing a group's creativity involves the ability to break down the general roles of group or team members into the specific cognitive and interactive processes required to implement or fulfill that role. For example, goals that stimulate creativity are usually set towards something in the future. In the Dreamer phase, they are more long term. At the Realist phase, they are more short term.

In the processes of evolving, encouraging and drawing out the creativity of others it is important to be able to identify and adapt to both physical and psychological constraints. Managing the creative cycle of a group involves establishing physical and psychological constraints which direct the group's process in relation to the phase of the creative cycle they are in.

Different stages of the creative cycle involve constraints relating to different types of evidences. An evidence for dreaming might be the number of ideas generated. But, for the critic, having a lot of ideas is perceived as a problem.

Meta program patterns often relate to one another in natural clusters (e.g., shortening a time frame for a project tends to focus people on the task instead of the relationship). As we pointed out earlier, there are clusters of meta program patterns that can be associated with the Dreamer, Realist and Critic. Knowing about these clusters can allow you to recognize them in people or, to draw them out of people intentionally. The flexibility of a group can even be enhanced by assigning or encouraging different clusters of meta program patterns to individual group members.

For effective group creativity it is important to incorporate:

1. All three of the stages of the creative cycle (Dreamer, Realist, Critic)

   and

2. To incorporate the different points of view of the group members in all three stages.

One of the problems that can often happen during a meeting is that the Dreamer says something that is perceived as outrageous to which the Critic responds negatively. In reaction to the Critic, the Dreamer polarizes and starts defending the dream even more. The Critic complains and they go around and around in a vicious circle. Finally the Realist says, "We are running out of time. Let's get down to work." But it ends up as a chaotic mix of polarities. The cycle doesn't progress because the Dreamer is constantly being interrupted by the critic and so on.

In an effective group, each would support or complement each other's strengths by having the dreamer output a number of ideas to a realist who outputs a prototype to the critic, who evaluates the specific prototype, etc.

An important criterion for stimulating creativity in a group is to maintain balance. On the one hand, it is important to draw out as full a range of potential as possible in group members. On the other hand, it is also important to draw out and utilize individual strengths.

Disney's strategy acknowledges that there are different kinds of potentials within people. Some people have strengths as a Dreamer or Realist or Critic. One way to stimulate creativity is to try to develop the flexibility of everybody to cover the different phases. Another strategy is to identify and then utilize the particular strengths of certain individuals, but avoiding categorizing them in a way that 'pigeon holes' them.

Different processes are effective to stimulate creativity at the different stages of the creative cycle. Disney, as you recall, had different rooms for the Dreamer, Realist and Critic. He had one room that was a dreamer room which had pictures and inspirational drawings and sayings all over the walls. Everything was chaotic and colorful in this room, and criticisms were not allowed—only dreams! For their Realist space, the animators had their own drawing tables, stocked with all kinds of modern equipment, tools and instruments that they would need to manifest the dreams. The tables were arranged in a large room in which all of the animators could see and talk to other animators. For the Critic, Disney had a little room that was underneath the stairs where they would look at the prototype pencil sketches and evaluate them. The room always seemed cramped and hot, so they called it the 'sweatbox.'

One powerful form of team learning and creativity arises out of the fact that people have different maps of the world. The way that somebody else represents a particular individual's problem or idea can automatically provide a way of enriching and clarifying the idea or problem.

The next process is designed to apply Disney's strategies in a way that takes advantage of this natural process of team learning and co-creativity. It is called "inter-vision." In "supervision" there is an implied hierarchical relationship between people; the supervisor provides the 'right map' to the other person. In "inter-vision" it is assumed that people are peers and that there is no one right map. There is also an important implication in the term "vision." One of the goals of the exercise is to apply visual and symbolic thinking strategies in a group context.

The exercise has to do with the influence that different ways of representing and conceptualizing the 'problem space' of a plan or idea have on our ability to find potential solution space. It is best done in a group of four in order to get enough range of diversity.

The exercise is organized into three phases: 1) a Dreamer, 2) a Realist and 3) a Critic stage.

In the Dreamer phase, one of the group members, the 'explorer,' is to describe a plan or idea to the other group members. The content of the idea or plan is not restricted. Depending on the relationship of the group members, it could range from a business project to a plan for addressing the problems of a client to a family vacation.

As they are listening, the team members should make sure they are assuming the appropriate strategy and physiology associated with the Dreamer perspective. For instance, rather than judge or critically evaluate the idea or its feasibility, the goal of each group members at this stage is to "see clearly in his own mind how every piece of business in a story will be put." As they attempt to see the 'big picture,' group members will want to listen with their head and eyes up in a posture that is symmetrical and relaxed.

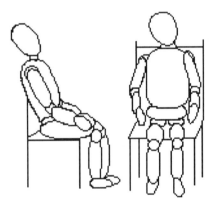

Dreamer State Physiology

When the explorer has finished describing the 'problem space', group members will want to consider whether the following 'Dreamer' questions have been answered and they are clear "how every piece of business will be put."

*"**What** do you want to do?* (As opposed to what you want to <u>stop</u> doing, <u>avoid</u> or <u>quit</u>.)"

*"**Why** do you want to do it?" "**What** is the purpose?"*
*"**What** are the payoffs?" "**How** will you know that you*
*have them?" "**When** can you expect to get them?"*
*"**Where** do you want the idea to get you in the future?"*
*"**Who** do you want to be or be like in relationship to the*
idea?"

The focus of the Dreamer stage of the intervision process is
on representing and widening the perception of the problem
space of a particular plan or idea. These questions can help
both the explorer and the other group members to widen,
enrich and clarify their mental picture of the problem space
of the idea or plan.

In the next phase of the exercise, each group member
(including the explorer) is to make a simple 'storyboard' of
the plan or idea. This 'first approximation' should be very
general and synthetic, encapsulating the whole plan or idea.
It can be any kind of a diagram or a sketch. It may be best to
make a symbolic or metaphoric picture of the plan or idea.
For example, somebody might draw a kind of landscape;
another person may just draw a group of symbols like
rectangles, circles and stars and connect them with lines and
arrows.

Each person is to make his or her own representational
map individually without looking at the other drawings. So,
each draws his or her own individual picture of what this
problem space is, including the explorer, making a total of
four pictorial maps of the problem space. Then group members share their pictures and discuss the assumptions and
criteria behind the various drawings and interpretations.
Contrasting different peoples' maps and assumptions about a
problem space is a way to enrich perceptions about that
space.

"Intervisors" are to explain their drawings without giving
any specific suggestions or solutions. They are simply explaining their representation and what assumptions they

made. That is, intervisors don't try to tell the explorer how to manifest the idea or plan; they simply show and explain their "storyboard" of that plan or idea.

Group members may then explore the following 'Realist' questions.

> *"**How** specifically will the idea be implemented? **How** will you know if the goal is achieved? **How** will the performance criteria be tested?"*
>
> *"**Who** will do it?"* (Assign responsibility and secure commitment from the people who will be carrying out the plan.)
>
> *"**When** will each phase be implemented?" "**When** will the overall goal be completed?"*
>
> *"**Where** will each phase be carried out?"*
>
> *"**Why** is each step necessary?"*

During the discussion, group members should be sure they are assuming the strategy and physiology of the Realist. As they are discussing, individual group members may want to sit with their head and eyes straight ahead or slightly forward with a posture that is symmetrical and slightly forward. Their cognitive focus should be to act 'as if' the dream is achievable and consider how the idea or plan can be implemented; emphasizing specific actions and defining short term steps. Group members may want to put themselves into 'second position' with the people involved in the plan and perceive it from several points of view.

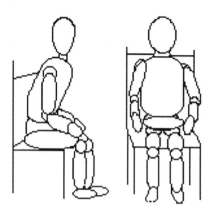

Realist State Physiology

In the Critic stage of this 'intervision' process, the separate 'storyboards' are to be synthesized together into a common storyboard. Typically this is done by the explorer who is to give feedback to the group in terms of how his or her own map of the problem space has been enriched by each member. The explorer restates the plan or idea and makes a 'next approximation' by creating a new or combined storyboard.

The group is then to take "a second look" at this 'storyboard'. As Disney advised, the group should get "far enough away" to be able to take this second look effectively. This may involve the group physically changing location or moving the representation of the storyboard somewhere else. Group members may then consider the following 'Critic' questions:

> *"Does this plan match the criteria and purpose for which it was intended?"*
>
> *"**Why** might someone object to this new idea?"*
>
> *"**Who** will this new idea effect and who will make or break the effectiveness of the idea and what are their needs and payoffs?"*
>
> *"**What** positive things are derived from the current way(s) of doing things?"*

*"**How** can those things be kept when you implement the new plan or idea?"*
*"**When** and **where** would you <u>not</u> want to implement this new idea?"*

As Disney did, the group may want to consider several different perspectives and criteria as they evaluate the storyboard - 1) the whole plan, 2) the characters or individuals involved in implementing the plan or who will be affected by the plan and 3) the specific actions of those individuals.

While taking the second look, group members will want to employ the appropriate strategy and physiology related to the 'Critic'. Their purpose is to help avoid problems by taking different perspectives and finding missing links by logically considering 'what would happen if' problems occur. This may be facilitated by assuming an angular posture in which the eyes and head are down and slightly tilted.

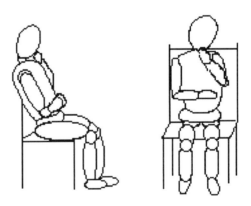

Critic State Physiology

In order to be 'constructive' as critics, group members will want to first acknowledge which criteria have been met, and formulate their 'criticisms' as questions as much as possible.

When the questions have been collected, the group may switch to another 'explorer' or may keep cycling through the phases to make successive approximations of the plan.

To summarize the steps of the process:

1. The explorer describes (in 5 minutes or less) a plan or idea. Group members assume Dreamer strategy and physiology.

2. Group members explore Dreamer questions to clarify and enrich their perception of the 'problem space' of the plan or idea.

3. Each person, including the explorer, draws a simple 'storyboard' or visual map of the problem space (to be done in 5 minutes or less).

4. Group members compare the pictures, explain them and discuss the criteria and assumptions behind them. The discussion should also be kept within a time limit of approximately 5 minutes per person.

5. Group members then explore the Realist questions, assuming the strategy and physiology of the Realist, in order to clarify specific steps and actions.

6. The separate 'storyboards' are synthesized together by the 'explorer' and the Critic questions are considered employing an appropriately 'distant' strategy and physiology.

7. The group may keep cycling through the phases to make successive approximations of the plan.

Conclusion

Disney's strategy of cycling between Dreamer, Realist and Critic provides a powerful basis for almost any creative or productive endeavor.

Disney's process of creative dreaming primarily took place through visual imagination but also involved the overlapping and synthesizing of the senses. The 'Dreamer' focused on the 'big picture' with the attitude that anything is possible. The Dreamer phase tends to be oriented towards the longer term future. It involves thinking in terms of the bigger picture and the larger chunks in order to generate new alternatives and choices. Its primary level of focus is on generating the content or the 'what' of the plan or idea - the 'final causes'.

Disney's process of 'realizing' his dreams took place through the physical association into the characters of the dream and through the 'storyboarding' process of chunking the dream into pieces. The Realist acts "as if" the dream is possible and focuses on the formulation of a series of successive approximations of actions required to actually reach the dream. The Realist phase is more action with respect to the future, operating within a shorter term time frame than the Dreamer. The Realist is often more focused on procedures or operations. Its primary level of focus is on 'how' to implement the plan or idea - the 'formal' and 'precipitating' causes.

Disney's process of critical evaluation involved separating himself from the project and taking a more distant 'second look' from the point of view of his audience or customers. Its primary level of focus is on the 'why' of the plan. The Critic seeks to avoid problems and ensure quality by logically applying different levels of criteria and checking how the idea or plan holds up under various "what if" scenarios. The Critic phase involves the analysis of the plan in order to find out what could go wrong and what should be avoided. The Critic phase needs to consider both long and short-term issues, searching for potential sources of problems in both the past and the future - the 'constraining' causes.

Footnotes to Chapter 3

1. Thomas, F. & Johnson, O.; *Disney Animation; The Illusion of Life* ; Abbeyville Press, New York, New York, 1981, p. 379

2. Disney, W., *Growing Pains* (1941), reprinted in *SMPTE Journal*, July 1991, pp. 547-550

3. Thomas, F. & Johnson, O.; *Disney Animation; The Illusion of Life* ; Abbeyville Press, New York, New York, 1981, p. 85

4. Disney, W., *Growing Pains* (1941), reprinted in *SMPTE Journal*, July 1991, pp. 547-550

5. Culhane, J.; *Walt Disney's Fantasia* ; Harry N. Abrahms Inc., New York, New York, 1983, p. 29

6. *ibid*, p. 36

7. Finch, C.; *The Art of Walt Disney* ; Harry N. Abrahms Inc., New York, New York, 1973, p. 155

8. Disney, W., *Growing Pains* (1941), reprinted in *SMPTE Journal*, July 1991, pp. 547-550

9. Thomas, F. & Johnson, O.; *Disney Animation; The Illusion of Life* ; Abbeyville Press, New York, New York, 1981, p. 25

10. *ibid*, p. 159

11. *ibid*, p. 186

12. Disney, W., *Growing Pains* (1941), reprinted in *SMPTE Journal*, July 1991.

13. *ibid*

14. Thomas, F. & Johnson, O.; *Disney Animation; The Illusion of Life* ; Abbeyville Press, New York, New York, 1981, p. 62

15. *ibid*, p. 71

16. *ibid*, p. 47

17. McDonald, J.; *The Game of Business*, Doubleday, Garden City, New York, 1974, pp. 170-171

18. Disney, W., *Growing Pains* (1941), reprinted in *SMPTE Journal*, July 1991, pp. 547-550

19. *ibid*

20. Thomas, F. & Johnson, O.; *Disney Animation; The Illusion of Life* ; Abbeyville Press, New York, New York, 1981, p. 77

21. *ibid*, p. 186

22. Disney, W., *Growing Pains* (1941), reprinted in *SMPTE Journal*, July 1991, pp. 547-550

23. Culhane, J.; *Walt Disney's Fantasia* ; Harry N. Abrahms Inc., New York, New York, 1983, p. 198

24. McDonald, J.; *The Game of Business*, Doubleday, Garden City, New York, 1974, pp. 170-171

25. Thomas, F. & Johnson, O.; *Disney Animation; The Illusion of Life* ; Abbeyville Press, New York, New York, 1981, p. 84

26. *ibid*, p. 86

27. Disney, W., *Growing Pains* (1941), reprinted in *SMPTE Journal*, July 1991, pp. 547-550

28. McDonald, J.; ***The Game of Business***, Doubleday, Garden City, New York, 1974, pp. 220-245

29. *ibid*

30. *ibid*

31. Thomas, F. & Johnson, O.; ***Disney Animation; The Illusion of Life*** ; Abbeyville Press, New York, New York, 1981, p. 188

32. *ibid*, p. 153

33. Finch, C.; ***The Art of Walt Disney*** ; Harry N. Abrahms Inc., New York, New York, 1973, pp. 170-171

34. Disney, W., *Growing Pains* (1941), reprinted in *SMPTE Journal*, July 1991, pp. 547-550

35. Thomas, F. & Johnson, O.; ***Disney Animation; The Illusion of Life*** ; Abbeyville Press, New York, New York, 1981, p. 367

Wolfgang Amadeus Mozart

Chapter 4

Wolfgang Amadeus Mozart

Songs From the Spirit

Overview of Chapter 4

- Musical Dreams
- Similarity of Mozart's Strategy to Other Musicians and Composers
- Mozart's Creative Process and Self-Organization Theory
- Implementing Mozart's Strategy
- Application of Mozart's Strategy to Areas Other Than Music

    The 'Musical S.C.O.R.E.' Format

- Guided Meditation Using Mozart's Strategy
- Conclusion
- Footnotes to Chapter 4

Wolfgang Amadeus Mozart: Musical Dreams

For over two centuries Wolfgang Amadeus Mozart (1756-1791) has represented the pinnacle of musical genius. His abilities have seemed far above the capabilities of the average, or even the above average human being. Numerous anecdotes exist about Mozart's abilities and prowess: how he could play billiards and write down measures in between shots; how he wrote the overture to the opera Don Giovanni in two hours on the day of the performance; how he wrote down the fugue to a piece while he was composing the prelude; how he was able to note from memory the entire "Miserere" of the Sistine Chapel after only two hearings.

Yet, according to the principles of Neuro-Linguistic Programming,[1] Mozart's incredible abilities were not just some mystical, magical fluke, but rather the product of some very concrete and highly developed cognitive abilities that can be understood and even replicated by the average person. Using the modeling methods and distinctions we have been developing in this book (and a bit of 'detective work' in the style of Sherlock Holmes) we can gain some new and practical insights into Mozart's exceptional strategies.

One of the best insights into how Mozart's creative process functioned comes from a letter he wrote in 1789. In this letter Mozart describes his strategy for composing music with impressive detail, outlining four basic stages in the composition process. He begins with the following description:

"When I am, as it were, completely myself, entirely alone, and of good cheer - say, traveling in a carriage, or walking after a good meal, or during the night when I cannot sleep; it is on such occasions that my ideas

flow best and most abundantly. Whence and how they come, I know not; nor can I force them. Those pleasures that please me I retain in memory, and am accustomed, as I have been told, to hum them to myself." [2]

Mozart starts by describing the psychological and emotional state from which his musical inspirations sprang. He begins by saying, "When I am...completely myself..." Being 'completely oneself' bespeaks some sort of internal harmony and congruence on the identity level. There is no inner conflict or confusion about who one is. Being "entirely alone" indicates that he is not in any immediate relationship with another person. He is free to have an uninterrupted relationship with his own inner world. Mozart also specifies being "of good cheer" - being in a positive feeling state.

So, Mozart identifies three psychological conditions: being 1) congruent, 2) in an undisturbed inner relationship with himself and 3) in a positive feeling state.

He then identifies some physical conditions, giving the examples of "traveling in a carriage or walking after a good meal". These seem to imply some type of physical motion. Mozart does not just sit and think, there is some kind of accompanying movement.

Mozart continues by saying, "...it is on such occasions my ideas flow best and most abundantly". It is important to note that he does not say, "on such occasions *I make* my best music". The term "flow" indicates that the ideas arise naturally and without conscious control. It is almost as if he perceives his neurology as a kind of musical instrument that plays itself, and that by adjusting it correctly, the music will come out on its own. Mozart seems to focus on setting up the psychological and physical conditions that will allow musical ideas to emerge spontaneously and automatically.

Mozart points out that, "Whence and how they come, I know not, nor can I force them." This is clearly indicating that Mozart's creative process is largely unconscious and is a very systemic process rather than a direct cause-effect operation. Whatever conscious actions he does take do not cause or make musical notes appear in his mind in a linear fashion. Instead, Mozart's conscious actions adjust the state of his neurological system so that musical ideas are released or allowed to emerge naturally.

He then states that, "Those pleasures that please me I retain in my memory". Here he is describing a very fundamental and important relationship between "pleasure" and "memory." "Pleasure" in this case would undoubtedly relate to feelings, "memory" would relate to the recollection of sounds. It would seem that, on the micro-level, Mozart's feelings form a *synesthesia* with sound in a kind of self-reinforcing positive feedback loop or T.O.T.E. The degree to which something feels 'pleasurable' is the *test* in this loop. The *operation* involves transforming body sensations into sounds. Thus, Mozart's feelings generate internal representations of sound within his neurology. The sounds that fit with the feelings of pleasure or reinforce those feelings are naturally retained.

Mozart's basic generative process seems to be a clear example of Aristotle's basic 'pleasure principle'. Mozart's behavior and the quality of contact with his external environment, stimulate or release internal auditory representations. The qualities of the auditory representations in turn stimulate or release feelings. If the feelings stimulated by his musical ideas fit with or enhance the congruent, positive feeling state he is in, they become more strongly associated together.

Mozart next says he is, "accustomed, as I have been told, to hum them to myself."

If the feeling that is triggered by his inner music 'resonates' with the generative positive feeling, then Mozart outputs that music by humming it. Humming involves another kind of combination of feeling and sound - muscles in the throat and chest are activated to produce and externalize sound. The fact that Mozart mentions that he has been told that he hums is a clear indication that this is actually a process that he is not consciously aware of at the time he is doing it.

In the language of NLP, we can outline the micro structure of this first, most basic stage in Mozart's strategy in the following manner: Mozart's composition process seems to begin from a positive, congruent kinesthetic feeling state combined with some kind of physical movement. Internal feelings arise from this state which produce sounds or tones through a natural overlap between the kinesthetic and auditory senses (K—>A^i). This linking is known as a "*synesthesia.*" If these sounds fit with or reinforce the positive feeling state they are hummed (K^e/A^e) and retained in memory, otherwise they are discarded.

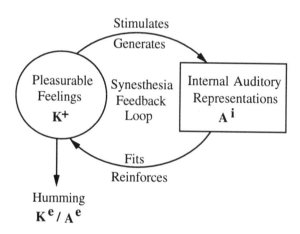

Diagram of the First Stage of Mozart's Strategy

Once enough of these basic musical patterns are gathered together, Mozart proceeds to a next stage. He writes:

> *"If I continue in this way, it soon occurs to me how I may turn this or that morsel to account, so as to make a good dish of it, that is to say, agreeably to the rules of counterpoint, to the peculiarities of the various instruments, etc."[3]*

Mozart states, "If I continue this way, it soon occurs to me how I might turn this or that morsel to account so as to make a good dish of it." The indication is that the sounds he has retained in memory form into larger chunks made of sound clusters, or "morsels." Once Mozart has gathered enough of these chunks, he jumps to another level of neurological organization in order to combine the bigger pieces together. He uses the analogy of making "a dish" out of them - a meal. While the reference to eating is clearly a metaphor, it is not out of the question to hypothesize that it might also indicate the inclusion of the senses of taste and smell into Mozart's creativity strategy via another synesthesia relationship.

At this stage Mozart has selected small groups of "musical ideas" through the feedback loop between feelings and sounds. When he has enough of these groups - when they have reached a kind of 'critical mass' - he shifts to another level of neurological organization: making a meal out of the morsels. To do this, he employs "the rules of counterpoint" and begins to take into account "the peculiarities of the various instruments." It is as if Mozart has to collect enough ideas together to reach a threshold where he can make a kind of mental 'first draft' of a composition before he can begin to apply these other filters; in the same way a writer would make a first draft before applying the rules of spelling, grammar and style.

This new level of processing involves working with bigger chunks of information and it would make sense that it necessitates the mobilization of other neurological systems than his initial creative process. Mozart mentions applying the "rules of counterpoint." Rule type thinking is most often associated with the left hemisphere of the brain (which processes language), whereas the kind of unconscious associative process Mozart described as his initial creative activity would be connected to right hemisphere type thinking. It seems reasonable to assume that, at this stage then, Mozart begins to involve the more logical 'dominant' hemisphere in his creativity strategy. His comment that it "occurs to *me* how *I* might turn this or that morsel to account" also implies the perception on Mozart's part of his own conscious participation as a causal factor in the process at this point, which would be consistent with the involvement of the left hemisphere. Thus, while Mozart cannot "force" the original intuitive flow of musical ideas, he can consciously manipulate those ideas afterward.

It is important to remember that rules in and of themselves are only as meaningful to a particular individual as the personal reference experiences upon which they are based. Mozart's use of the metaphor of creating a dish out of morsels suggests the possibility that he might literally involve the senses of taste and smell as the intuitive base for his understanding of the rules of counterpoint. It is intriguing to speculate that Mozart may have encoded the rules of counterpoint, and the unique aspects of different musical instruments in terms of tastes and smells as opposed to abstract logical structures. There is a deep natural intuition we all have about how tastes and flavors fit together. You don't eat the sherbet at the beginning of a meal; its purpose is to balance out certain flavors. "Tasteful" music may actually require the sense of taste. One can imagine Mozart thinking, "Here is a sweet piece. Should it go with something bitter or something bland?"

In summary, at this phase of his composition strategy, Mozart is evaluating and working with the music on a larger level. He is taking his basic notes and melodies and combining and evaluating them in successively 'bigger chunks' as one might combine morsels of food into a dish. While his reference to the sense of taste through this analogy to food seems most likely to be primarily for descriptive purposes, it may very well be that, for Mozart, sounds also had a synesthesia or overlap to the sense of taste.

After this stage, the composition process continues with even larger chunks.

> *"All this fires my soul, and, provided I am not disturbed, my subject enlarges itself, becomes methodized and defined, and the whole, though it be long, stands almost complete and finished in my mind, so that I can survey it, like a fine picture or a beautiful statue, at a glance. Nor do I hear in my imagination the parts successively, but I hear them, as it were, all at once (gleich alles zusammen). What a delight this is I cannot tell! All this inventing, this producing, takes place in a pleasing lively dream. Still the actual hearing of the tout ensemble is after all the best."* [4]

Mozart claims, "All this fires my soul." This implies something beyond a simple positive feeling state. This description implies the activation of much deeper and even more pervasive systems of neurology. It seems that as more and more sound groups are pieced together the positive feeling state grows bigger and more intense along with them through the synesthesia overlap process. It is as if at this stage Mozart has reached a level of organization that requires the mobilization of neurology at an identity or even spiritual level. As the level of organization of the musical composition grows successively more expansive, the commitment of neurology required to represent, retain and manipulate the music also becomes more expansive. The feelings associated with this commitment of neurology would be quite deep indeed.

Mozart writes that, "provided that I am not disturbed, my subject enlarges itself." Once again, he does not say, "I enlarge it." The implication is, "I am the channel through which it is growing." It is as if the music is writing itself through some organic process of growth.

Mozart continues by saying that the composition, "becomes methodized and defined, and the whole even though it might be long stands almost complete and finished in my mind, so I can survey it, like a fine picture or a beautiful statue, at a glance." This stage of Mozart's strategy is probably the most surprising and interesting. It is clear that a new sensory system has been activated - that of vision. This is Mozart's first reference to the visual representational system. Mozart is implying that an auditory to visual synesthesia has developed, so that the combined sounds overlap to create a single constructed visual image representing the entire groups of sound blocks ($\mathbf{A{\longrightarrow}V^c}$). This image does not appear to be in the form of musical notes, but rather something more abstract like a painting.

It is relatively self-evident that each of the senses is able to process and represent information in a way that is unique from the others. Each sensory representational system has certain strengths in its ability to organize and evaluate our experience. Taste is really good for balancing things and putting them together. The visual representational system can hold many different kinds of information together simultaneously in a way in which they don't interfere with each other. For example, you can look at a whole group of people and see all of the individuals simultaneously without any interference by the sight of one individual or another. But if you listened to all of those individuals talking at once, it would be overwhelming. The auditory system is not particularly good at holding a whole lot of things simultaneously. It's strengths are in sequencing, harmony, timing, etc.

So, Mozart needs to mobilize his visual system at this stage. In doing so he seems to be activating a very powerful synesthesia. He adds, "Nor do I hear in my imagination the parts successively, but I hear them... all at once." It would appear that his image overlaps onto the auditory system producing some sort of auditory gestalt for the entire composition. And, as in the previous stages, these sounds overlap back onto the kinesthetic system as a positive reinforcement.

He says, "What a delight this is I cannot tell! All this inventing, this producing, takes place in a pleasing lively dream." Mozart's synesthesia patterns are so immediate and so unconscious that the whole process proceeds like a dream state (which also typically include many synesthesias) and requires no conscious effort. Once the process is started, it mobilizes so much of the nervous system that it continues by itself without any need for conscious prompting. It starts to take on a life of its own - like a dream.

This emphasizes the fact that it is the mental strategy that is the most important element of creative ability as opposed to conscious effort or inspiration. Once a strategy has become completely installed and automated, the program can run on its own without conscious interference. Mozart gives further testament to the elegance of this unconscious mental circuitry when he writes:

"What has thus been produced I do not easily forget, and this is perhaps the best gift I have my Divine Maker to thank for." [5]

Mozart states that, "What has thus been produced I do not easily forget." Here Mozart refers to his celebrated auditory memory, indicating that it is primarily an inborn natural "gift" from his "Divine Maker." Yet, if one takes into consideration all of the overlaps the music had made by this point with the other senses during the three stages of the composing process - including constant connections to very positive feelings and onto the single visual image (and even potentially onto the sense of taste) - it is not so surprising that these sounds would be difficult to forget. When something is hooked into other sensory representations, these connections leave their traces all over. It seems obvious that if you feel something, hear it, taste it, and see it, you would probably have to work rather hard to forget it! If you are sensing it in every part of your neurology where is it going to go? If you just hear it, it might be easier to forget. But when you have this incredible system of synesthesias, the music is so fully represented that it would seem to become almost holographic - so that every part of it contains every other part.

Mozart describes the final stage of his creative process in the following way:

> *"When I proceed to write down my ideas, I take out of the bag of my memory, if I may use that phrase, what has previously been collected into it in the way I have mentioned. For this reason the committing to paper is done quickly enough, for everything is, as I have said before, already finished; and it rarely differs on paper from what it was in my imagination. At this occupation I can therefore suffer myself to be disturbed; for whatever may be going on around me, I write, and even talk, but only of fowls and geese, or of Gretel or Barbel, or some such matters."* [6]

Mozart comments that, "When I proceed to write down my ideas, I take out of the bag of my memory...what has previously been collected into it in the way I have mentioned" Evidently, he "collects" musical ideas into the "bag" of his memory through the strategy of continually 'chunking up' - of using different parts of his nervous system to organize successively bigger and bigger 'chunks' or clusters of internal representations of music. Specific sounds represent the relationship between clusters of body sensations that make up his feeling state. Rules, or potentially tastes ("morsels" and "dishes"), represent the relationship between clusters of sounds. Vision represents the relationship between his musical "morsels" and "dishes". He keeps shifting representational systems in order to organize successively larger clusters of representations.

Because he has systematically chunked up in this way, retrieval is the function of simply reversing the process and chunking back down. To get to the individual pieces again Mozart just reverses the direction of the chunking process with which he organized the whole. He claims, "For this reason the committing to paper is done quickly enough, for...[it is] already finished and it rarely differs on paper from what it was in my imagination."

It is only at this final stage that the translation of the composition to the typical musical notes and symbols occurs. And since the gestalt is already there, this too does not require much effort. We could speculate that this translation to musical notation is probably a visual to visual mapping - a correspondence between the abstract constructed image and remembered counterparts of standard musical notation. If this is indeed the case, we can see how it would be possible for him to be making this translation while starting on another piece of music. The first couple of stages of his composition strategy seem to require primarily the kinesthetic and auditory senses which are free to do something new while the visual to visual mapping is taking place.

In fact, Mozart says, "At this occupation I can therefore suffer myself to be disturbed." Clearly, then, this is a different process from the one Mozart uses to create in which he needs to be "entirely alone." It requires much less of a commitment of neurology. He has one kind of picture and he is translating it into another kind of picture. As a result, his ears and his feelings and his tongue and nose are free to do something else. When you think of how well he was able to sort out and employ his representational systems, it is not so surprising that he was able to be writing down one piece at the same time as he was composing the next one. The visual system can be involved in writing down one composition while feelings and sounds are mobilized to start the next one.

He says, "I write, and even talk, but only of fowls and geese, or of Gretel or Barbel, or some such matters." The implication of this would appear to be that if the subject becomes too engaging, he has to start to commit too much of his neurology to the conversation and it begins to impinge on those neural circuits which have been devoted to transcribing the composition in his imagination.

In summary, we can describe Mozart's creative process in terms of the interweaving of a micro-strategy and a macro-strategy. The micro-strategy has to do with the successive connecting together of the senses in synesthesias. And the macro-strategy has to do with this chunking up process in order to encode larger and larger clusters of musical "ideas." Each successively larger 'chunk' involves the commitment of deeper and more pervasive neurological structures and seems to elevate the process to another 'neurological' level. Once Mozart has reached the highest and widest level of chunking (seeing an hearing the whole composition before him as a single entity), he chunks it back down again until he reaches the level of individual notes.

At the macro level, Mozart's strategy for creation is the inverse of Aristotle's strategy for analysis and induction and Holmes's strategy for observation and deduction. Both Aristotle and Holmes began with "rather confused masses" of information which they initially chunked down into more specific details and elements. Then they chunked back up from the details to infer or reconstruct the 'bigger picture'.

Mozart's strategy was more like Disney's cycle between Dreamer and Realist. Mozart and Disney would assemble together chunks of experience, primarily generated through synesthesias between the senses, until they were able to "see how every piece of business would be put." They would then chunk this larger vision back down into either a musical score or a 'storyboard'.

We can outline Mozart's creative process through the following steps:

1. The systemic interplay between Mozart's internal state, pattern of physical movement and stimulation from his environment create the conditions in which musical chunks or ideas are generated or released. Mozart's internal state (K^i) and the physical and environmental stimulation (K^e) are encoded primarily in terms of feelings and movement. Musical ideas in the form of constructed auditory representations (A^c) are produced through a process of synesthesia and filtered in relationship to their "fit" with pleasurable feelings.

2. Clusters of sounds and musical ideas ("morsels") are organized into larger structures ("dishes") by subjecting them to rules of counterpoint and associating them with the peculiarities of various musical instruments (A^r). It is at this stage that the music is evaluated by filtering it in accordance with beliefs and values related to musical structure and "taste," implying the activation of left hemisphere processes. The reference structures for the rules of counterpoint and the unique attributes of the various musical instruments are provided metaphorically, and perhaps literally, through the association of sound clusters with food and potentially qualities of taste and smell (G/O).

3. The "dish" begins to take on a life or identity of its own, transcending Mozart's sense of self and requiring no more conscious intervention. A completed whole emerges through a dreamlike state as a kind of vision (V^c) that represents the gestalt of the entire composition. At this stage the visual representational seems to play a key role, but synesthesias with feelings (K^i - "fires my soul" "what a delight") and sound (A^c - "I hear it all at once") are essential to mobilize the neurology necessary to produce the gestalt.

4. The final stage of writing down the composition is a function of reversing the chunking process and unfolding or decoding what has been enfolded or encoded together through the previous three stages. The transcription of the multi-sensory musical gestalt most likely occurs through the mapping of elements of the abstract constructed visual image (V^c) to the standard musical notational system held in memory (V^r).

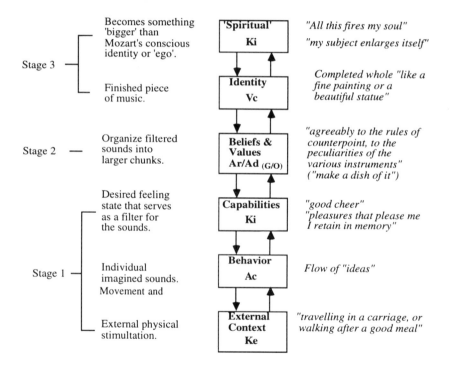

Stage 3 — Becomes something 'bigger' than Mozart's conscious identity or 'ego'.

Finished piece of music.

Stage 2 — Organize filtered sounds into larger chunks.

Desired feeling state that serves as a filter for the sounds.

Stage 1 — Individual imagined sounds. Movement and

External physical stimultation.

Box	Label
'Spiritual'	Ki
Identity	Vc
Beliefs & Values	Ar/Ad (G/O)
Capabilities	Ki
Behavior	Ac
External Context	Ke

"All this fires my soul"
"my subject enlarges itself"

Completed whole "like a fine painting or a beautiful statue"

"agreeably to the rules of counterpoint, to the peculiarities of the various instruments" ("make a dish of it")

"good cheer"
"pleasures that please me I retain in memory"

Flow of "ideas"

"travelling in a carriage, or walking after a good meal"

Stages and Levels of Mozart's Strategy

On the level of meta strategy, one of the most fascinating things about Mozart's process is the degree to which he so clearly distinguishes the various stages and levels of creativity according to different senses and metaphors. For example, Mozart's reference to "making a dish" at the second stage of his composition process implies the micro-strategy of taste and smell, but it also implies the use of the metaphor of a meal for a musical composition as a macro-strategy. His reference to painting and sculpture at the third stage of his composition process not only indicates the addition of a different sense in the micro-strategy, but the metaphor also introduces a different set of relationships at the level of macro strategy.

The kinds of relationships we pay attention to while appreciating a painting or sculpture are different from those we notice while tasting or appreciating a dish or meal. It is as if each level incorporates a different set of what Aristotle called "common sensibles." Common sensibles are qualities that are shared by all of the senses. Aristotle identified them as features such as "movement, rest, number, figure, magnitude, unity." Sound shares different kinds of commonalities with feeling and movement than it does with the sense of taste or sight.

Metaphors are one of the main mechanisms by which we apply "common sensibles." Thus, Mozart's choice of metaphors is not trivial. As a contrast, imagine if he had used the metaphor of seeing the whole composition as a well built machine; "I saw it before me like a well made clock." The metaphor is as important as the sensory system being employed because it implies certain kinds of interrelationships.

I once had the opportunity to listen to the performance of a mass composed by Mozart's father followed by Mozart's *Requiem*. There was really no comparison between the piece that Leopold Mozart wrote and his son's Requiem. Not that the elder Mozart's composition wasn't a nice piece. He was clearly familiar with all of the mechanics of how to write music. But there was not the same kind of personality, complexity nor richness in his mass that characterized his son's work. It was indeed more like a well made 'clock' than a 'painting' - technically flawless but lacking the richness of identity and spirit of his son's Requiem. You could tell that the younger Mozart's Requiem was like a painting. The pieces of the composition fit together with a kind of nonlinear coherence that a painting would have.

Mozart's creativity strategy is more akin to the process people go through when they fall in love than a technical process of analysis and criticism. In fact, Mozart once described the meta strategy for the whole of his creative process by stating, *"I am constantly searching for two notes who love each other."*

Similarity of Mozart's Strategy to Other Musicians and Composers

Mozart is not the only famous composer who described his process for creating music in these kinds of terms. Beethoven, for instance, used language remarkably similar to Mozart's in describing his own strategy for composing:

> *"I begin to elaborate the work in its breadth, its narrowness, its height and depth, and, since I am aware of what I want to do, the underlying idea never deserts me. It rises, it grows, I hear and see the image in front of me from every angle, as if it had been cast, like a sculpture, and only the labour of writing it down remains..."*[7]

Amazingly, Beethoven's description echoes Mozart's in almost every key detail: the composition "grows"; it is "heard" and "seen" before him "like a sculpture"; and in the end, only the "labour of it writing down remains."

Similarly, composer Paul Hindemith maintained:

> *"A genuine creator...will...have the gift of seeing - illuminated in the mind's eye, as if by a flash of lightening - a complete musical form...he will have the energy, persistence and skill to bring this envisioned form into existence, so that even after months of work, not one of its details will be lost or fail to fit in to his photographic picture."* [8]

Like Mozart, Hindemith refers to the vision of "a complete musical form," although he uses the analogy of a photographic picture as opposed to a painting or statue. Since photography did not exist in the times of Mozart or Beethoven it is difficult to assess if the artistic implications of painting and sculpture are essential, or if Mozart and Beethoven would have shifted to more modern metaphors.

What is clear is that the visual form of the music is not that of standard musical notation but of a more abstract quality. Pulitzer prize winning symphony composer Michael Colgrass described the role these kind of synesthesias and special imagery played in his creative process in the following way:

> "Once you set up your idea of the material, you kind of sit back. You look at it. You think about it, and you feel it. And then, if you're sensitive to it, it starts to tell you what it wants to do. It's like it starts to move in a certain direction. If you're sensitive, you'll just kind of say, 'um humh,' and then you'll just start writing it down...

> When I'm like this, in an important moment, writing it down, I'm feeling it, I'm hearing it, and I'm seeing the mathematical subdivisions of the rhythms that have to be written down...

> Sometimes people say, 'How do you write pieces?' And I'll say, 'You build them.' You do write with a pencil, that's the mark you make. But you do build, you construct. And as these pieces start to go in, then they suggest other pieces.

> And a certain detachment begins to take place too. Because as you detach yourself, you are getting a gestalt view of what's going on here, see. Because this piece is going to last twenty minutes but you've got to be able to see it, 'Swooch,' as finished. You've got to be able to see from here to here. You can't sing through twenty minutes every time you want to check something here at the seventeenth minute. So you've got to be able to go, 'Zzzuh,' like that and take in the emotional runnings, things, feelings and events. Events and

feelings that have to take place fast. So that you can get to this point and not have to waste a lot of time...

These are amorphous images that I am speaking of now, not the eighth notes or sixteenth notes or b-flats. It's kind of like a painting, but not exactly. It's an abstract image." [9]

Elements of Mozart's strategy appear to be important for almost all aspects of music, not simply creativity and composition.   I once assisted in a study of the strategies of exceptional music students conducted at two of the most prestigious music schools in England.[10] These students had demonstrated ability in skills such as memory for rhythm and pitch, and chord discrimination tasks. Like Mozart, the exceptional students used a great deal of synesthesia, transforming sounds into feelings and imagery to represent the music as a whole. They would visualize sounds generally not as notes, but as shapes and colors, like an abstract painting which they referred to as "musical mappings" or "graphs". They were able to use this type of abstract imagery to remember unusual or extended melodies and rhythms.

It is interesting to note that Mozart's strategy is not limited to the composition of classical music either. Some of the most successful and prolific composers of modern popular music have also mentioned a dreamlike, largely unconscious, quality described by Mozart as part of their creative process. For example, in an interview with *Rolling Stone* magazine in 1983, popular music composer and performer Michael Jackson reported:

"I wake up from dreams and go, 'Wow, put this down on paper.' You hear the words, everything is there in front of your face...That's why I hate to take credit for songs I've written. I feel that somewhere, someplace, it's been done and I'm just a courier bringing it into the world."

Paul McCartney, another famous popular music composer (who has also written classical pieces) mentioned a similar experience in a television interview. He described how, when he was a member of the Beatles, he dreamt that he heard the Rolling Stones, a rival musical group, performing a song that he was quite jealous of. When he awoke, he realized that they had never actually recorded or performed the song that he had dreamt about, so he wrote it down and recorded it. It was one of the groups' most successful hits - *Yesterday*.

Key aspects of Mozart's strategy also appear in the creative processes of non-musicians. For instance, Albert Einstein's perception of mathematical equations for representing his theories strongly echoes Mozart's description of the role of musical notation in his creative process.

> *"No really productive man thinks in such a paper fashion...[The theory of relativity] did not grow out of any manipulations of axioms...These thoughts did not come in any verbal formulation. I very rarely think in words at all. A thought comes, and I may try to express it in words afterward.*
>
> *"The words or the language, as they are written or spoken, do not seem to play any role in my mechanism of thought. The psychical entities which seem to serve as elements in thought are certain signs and more or less clear images which can be 'voluntarily' reproduced and combined...The above mentioned elements are, in my case, of visual and some of muscular type. Conventional words or other signs have to be sought for laboriously only in a secondary stage, when the mentioned associative play is sufficiently established and can be reproduced at will."* [11]

Perhaps the most important thing to be learned from Mozart's strategy in relationship to the process of composing, performing and appreciating music is the significance of synesthesias between the senses and the constant anchoring of the whole process to positive feelings. The actual knowledge of musical notation only comes into play at the very end of the strategy. Yet, ironically, it is this knowledge that always seems to be taught to music students first. And unfortunately it is often done in a way that interferes with the connection of sound patterns to positive feelings and creative synesthesias to the other senses. Perhaps if we revised the sequence and structures with which we teach music students to match the strategy of Mozart, we would have more potential Mozarts in the field of music today.

Mozart's Creative Process and Self-Organization Theory

'Self-organization' theory[12] relates to the process of order formation in complex dynamic systems. Paradoxically, it arose from the study of chaos. Scientists studying chaos (the absence of order) noticed that when enough complexly interacting elements were brought together, rather than create chaos, order seemed to 'spontaneously' form as a result of the interaction.

In many ways, Mozart's description of his creative process seems to reflect this phenomenon of self-organization. Mozart wrote about how his musical ideas "flowed" without conscious effort and that his process of composing took place "in a pleasing lively dream." Other composers also talk about how their music seems to arise on it's own, appear in dreams or otherwise 'write itself'. The implication is that somehow the music 'organizes itself' within the nervous system of the musician or composer.

In our nervous system, self-organizing processes are thought to be the result of associative connections between our nerve cells. These associations are thought to be established and elaborated according to the 'Hebb' rule. Hebb was a Nobel prize winning neurologist that discovered if two interconnected neurons in a similar state respond simultaneously, their connection is strengthened. In other words, rather than a 'beaten path' established by physical force, the strength of the associative connections between the parts of our brain and nervous system is determined by a kind 'rapport' between the nerve cells. This principle is deeply reflected in Mozart's comment that he was "constantly searching for two notes who love each other." (The Hebb rule may even be at the root of the basic strategy for establishing rapport in NLP, which involves the 'mirroring' of another person's behavioral or cognitive patterns.)

According to 'self-organization' theory, order in an interconnected system of elements arises around what are called 'attractors' which help to create and hold stable patterns within the system. These attractors form a kind of 'landscape' that shape and determine patterns of interaction within the system. Perceptual "attractors," for instance, are the focal point in a phenomenon around which the rest of our perceptions become organized. As an example, consider the well-known picture below. Is it an image of a young woman wearing a necklace or old woman with her head bowed?

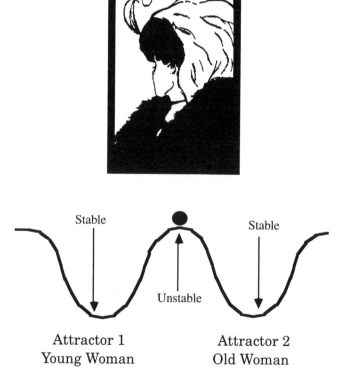

Attractor 'Landscape' of the Picture Above

Of course, the picture itself is simply a complex combination of lines and light and dark areas. The images of the women, young or old, are not really on the paper, but rather in our minds. We "see" a "young" or "old" woman because of basic assumptions and forms deep within our own nervous systems - what Aristotle referred to as "formal causes." To move between the 'images' in the 'landscape' we need to first *destabilize* our focus on one attractor and subsequently *restabilize* around a new attractor.

Some other examples of 'attractor landscapes', related to visual and verbal 'formal causes', are shown below. The first group shows the face of man transforming or "morphing" into the body of a woman. The intermediate images become progressively more ambiguous. Again, the experience of "man's face" or "woman's body" are not in the marks on the paper but in our own nervous system (a bee or a dog would not be likely to recognize either image).

The Face of Man or the Body of a Woman?

The following set of words show a transformation between the words "endure" and "change" as the two verbal 'attractors'.

endure
endure
chance
chance
chance

"Endure" or "Change"?

Of course, attractors are not only a visual phenomenon. They occur in the senses of hearing, taste and feeling as well. In fact, music itself could be considered to be a very intricate attractor 'landscape', 'destabilizing' and 're-stabilizing' our awareness; drawing out and directing the flow of attention within our internal sensory experience. What makes Mozart's music powerful and compelling are the attractors which stimulate and mobilize patterns within our own nervous systems.

In self organization theory, order is often 'unveiled' by the process of *iteration*. Self organizing systems tend to reproduce their own order and patterns by applying internally generated principles and rules. Looked at from this perspective, Mozart's music emerged organically through this type of iterative process. Mozart's positive feeling state and pattern of movement functioned as the initial "attractors" for his auditory representational system; first drawing out internal sounds and then collecting them together in memory. These collections of sounds then become an "attractor" themselves for the next level of organization. Each stage of his creative process built upon the others until a coherent and beautiful whole was produced much like organic growth in nature (a quality that one can easily hear in Mozart's music).

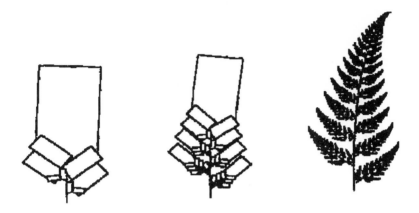

**Mozart's Strategy for Composing Music
Resembles The Formation and Growth of a Living
Thing Such as a Leaf**

In the next section, we will explore some ways in which we can develop and encourage some of the 'self organizing' capabilities underlying Mozart's unique abilities.

Implementing Mozart's Strategy

One issue that might legitimately be raised, as we consider how to apply what we have learned about Mozart's strategy, is whether the kinds of mental processes described by Mozart and other exceptional composers and musicians are even possible to teach or transfer. It could be contended that the ability to form synesthesias and create these types of abstract visualizations of music are inborn traits or talents that are not possible for the average person to develop. It could also be maintained that Mozart's strategy was a result of years and years of practice and immersion in music which he began at a very early age.

There is certainly no contending the important influence of physiology, environment and practice in the development of exceptional abilities. The belief system of NLP, however, is that the fundamental neurological capabilities that form the basis of Mozart's strategy are latent in every human being. And that while practice and experience on the one hand and physiological make up on the other certainly influence the limit to which such abilities may be developed, these kinds of 'self-organizing' skills can be released in people of average ability in a way that greatly enhances their competence. Obviously, there will never be another person exactly the same as Mozart. There were many influences at work to produce him as a specific individual. Our goal is not to make an exact "clone" of Mozart who produces the exact same compositions of Mozart, but rather to extract key elements that can significantly enhance the performance and experience of other people.

Another objection might be raised that the amount of detail we are able to derive from Mozart's letter is not specific enough to tell us exactly "how to" think like Mozart. Certainly Mozart's letter gives only very broad hints about an undoubtedly very complex and sophisticated process. There are many missing links to be filled in. Some have even argued that the letter is a forgery. It is important to keep in mind that NLP begins from the assumption that the map is not the territory. Even if Mozart were alive today and could be interviewed in great detail, his actual neurological process would still be unconscious, invisible and so immensely complex that it would be impossible to describe. In terms of transferability it is not even desirable that such generative processes be described in minute detail. In order for them to be adapted to the many different possible types of nervous systems possible in human beings, a certain amount of flexibility must be built in.

The ultimate purpose of modeling in NLP is to produce a map that is rich in quality, with enough structure and flexibility to be of practical value to those who choose to utilize it. Once you have identified enough of the key elements of the micro and macro strategy of your model, you can start to fill in the missing pieces by inference. In other words, if I know that I have to go from point **A** to point **B**, I can use other tools to fill in the pathway to get there. Furthermore, once I have identified the general framework employed by a person like Mozart, I can fill in missing links and define the more mechanical aspects of the process by modeling other exceptional people in the area of music and composition. You can then piece the strategic details drawn from these other models together with what has been derived from Mozart in order to fill in the blanks, and create something that has very practical applications.

A beautiful example is provided by Michael Colgrass, the Pulitzer prize winning composer I quoted earlier, who developed a program to teach musical composition based on the strategy we have been exploring. With it he is able to take people as young as seven and eight years old on up to adults and teach them how to write and compose music in about forty five minutes. The following is a description of how he is able to help them develop the specific types of self organizing capabilities involved in Mozart's strategy.

"I may start warming them up by telling them to move around, change their posture and position and start making any old sounds. (I myself will often stand on my head when I'm preparing to compose.) And the room becomes cacophonous with noise from people howling and screeching and grunting, and clicking their mouths. And I ask them to think of a mark they could put on the blackboard that would represent that sound.

They don't know how to write pitches and all that. If you were going to teach them that it would take months. So you don't do that, you just say, 'Make a mark that represents a sound.' Anybody can make a mark on a blackboard. So when somebody has a sound in their mind I instruct them to hear the sound, and go to the blackboard. Then I tell them to think of the left side of the blackboard as the beginning and the right side of the blackboard as the end; the top of the blackboard as high and the bottom of the blackboard as low. And make a mark that represents your sound.

So the person goes up to the blackboard and makes a mark. Of course, you could talk about that mark for a long time. You could say, 'Well, exactly how high or low is it?' But you'd go nuts because there is no way of measuring it. So I say, 'Well, we'll let that go for a moment and approach it differently.' If the person has made a mark that looks like a little curly-cue, I'll ask, 'Can you sing that?' And he might go, 'Buuwhuit,' because the mark kind of went like that.

Then I'll say, 'Will somebody else come up here and make a mark?' You could also have the same kid working, but it's fun to have different people doing it. It's a good idea to do a collective piece. So I'll ask somebody else come up and make a mark, but now there's one big difference. I'll point out, 'You already have one sound there and the second sound you're going to make has got to be in relation to that sound, but independent of it. It's got to come before it or over it or below it or after it. It may be quite different from it, or extremely similar to it.'

So a person says, 'Yeah I've got a sound.' And they go up there, and they might make something like, 'Whup whup whup whup whup,' like little inverted apostrophes or something like that.

So the first person made this 'Buuwhuitt.' The second person made 'Whup whup whup whup whup' underneath that, or just after it. Now we have two things there. Now the third person comes up and I ask him, 'What do you want to hear? What do you think belongs there?' He might say, 'Well, right after that I want to hear 'click click click click click click click click.' By now they are seeing too. I think this is important because people often have a lot of trouble hearing. As you have pointed out, we're more visual than auditory in North America. So, when they can see the sound, as it were, then they can hear the sound better. That's why I go to the blackboard with it.

And so, the child hears, 'Click click click click click click.' So I'll ask, 'What mark would represent that well on the blackboard?' Maybe he makes a big mistake, given what's already there. Maybe he'll draw a bunch of little circles. So I'll ask, 'Does everybody understand that to be 'Click click click click click click?'' And the rest of the group will say, 'No, that's 'Bewitt bewitt bewitt bewitt bewitt bewitt.' It's great the sounds you'll get. And so I'll say, 'What will make 'Click click click click click click?'' And somebody will say, 'Well the sounds all have to be all like little dots.' And I'll go, 'OK., did you hear what your colleague said, go make dots instead of circles.'

In this process, incidentally, I like them to do it. I don't ever go to the blackboard and make the marks for them. I don't tell them what to do. Instead I'll ask the group, 'Are you satisfied with what he's done?' Because in this way the whole group's learning at the same time.

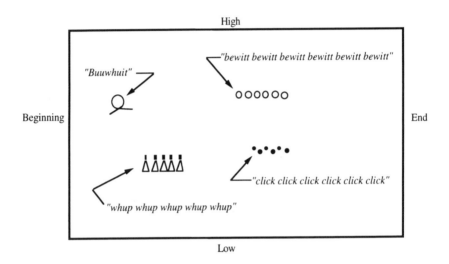

Example Drawings of Sounds

To help them complete the piece, I might act like a little bit of a rudder. I'll ask, 'Does anybody want any more on the piece? Is it finished?' When they're finished, I might have them discuss what they hear and see that lets them know that it was completed.

Then I ask them, 'Now how are we going to perform this?' This is very important because they have created a work now, but it hasn't come to life yet. And to understand the whole process, they've got to perform it. Now if I tell them how to perform it, then they will not have divined for themselves how a performance can take place. They will not have fully understood what the composing process is.   So I say, 'Anybody got any ideas?   Come on, we're gonna all make these noises together now.'

So someone might say, 'I got an idea,' and they go up to the board and they'll try it their way.   One person might say, 'All of you on the left side of the room do the first song, and all of you on the right side of the room do the second song.' Somebody else might say, 'I'm going to run my finger across the board. Wherever my finger touches, everybody just sing what you see.' One kid, one time, said, 'Everybody do anything they want, whenever they want to.   Look at the sounds that are there and finish when you are finished.' I thought that was a wonderful one.   The piece sounded terrific when they did that.   It had all kinds of parameters that the written one didn't have.

This is one way of teaching conducting.   Another way is saying, 'You do this and you do that.' You basically teach it.   You elicit the performance by leading them in a certain direction.

So now what they've done then is: they've heard sounds, put those sounds together in a composition by creating their own notation for it, conducted it, and performed it.   In that one period of forty or fifty minutes, the past thousand years of music history has been re-created for them.

I like to point out to them, 'Now, what you have done here is exactly what a composer does, no different.   Except, you have not specified exactly how high or how low the sounds are.   How long, how short, how dark, how thin, how loud, how soft. A composer has notations for those and those notations can be easily learned.' I might take the mark for the 'Buuwhiip' mark and write some quick musical notes, and put the beams on the tie and add a little crescendo mark or something and it looks like 'real' music then. And they see how that abstract mark can be transferred into the notation which is usually a foreign language to them. I'll go through the whole piece that way, kind of like just quickly. Then they see a whole score right in front of them, and they understand the essence of the score.

People say, 'How do you compose music, what do you think of first, aren't you a genius to do that?' and all that sort of thing. And I like to point out to them that the process we've gone through is exactly the process a composer goes through.

As a composer you've got to think of how to start, what to do next, and how to finish. That's what really is involved. If you can do that, you can compose. Someone might say, 'Well I don't know anything about music.' That doesn't make any difference. If you can do the process I was just describing with blocks of sound, you can compose. The learning of the musical linguistics, as it were, is just a question of time and sophistication. And it does take time and all that.

But I've seen professional composers try and do this exercise and they don't do it very well. I've seen some non-composers that have never written a line of music go up to the blackboard and they'll be fearfully imaginative. And I'll say to them, 'I sure wish you would learn notation and start studying some of this, and sit in orchestras and play an instrument and so forth because you sound like a composer to me.' [13]

By developing a simple strategy based on principles of self-organization and the establishment of elemental synesthesias between feelings and sounds, and then sounds and pictures, Michael's students are able to write a piece of music, conduct it, score it, and perform it - in less than forty five minutes! The orchestration of the piece would come by matching the oral sounds from which the composition has been initially performed to the "peculiarities of the various instruments." For instance, you would ask, "What instrument would make a 'buuwhitt' sound?" "What instrument makes a good 'whup, whup, whup' sound?" And so on.

As Michael points out, it is only at the very end that you need to know how to break the abstract, intuitive representation down into standard notation. But that skill isn't necessary in order to begin to compose, write and conduct music in a manner similar to that employed by Mozart. I have taught this strategy many times myself and it is surprising what an eight year old can do if you give him a few simple creative tools such as these.

Michael's process is a specific way of putting many of the pieces together that we have identified in Mozart's process. Minimally it offers a child or an adult a way of experiencing the creative cycle involved in composing music that can then be refined through practice and experience. And Michael is operating without some of the powerful tools that are available to us with modern technology. It is relatively simple to imagine how one could use readily available computer technology to enhance this strategy immensely.

Most personal computers, for example, can create sounds or can be connected to music synthesizers. Programs can be easily written that would connect visual shapes, colors and locations to specific types of sounds, timbres and pitches in a manner matching Mozart's strategy. In this way, people could literally draw abstract pictures on the computer and have them played by the computer. Whole pieces could be composed and performed through this intuitive, organic approach. The computer itself could then be programmed to translate the abstract picture into formal musical notation.

Of course, in the same way that Mozart's creative strategy has been modeled, it is possible to model strategies for streamlining the ability to learn musical notation and to play musical instruments. Certainly, Mozart's prowess as a performer was as legendary as his ability to compose music. And while Mozart himself left no record giving any clues to his strategy for learning to play a musical instrument, we might gain some insight through studying the strategies of exceptional musicians of today.

For example, I was once involved in the modeling of a piano player who could immediately sight read and beautifully perform any piece of music that was placed in front of him, as if he had played it many times before. By exploring his internal strategy, we discovered that, when he was learning to play the piano, he would visualize the piano keyboard in his mind. As he was learning to sight read he would look at individual notes in their written form and would picture which of the keys on his mental keyboard was to be depressed to make that note. He would look at a particular note, and imagine which key was to go down. After a while he could look at any particular written note and see the corresponding key automatically going down on his mental keyboard. Pretty soon he could look at two or three notes at once and see the corresponding keys being depressed. He was eventually able to see the notation for whole chords and imagine the cluster of keys being depressed that made up that chord. By overlapping his mental image of the piano keyboard with the actual piano keys, he would then use his fingers to press on the keys that he saw were supposed to be depressed. He explained that, "Now when I sight-read music its very easy - it is like playing a player piano. I look at the notes, see the keys going down and I just stick my fingers in the slots."

This is a strategy based on the development of associations between an externally represented code (musical notation) and a personal internal image (the imaginary keyboard). There is then an association made from activity on the mental keyboard (notes being depressed) to the kinesthetic act of pressing the corresponding key on the actual physical keyboard.

It is intriguing to note that in the study of exceptional music students that I mentioned earlier, it was discovered that students who had perfect pitch used a strategy very similar to this - but in reverse. They reported that they mentally saw piano keys go down for notes and chords when they heard music. The internal image was automatically triggered by the sound. Using the internal image as a reference they were able to determine what the exact notes were.

Thus, it would appear that sight-reading follows a strategy of: 1) see specific note; 2) picture key on imaginary keyboard; 3) move finger to corresponding position on actual keyboard; 4) produce sound. The strategy employed by individuals with perfect pitch went in the reverse direction: 1) hear sound; 2) picture key on imaginary keyboard; 3) determine specific note.

While the models who had developed this kind of strategy on their own undoubtedly had to possess a relatively high degree of motivation and had to devote some amount of time to develop these skills, modern technology can be used to streamline and enhance the development of these kinds of associations.

For example, I used this kind of strategy as a basis to develop a computer program to teach people to type.[14] In this program, the computer screen shows a picture of your hands and of the computer keyboard. It begins by displaying individual letters, and highlights which key on the keyboard corresponds to that letter and which finger should be used to depress that key. So you see the letter, the location on the keyboard and the finger to be used. Keeping your eyes on the computer monitor, you are to try to press the highlighted key with the indicated finger. If you hit the wrong key, that key is highlighted in a different color than the target key, so you can see where your finger is with respect to where it should be, without having to look down at the keyboard.

In order to encourage the self-organizing processes required to effectively acquire any psychomotor skill, such as typing or playing a musical instrument, you need to provide *feedback*. The problem is that the most direct way to get feedback while typing or learning a musical instrument is to look at what you fingers are doing. Unfortunately this is disruptive and inefficient because 1) you have to look away from the written source for what you are trying to type or play, and 2) it does not facilitate the development of an internal representation of the keyboard or musical instrument. This computer program encourages you to fumble around kinesthetically by continuing to press the keys with your fingers until you see that you hit the right key. It keeps showing you the relationship between the target key, the finger to use and the key you've actually hit. As a result you naturally build an image of the keyboard and develop the synesthesia between eye and hand without having to look down. As your skill increases, individual letters are extended to form words, sentences and finally whole paragraphs.

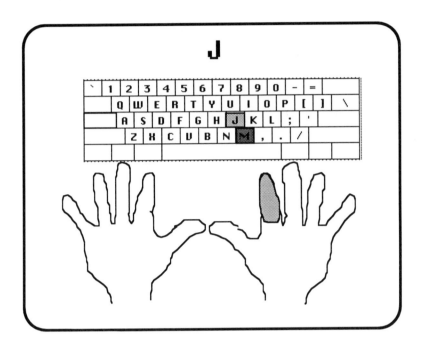

Sample Screen From 'Typing Strategy' Program

Obviously, a similar kind of program could be developed to help people to learn the strategy to sight-read for musical instruments. Notes could be displayed on the computer screen together with a replica of the instrument to be played and a pair of hands. Individual notes could be shown and the key, string or valve required to produce that note could be highlighted in some way along with the finger(s) to be used. The actual instrument could be connected or wired to the computer in some way so that it was able to ascertain which note you were actually playing in order to complete the feedback loop.

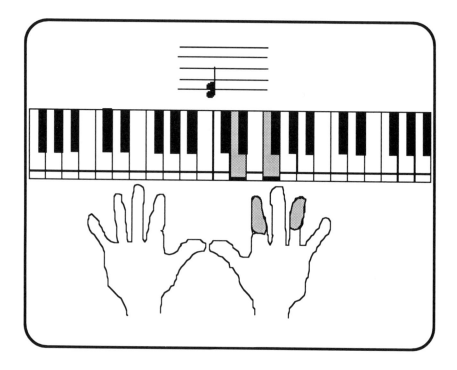

Example of Music 'Sight Reading' Program

By discovering and understanding the basic skills behind complex behaviors we can create tools that enhance the development of those skills in ways that can be easy and even fun.

Another computer tool I have developed for enhancing 'strategies of genius' is the *NeuroLink*, a type of biofeedback device which simultaneously monitors and records activity in heart rate, body temperature and the brain hemispheres via patterns of electrical activity on the left and right sides of the body. Mozart's Strategy acknowledges the powerful influence of one's physiolgical state in creativity. The NeuroLink comes with software which combines these key measurements of nervous system activity with artificial intelligence and NLP methods and principles to help people achieve optimal states of health, learning and personal performance.

Application of Mozart's Strategy to Areas Other Than Music

One of the most valuable things about using NLP to model strategies such as Mozart's, is that the basic form of the strategy may be transferred to areas other than those for which it was initially developed. For instance, Mozart's strategy has interesting applications beyond music. It is essentially a strategy for applying the natural self-organizing capabilities of our nervous system to systemically represent and organize complex patterns of interaction. On its most fundamental level, Mozart's strategy mobilizes vast amounts of neurology and stimulates unconscious processing. These can be extremely valuable for any number of applications involving creativity or problem solving.

Many people listen to music when they are working on a problem. It is quite possible that on a physiological level, music even activates neural circuits that become available to facilitate or participate in creativity or problem solving. It is even quite possible that Mozart himself, as has been suggested by some of his biographers, worked out his personal problems through his music. Certainly Mozart was familiar with thinking in metaphors.

I have already mentioned the similarity between Mozart's creative process and that described by Albert Einstein. Our study of Walt Disney also turned up a highly systematic use of synesthesia and chunking. In fact, Disney's *Fantasia* is an exquisite example of mapping music into imagery. I have also modeled and described a similar strategy, involving metaphorical visualization, employed by the teacher and healer Moshe Feldenkrais to work with patients who had physical problems.[15]

Certainly, many people use music as a stimulus and a metaphor to help with problem solving. For instance, I know of a chief executive officer of one of the largest automobile manufacturers in Europe who had two hobbies; neurophysiology and music. Whenever he was confronted with a difficult organizational problem he would create a metaphor for the problem in terms of these other two fields. For example, he might think of people as notes, teams as chords, projects as musical pieces, etc. Then he would try to "hear" the problem in the terms of the music. Were there discordant notes? Were there two chords in harmony? And so on.

One formulation of Mozart's strategy into a more general method for involving unconscious processes and stimulating lateral thinking during creativity and problem solving could be stated as follows:

1) Think of a problem you are trying to solve or an outcome you want to achieve. Introspectively pay attention to how you are currently thinking and feeling about the problem or outcome and which choices you perceive available to you.

2) Put yourself into a positive feeling that represents your desired state for the issue you are working with.

3) Allow the feeling to transform into sounds that fit with or enhance your desired state feeling.

4) 'Hear' the problem as a kind of sound. It may initially interfere with the desired state 'music'.

5) Allow the sounds representing the desired state and problem to transform into tastes and smells that you might associate with food.

6) Find 'counterpoints' for the problem sounds and taste (i.e., sounds and tastes from the desired state music and flavors that balance or offset the problem sounds).

7) Make the sounds and tastes into imagery (shape, color, brightness etc.) and see how they interact as a whole. Allow the image to form an abstract representation that metaphorically embodies a solution to the problem.

8) Return to your typical conscious thinking process in relation to the problem and notice how it has changed.

The 'Musical S.C.O.R.E.' Format

This basic problem solving format can be enriched and enhanced through a process I call the "Musical S.C.O.R.E." which applies the principles and structure of the S.C.O.R.E. model that we applied in the chapter on Aristotle. There is a charming and intended association in the letters defining the S.C.O.R.E. model. An actual 'musical score' is the arrangement of a musical composition including the notes to be performed and the parts for the different musical instruments or voices. The term "score" is also used for the description of a dance composition in choreographic notation.

In the "Musical S.C.O.R.E." process we will be making use of both of these implications. It is a problem solving method that incorporates many of Mozart's creative processes.

1. Think of a problem you are trying to solve or an outcome you want to achieve. Notice how you are currently thinking and feeling about the problem or outcome and which choices you perceive available to you.

2. Lay out four locations in a sequence representing the cause, symptom, outcome and desired effect related to the problem. Resources will be explored in a later stage of the exercise. Recall that:

   Symptoms are the most noticeable and conscious aspects of a presenting problem or problem state.

   Causes are the underlying elements responsible for creating and maintaining the symptoms. They are usually less obvious than the symptoms they produce.

   Outcomes are the particular goals or desired states that would take the place of the symptoms.

Resources are the underlying elements responsible for removing the causes of the symptoms and for manifesting and maintaining the desired outcomes.

Effects are the longer term results of achieving a particular outcome.

3. Physically associate into the experience and internal state related to each location. Pay special attention to the pattern of movement associated with each location, intensifying it a little to help build your sense of the physiology associated with each element.

4. Let each pattern of movement become a sound. Listen to the sound and notice how well it fits the feeling. Allow the feeling/movement/sound to become a taste. Notice if it is sweet, bitter, acidic, etc. Finally, let the feeling/ movement/sound/taste become an abstract or symbolic visual image, so that each location is fully represented in all the senses.

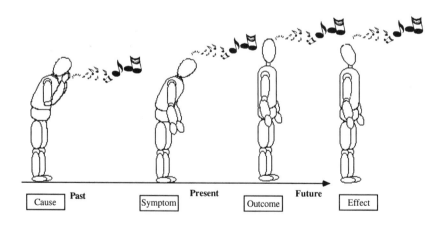

Pay special attention to the effect location. It is important to build the representation of this space as strongly
as possible so that it becomes an "attractor" or "final
cause" for the whole S.C.O.R.E.

6. Starting in the 'cause' location, walk slowly through
   entire sequence, feeling, hearing and seeing the sensory
   experiences of each location. Notice how they fit together, change and intermingle at each step. Listen for
   'counterpoints' to the problem sounds and taste (i.e.,
   sounds and tastes from the desired state music and
   flavors that balance or offset the problem sounds). Pay
   attention to the 'story' that is being told. Repeat this
   process several times until there is a sense of a single
   movement from cause to desired effect.

7. Go to a physical meta position and let your body lead
   you to a special movement representing the appropriate
   resource to bring into the S.C.O.R.E. sequence. Allow
   this movement to also become a sound, a taste and into
   imagery (shape, color, brightness etc.) and see how they
   interact as a whole. Allow the image to form an abstract
   representation that metaphorically embodies a solution
   to the problem.

8. Starting in the cause location, incorporate the resource
   movement/sound/taste/image into the other sensory representations associated with that location. Walk through
   the other locations adding the resource to the other
   movements until you have reached the effect space.

9. Repeat the movement through cause, symptom, outcome
   and effect until you have transformed it into a kind of
   song, 'dance', meal, painting and story that metaphorically embodies a solution to the problem.

Guided Meditation Using Mozart's Strategy

Another way to implement the elements of Mozart's strategy is in the form of a meditation. This helps to enhance the spontaneous and dreamlike quality described by Mozart. I have often applied Mozart's strategy in this way to my own work in the areas of creativity and health.[16] The following is a transcript of an example of a guided meditation for creativity based on Mozart's process.

> *Take a moment and relax. Put your body in a balanced and symmetrical posture. As Mozart said, 'Be completely yourself'. For a moment, you don't have to worry about anything or anybody else. You can just be alone with yourself.*
>
> *Allow your attention to focus on an outcome you would like to achieve or a problem you are trying to solve. As you do, focus on your desired state. What would you really like to get from solving that problem or reaching that goal? What is it that seems to draw you towards it as you imagine resolving this issue? Begin to fully sense and feel the positive desired effects and benefits you would like to achieve.*
>
> *As you become strongly in touch with your desired state, be aware of what is going on inside of you. Notice how these positive feelings affect your inner body sensations or your physiology. When you really experience this good feeling, does it change your breathing? In what way does it affect your posture? Is there a kind of feeling of circulation or warmth? What kind of subtle movements are you aware of? Allow your body to move with the sensations you feel, solidifying and exaggerating them.*

Now, imagine that each part of your body was a kind of a musical instrument that could make a different kind of sound. Imagine that your heart could make a certain kind of a sound, your lungs another. Fantasize that the muscles in your shoulders, your tongue, your hands, your stomach, your throat, your eyes and your spine are each musical instruments that make their own special kinds of sounds.

And as you experience that special feeling associated with your desired state, listen to which of these instruments are involved in producing that feeling. What sounds do they each generate as they create this positive feeling? What kind of inner sounds come from your heart? Your brain? Your stomach?

Is there a certain rhythm to this feeling? Is it fast or slow? Is it high pitched? Are there some parts of your inner body's musical instruments that play louder? Perhaps your heart plays a bit louder than your throat. Just listen to your body. Listen to the natural music that is already there. The kind of music that expresses this special feeling and the relationship with which it is associated.

Gently play with the sounds, tones and melodies that arise from your body and notice what kind of sounds deepen the feeling that you have. What kind of inner music seems to fit with and expand that feeling?

As you let your body's music continue to build, begin to imagine that these sounds, and this music could become tastes and smells. As you hear the music coming from your heart, realize that you can smell it and taste it as well. As you inhale, act as if you could breath in that special sensation and not only hear it and feel it, but taste what is so special about it. What does it smell like? What does it taste like? Is it kind of bittersweet? Or light and fluffy? Perhaps it tastes like a very old and well-aged wine. How could you make a meal out of that? A movable feast?

Savor and cherish the tastes and smells that go with this feeling and with this inner music. As your body continues to move in rhythm with that feeling, and the sounds circulate in your inner ears, and the tastes really come alive on your tongue like the best meal that you have ever eaten, perhaps these tastes can almost begin to explode into colors and into vision. So that you can see this feeling, these sounds, these exquisite flavors and tastes that represent the most positive qualities of that desired state. You can almost see a painting of light dazzling and dancing with colors that really represent and deepen that feeling and those sounds and those tastes all together.

The vibrancy of the colors and shapes you see can deepen the taste and feeling. The image spreads before you like a beautiful landscape and allows you to taste even more richly and hear even more concretely and feel your desired state even more fully. So that all of your inner senses are alive with this feeling. Your breathing expresses it. Your heart expresses it. Your entire neurology expresses it. It is like a hologram of the senses that imprints that experience deeply in you.

Now begin to listen for any problems or interferences to reaching your desired state or solution. At first they may sound rough or discordant; but as you continue to listen, you can hear, feel, taste or see the ways in which to incorporate, balance, transform or absorb any unpleasant sounds into the powerful beauty of your internal music. If you want, you can allow resources and solutions in the form of other types of songs and music. Perhaps you can even hear some of Mozart's music gently drifting in and out as a guiding inspiration.

Imagine that your inner music is a kind of 'holographic' resource - a resource in which all other resources are contained. From it, confidence, capabilities and solutions seem to flow easily and naturally. As you feel, listen, taste and watch, many new choices and alternatives begin to open to you, even if you are not consciously aware of them at this time. You can trust that they will be available in the "bag of your memory" when you need them.

And then, think of what kind of unique way you could tangibly embody that hologram of resources and solutions. If you don't consciously know what they will be in reality yet, you can express them in the form of a symbol, metaphor or music as Mozart did. Maybe you would express it through a drawing or a dance or a poem. Perhaps you would simply express it with a particular posture of your body or a look in your eyes.

What is something that you could physically make that would express this feeling? What song might you sing? What drawing could you make? What is something that would come out of your own hands or your own mouth or your own neurology that would represent your desired state?

Allow the natural and powerful self-organizing capabilities of your nervous system to dream something up. Let it happen as if it were some 'pleasing lively dream.' Perhaps even in your dreams tonight some element of these special feelings, sounds, tastes or vision could be there and continue to bloom whether you are consciously thinking about them or not.

Even as you begin to become consciously aware of the room around you, this dream can continue in the back

*of your mind. Feel the parts of your body touching the
chair or the floor, and hear the sounds drifting through
the air surrounding you, and open your eyes to see the
concrete objects before you.   Yet in some way, the
elements of this inner sensory hologram can be reflected
back to you from your external reality. Realize that you
actually sense parts of that music and that dream in
everyday experience. Maybe at your meal tonight you
will suddenly taste something that reminds you of
your inner feast. Perhaps in the eyes or the voice or the
movements of someone you are with, you will be able
see your vision or hear your music. Most importantly,
manifest and embody it through your own creations
and actions. For "the actual hearing of the tout ensemble
is after all the best."*

Conclusion

Like the music he generated with it, Mozart's strategy is full of the organic richness of life. Our knowledge of its structure can not only offer fresh insights into his creations, but by filling in missing links through the study of the processes of other composers and musicians, it can help to enhance the skills and appreciation of musicians (and latent musicians) young and old. Ultimately, it can offer guidance in how to utilize all levels of our neurology, mobilizing intuition and unconscious abilities as well as conscious skill.

Footnotes to Chapter 4

1. Dilts, R., Grinder, J., Bandler, R. & DeLozier, J., *Neuro-Linguistic Programming Vol. 1*, Meta Publications, Cupertino, CA, 1980.

2. E. Holmes, *The Life of Mozart Including His Correspondence,* Chapman & Hall, 1878, pp. 211-213

3. *ibid.*

4. *ibid.*

5. *ibid.*

6. *ibid*

7. Hamburger, M.; *Beethoven: Letters, Journals and Conversations;* Pantheon Books, 1952

8. *A Composer's World: Horizons and Limitations,* Harvard University Press, 1952

9. Dilts, R., Epstein, T. & Dilts, R., *Tools for Dreamers*, Meta Publications, Cupertino, CA, 1991, pp. 96-104.

10. O'Connor, Joseph; *Listening Skills in Music;* Lambent Books, London, 1989

11. Dilts, R., *Albert Einstein: A Neuro-Linguistic Analysis of a Genius*, Dynamic Learning Publications, Ben Lomond, CA, 1990.

12. H. Haken & M. Stadler (Ed.), *Synergetics of Cognition*, Springer-Verlag, Berlin, Germany, 1989.

13. Dilts, R., Epstein, T. & Dilts, R., *Tools for Dreamers*, Meta Publications, Cupertino, CA, 1991, pp. 105-110.

14. Dilts, R., *Strategies of Excellence; Typing Strategy*, Behavioral Engineering, Scotts Valley, CA, 1982.

15. Dilts, R., *Moshe Feldenkrais; NLP of the Body*, Dynamic Learning Publications, Ben Lomond, CA, 1990.

16. Dilts, R., Hallbom T. & Smith, S., ***Beliefs: Pathways to Health and Well-Being***, Metamorphous Press, Portland, OR, 1990, pp. 193-196.

Chapter 5

Conclusion

Some Patterns of Genius

In the opening chapter of this book I outlined an approach for finding "basic conditions" and "first principles" of genius based on Aristotle's strategy of analysis. The approach essentially involved an 'inductive' method for finding common patterns of genius consisting of:

1) Collecting a group of individuals who were acknowledged to have been 'geniuses'; and

2) Comparing the cognitive processes and strategies of these individuals and looking for qualities and characteristics that they all had in common.

In this volume, we have examined some of the key cognitive processes of four remarkable individuals: Aristotle, Sir Arthur Conan Doyle's Sherlock Holmes, Walt Disney and Wolfgang Amadeus Mozart. On the surface, these four people would appear to be quite different:

Aristotle was a philosopher and scientist. His key strategy revolved around the core values of 'order' and 'understanding' and involved finding first principles through induction and analysis.

Sherlock Holmes was a fictitious detective. His key strategy involved solving environmental riddles through observation and deduction, and then employing the capability of metacognition to 'explain how' the riddles were solved.

Walt Disney was a filmmaker and producer. His key strategy involved manifesting dreams and ideas through successive approximations in order to sustain his core value of 'continual improvement'.

Mozart was a musician and composer. His key strategy involved synthesizing multiple levels of processes in the service of the core values of 'harmony' and 'wholeness'.

Although there are many differences between these individuals, some common patterns begin to emerge as we reflect upon the information we have gathered about them. The following is a summary of ten main elements that seem to be common to all of the geniuses covered thus far in this study.

1. Have a well developed ability to visualize.

All of our geniuses seem to have had a well developed ability to visualize. Certainly, they used their other senses too, but vision seems to have been a central guiding element. Aristotle maintained that "To the thinking soul, images serve as if they were contents of perception...just as if it were seeing, it calculates and deliberates..." Holmes almost exclusively emphasized visual observation and imagination. Disney claimed it was essential for a person to "see clearly in his own mind how every piece of business in a story will be put." Mozart saw his finished compositions in his mind's eye as if they were a "painting" or "statue."

2. Have developed numerous links between the senses.

While vision may be a central focus, geniuses tend to use all of their senses, and to create synesthesias between the senses. Mozart is probably the best example of this - he felt, saw, and even tasted his music. Disney also had a remarkable ability to overlap his senses, as is demonstrated in works like *Fantasia*. Aristotle coined the term "common sensibles" to describe the ability to share information between the senses. Holmes maintained that "all life is a great chain, the nature of which is known whenever we are shown a single link of it," implying the interconnection between what is seen, heard, felt and tasted in the world around us.

3. Use multiple perspectives.

One of the most common characteristics of genius is to be able to entertain more perspectives of a particular subject or process than is typical, and to find the perspective(s) that no one else has taken. Aristotle, for instance, sought several different types of 'causes' in his analyses and checked his premises and syllogisms through various verbal "conversions." Holmes used not only knowledge about cultural patterns and world events but also relatively obscure and esoteric knowledge to make inferences and draw conclusions. Disney systematically used different perspectives, such as taking a "second look" at his stories and plans. Mozart employed different senses and metaphors for each stage of his creative process.

4. Highly developed ability for switching between perceptual positions.

In addition to being able to take different points of view, geniuses have the ability to identify with different perceptual positions - i.e., 1st (self), 2nd (other) and 3rd (observer) position. Disney, for example, could not describe the behavior of his animated characters without simultaneously acting them out himself. He also had the ability to leave his own perceptual position behind and assume the world view of his audiences. Holmes would put himself into the perceptual position of his quarry as he was investigating them. In fact, a commonly reported characteristic of geniuses is the ability to identify (take second position with) whatever they are working with, even if they are inanimate objects. People who are geniuses with computers claim to be able to view the world as a computer would. Michelangelo could go to second position with a piece of stone. He maintained, "I don't make the statue. The statue is already in the marble waiting for me to release it. I just keep chiseling until it is free." Mozart claimed his symphonies more or less wrote themselves after a certain point was reached.

5. *Ability to move back and forth between different chunk sizes and levels of thinking.*

All of our geniuses were able to move easily between the broader vision and specific actions and elements required to reconstruct or manifest the bigger picture. They could work with the little pieces and yet not become caught up in all the details. They were also able to see the big picture without losing sight of the little pieces. Aristotle, Holmes, Disney and Mozart seemed to be uniquely able to balance both big and small chunks. For instance, both Aristotle and Holmes began with "rather confused masses" of information which they initially chunked down into more specific details and elements. Then they chunked back up from the details to infer or reconstruct the 'bigger picture'. Mozart and Disney, on the other hand, would assemble together chunks of experience, primarily generated through synesthesias between the senses, until they were able to "see how every piece of business would be put." They would then chunk this larger vision back down into either a musical score or a 'storyboard'.

6. Maintain a feedback loop between the abstract and the concrete.

Our geniuses were also able to move between abstract models and principles and specific concrete expressions of those abstractions. They were able to find the higher level principles and qualities ("common sensibles") in the concrete examples they were working with, and to embody abstract relationships in specific examples. This formed a kind of loop that allowed them to refine their ideas or theories through feedback from the concrete world, and at the same time refine their physical works through feedback from more abstract principles.

7. Balance of cognitive functions: Dreamer, Realist & Critic.

Geniuses are not only dreamers. They have the ability and the skills to manifest their dreams in concrete expressions and to think critically about their ideas. In some ways, the ability to think critically is as important to the process of genius as the ability to dream. It is what insures that the genius' ideas are truly above average. The key seems to be in not letting the critical thinking squelch the dream. Certainly, a key pattern of genius is to end up with some external product or representation. An act of genius always culminates in some kind of mapping into an external form. Aristotle expressed his ideas in writing. Holmes directed his mental powers to the solution of an environmental problem or riddle. Disney's main strength was his ability to turn his dreams into tangible expressions. Mozart wrote down his musical dreams in the form of notes. If these people had merely kept their ideas in their heads the world would have never known about their genius.

8. Ask basic questions.

Geniuses tend to emphasize questions more than answers. They are typically very bold about their questions and humble about their answers. Certainly, a key characteristic of all geniuses is their high degree of curiosity and fascination. Rather than try to confirm and hold onto what they already know, they seek where their knowledge is incomplete. They also have a unique ability to perceive lack of success not as failure but as feedback for where to look next. Aristotle, for instance, defined four basic questions that he continually asked and a process by which he checked his assumptions and premises. Holmes warned against the tendency to "twist facts to suit theories, instead of theories to suit facts." Disney commented, "I must explore and experiment...I resent the limits of my own imagination." Mozart's music was a result of a constant query as to whether 'two notes loved each other'.

9. Use metaphors and analogies.

Geniuses are constantly using metaphors and lateral or nonlinear thinking strategies. In fact, metaphor or analogy seems to be at the core of every act of genius. Aristotle constantly illustrated his ideas with examples and analogies. Holmes claimed that his methods were based upon the "mixture of imagination and reality." Mozart used metaphors and analogies such as 'putting together morsels to create a meal' and comparing his music to a "painting" or "statue" to describe his process of composition. Disney's business *was* that of creating metaphors. It would seem that the use of metaphor allows the genius to focus on 'common sensibles' and the deeper principles within the world around and inside of them and not get overly caught up in the content or the constraints of reality.

10. Have a mission beyond individual identity.

Aristotle sought the 'first principles' in all of nature. Holmes desired to apply the links in the 'great chain of life'. Of his work, Disney maintained, "This is not the cartoon medium, we have worlds to conquer here...Whatever the mind of man can conceive, animation can explain." Mozart claimed that writing music 'fired his soul' and thanked his "divine maker" for his creative gifts.

One common characteristic of all geniuses is that they perceive their work as coming from something and serving something larger than themselves. There have been many 'brilliant', 'creative' people who were not 'geniuses'. Perhaps this connection with something larger is what separates the geniuses from those who are simply creative or innovative.

I stated in the introduction to this volume that my mission was to apply the tools of NLP to unveil some of the key strategies of important historical figures who have been acknowledged as geniuses. The purpose was to help enrich our perceptions of reality in a way that offers more choices for us to act effectively and ecologically in our own lives. This volume represents a first step in that overall mission.

I mentioned in the preface that this work is the culmination of a twenty year journey into the minds and hearts of many exceptional individuals. I hope the first 'leg' of this journey has been as stimulating for you as it has been for me.

Afterword

I hope you have enjoyed this exploration into the *Strategies of Genius*. As I indicated during the course of the book, many tools and resources exist to further develop and apply the models, strategies and skills described within these pages. In addition to the tools already mentioned, I am currently planning a collection of tapes, workbooks, computer software and multi media programs to help illustrate and support the types of strategies described in this book. I am also conducting seminars and workshops on *Strategies of Genius* in various parts of the United States and Europe as well as training programs on the applications of NLP for Creativity, Health, Leadership, Effective Presentations Skills, and Modeling.

If you would like to receive further information regarding these tools and resources or any future developments related to *Strategies of Genius*, please contact:

Strategies of Genius
P.O. Box 67448
Scotts Valley, California 95067-7448
Phone & Fax: (408) 438-8314

Appendix A: Background and Principles of NLP

NLP was originated by John Grinder (whose background was in linguistics) and Richard Bandler (whose background was in mathematics and gestalt therapy) for the purpose of making explicit models of human excellence. Their first work *The Structure of Magic Vol. I & II* (1975, 1976) identified the verbal and behavioral patterns of therapists Fritz Perls (the creator of gestalt therapy) and Virginia Satir (internationally renowned family therapist). Their next work *Patterns of the Hypnotic Techniques of Milton H. Erickson, M.D. Vol. I & II* (1975, 1976) examined the verbal and behavioral patterns of Milton Erickson, founder of the American Society of Clinical Hypnosis and one of the most widely acknowledged and clinically successful psychiatrists of our times.

As a result of this earlier work, Grinder and Bandler formalized their modeling techniques and their own individual contributions under the name "Neuro-Linguistic Programming" to symbolize the relationship between the brain, language and the body. The basics of this model has been described in a series of books including *Frogs Into Princes* (Bandler & Grinder, 1979), *Neuro-Linguistic Programming Vol. I* (Dilts, Grinder, Bandler, DeLozier, 1980), *Reframing* (Bandler & Grinder, 1982) and *Using Your Brain* (Bandler, 1985).

In essence, all of NLP is founded on two fundamental premises:

1. *The Map is Not the Territory.* As human beings, we can never know reality. We can only know our perceptions of reality. We experience and respond to the world around us primarily through our sensory representational systems. It is our 'neuro-linguistic' maps of reality that determine how we behave and that give those behaviors meaning, not reality itself. It is generally not reality that limits us or empowers us, but rather our map of reality.

2. *Life and 'Mind' are Systemic Processes.* The processes that take place within a human being and between human beings and their environment are systemic. Our bodies, our societies, and our universe form an ecology of complex systems and subsystems all of which interact with and mutually influence each other. It is not possible to completely isolate any part of the system from the rest of the system. Such systems are based on certain 'self-organizing' principles and naturally seek optimal states of balance or homeostasis.

According to NLP, the basic process of change involves 1) finding out what the *present state* of the person is, and 2) adding the appropriate *resources* to lead that person to 3) the *desired state*.

Present State + Appropriate Resources —> Desired State

The distinctions and techniques of NLP are organized to help identify and define present states and desired states of various types and levels and then to access and apply the appropriate resources to produce effective and ecological change in the direction of the desired state.

The Nervous System

Higher organisms coordinate their behavior and organize their experience of the world through their nervous systems. In human beings, the nervous system may be viewed as consisting of three primary subsystems: 1) the Central Nervous System 2) the Peripheral Nervous System and 3) the Autonomic Nervous System.

The *Central Nervous System* is made up of the brain and spinal cord. It controls our muscles and movement and is associated with conscious thought and action.

The *Peripheral Nervous System* is made up of the branches of the spinal cord and the sense organs. It relays information about the environment from the organs, muscles and glands to the central nervous system and back again.

The *Autonomic Nervous System* deals with a network of nerves outside of the spinal cord that deals with many unconscious activities such as temperature regulation, circulation, salivation, the initiation of the "fight-flight" reaction and other emotional and attentional states.

The Central Nervous System executes mental programs, plans and strategies via the Peripheral Nervous System. The Autonomic Nervous System determines the state of the biological "hardware" within which those programs are carried out. While most people are consciously aware of their sensations, thoughts and actions, the functions of the Autonomic Nervous System generally take place outside of conscious awareness.

Whether it be talking, thinking, eating, understanding, working or sleeping; all human action and experiences are mediated and manifested through the interplay of these three parts of the nervous system. Learning is a function of the establishment of coherent patterns of organization and interaction within these three neurological subsystems.

The Fundamental Structure of Behavior: T.O.T.E. Model

A mental strategy is typically organized into a basic feedback loop called a T.O.T.E. (Miller, et al, 1960). The letters **T.O.T.E.** stand for *Test-Operate-Test-Exit*. The T.O.T.E. concept maintains that all mental and behavioral programs revolve around having a *fixed goal* and a *variable means to achieve that goal.* This model indicates that, as we think, we set goals in our mind (consciously or unconsciously) and develop a TEST for when that goal has been achieved. If that goal is not achieved we OPERATE to change something or do something to get closer to our goal. When our TEST criteria have been satisfied we then EXIT on to the next step.

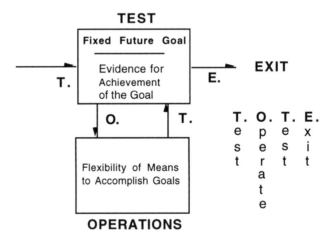

So the function of any particular part of a behavioral program could be to (**T**)est information from the senses in order to check progress towards the goal or to (**O**)perate to change some part of the ongoing experience so that it can satisfy the (**T**)est and (**E**)xit on to the next part of the program.

For example, one TEST for creativity might be that an idea is "unique". If the concept you have come up with is not unique enough you will OPERATE or go through a procedure to make the idea more unique or to come up with a better concept.

According to the T.O.T.E. model, effective performance comes from:

1. Having a fixed future goal.

2. Having the sensory evidence necessary to accurately determine your progress toward the goal.

3. Having a variable set of means to get to your goal and the behavioral flexibility to implement these choices.

Perceptual Positions

Perceptual positions refer to the fundamental points of view you can take concerning a relationship between yourself and another person.

1st Position: Associated in your own point of view, beliefs and assumptions, seeing the external world through your own eyes. Use first person language when talking about yourself - "I am seeing," "I feel," etc.

2nd Position: Associated in another person's point of view, beliefs and assumptions, seeing the external world through his or her eyes. Use second person language when talking about your self in first position - "You are", "You look," etc.

3rd Position: Associated in a point of view outside of the relationship between yourself and the other person with the beliefs and assumptions from both 1st and 2nd position. Use third person language when talking about yourself in first position or the other person (2nd position) - "He is," "She says," "They are," etc.

Meta Position: Associated in a 3rd position but with the beliefs and assumptions from only one of the other perceptual positions.

Observer Position: Associated in a 3rd position but suspending any beliefs and assumptions from 1st and 2nd position.

Levels of Processing and Organization

People often talk about responding to things on different *"levels"*. For instance, someone might say that some experience was negative on one level but positive on another level. In our brain structure, language, and perceptual systems there are natural hierarchies or levels of experience. The effect of each level is to organize and control the information on the level below it. Changing something on an upper level would necessarily change things on the lower levels; changing something on a lower level could but would not necessarily effect the upper levels. Anthropologist Gregory Bateson identified four basic levels of learning and change - each level more abstract than the level below it but each having a greater degree of impact on the individual. These levels roughly correspond to:

* *Environmental factors* determine the external opportunities or constraints a person has to react to. Answer to the questions **where?** and **when?**

* *Behavior* is made up of specific actions or reactions within the environment. Answer to the question **what?**

* *Capabilities* guide and give direction to behavioral actions through a mental map, plan or strategy. Answer to the question **how?**

* *Beliefs* and *values* provide the reinforcement (motivation and permission) that supports or denies capabilities. Answer to the question **why?**

* *Identity* factors determine overall purpose (mission) and shape beliefs and values through our sense of self. Answer to the question **who?**

* *Spiritual* issues relate to the fact that we are a part of a larger system that reaches beyond ourselves as individuals to our family, community and global systems. Answer to the question **who else?**

The environment level involves the specific external conditions in which our behavior takes place. Behaviors without any inner map, plan or strategy to guide them, however, are like knee jerk reactions, habits or rituals. At the level of capability we are able to select, alter and adapt a class of behaviors to a wider set of external situations. At the level of beliefs and values we may encourage, inhibit or generalize a particular strategy, plan or way of thinking. Identity, of course, consolidates whole systems of beliefs and values into a sense of self. While each level becomes more abstracted from the specifics of behavior and sensory experience, it actually has more and more widespread effect on our behavior and experience.

"Neuro-Logical" Levels

Each of these processes involves a different level of organization and mobilizes successively deeper mobilization and commitment of neurological 'circuitry'.

Spiritual -*Holographic* - Nervous system as a whole.
A. Identity - *Immune system and endocrine system* - Deep life sustaining functions.
B. Beliefs -*Autonomic nervous system* (e.g. heart rate, pupil dilation, etc.) - Unconscious responses.
C. Capabilities - *Cortical systems* - Semi conscious actions (eye movements, posture, etc.)
D. Behaviors - *Motor system (pyramidal & cerebellum)* - Conscious actions
E. Environment - *Peripheral nervous system* - Sensations and reflex reactions.

Cognitive Patterns: The R.O.L.E. Model

The goal of the R.O.L.E. modeling process is to identify the essential elements of thinking and behavior used to produce a particular response or outcome. This involves identifying the critical steps of the mental strategy and the role each step plays in the overall neurological "program". This role is determined by the following four factors which are indicated by the letters which make up the name of the **R.O.L.E.** Model - *Representational Systems; Orientation; Links; Effect.*

Representational Systems have to do with which of the five senses are most dominant for the particular mental step in the strategy: **V**isual (sight), **A**uditory (sound), **K**inesthetic (feeling), **O**lfactory (smell), **G**ustatory (taste).

Each representational system is designed to perceive certain basic qualities of the experiences it senses. These include characteristics such as *color, brightness, tone, loudness, temperature, pressure,* etc. These qualities are called "submodalities" in NLP since they are subcomponents of each of the representational systems.

Orientation has to do with whether a particular sensory representation is focused (**e**)xternally toward the outside world or (**i**)nternally toward either (**r**)emembered or (**c**)onstructed experiences. For instance, when you are seeing something, is it in the outside world, in memory or in your imagination?

Links have to do with how a particular step or sensory representation is linked to the other representations. For example, is something seen in the external environment linked to internal feelings, remembered images, or words? Is a particular feeling linked to constructed pictures, memories of sounds or other feelings?

There are two basic ways that representations can be linked together: sequentially and simultaneously. Sequential links act as *anchors* or triggers such that one representation follows another in a linear chain of events.

Simultaneous links occur as what are called *synesthesias*. Synesthesia links have to do with the ongoing overlap between sensory representations. Certain qualities of feelings may be linked to certain qualities of imagery - for example, visualizing the shape of a sound or hearing a color.

Certainly, both of these kinds of links are essential to thinking, learning, creativity and the general organization of our experiences.

Effect has to do with the result, effect or purpose of each step in the thought process. For instance, the function of the step could be to generate or input a sensory representation, to test or evaluate a particular sensory representation or to operate to change some part of an experience or behavior in relation to the goal.

Physiological Clues: Making the R.O.L.E. into a B.A.G.E.L.

The R.O.L.E. model elements deal primarily with cognitive processes.   In order to function, however, these mental programs need the help of certain bodily and physiological processes for consolidation and expression.   These physical reactions are important for the teaching or development of certain mental processes as well as for the external observation and confirmation of them.   The primary behavioral elements involved in R.O.L.E. modeling are:

> **B**ody Posture.
> **A**ccessing cues
> **G**estures.
> **E**ye movements.
> **L**anguage Patterns.

1. **B**ody Posture

People often assume systematic, habitual postures when deep in thought.   These postures can indicate a great deal about the representational system the person is using.   The following are some typical examples:

a. **Visual:** *Leaning back with head and shoulders up or rounded, shallow breathing*

b. **Auditory:** *Body leaning forward, head cocked, shoulders back, arms folded.*

c. **Kinesthetic:** *Head and shoulders down, deep breathing.*

2. Accessing Cues

When people are thinking, they cue or trigger certain types of representations in a number of different ways including: breathing rate, non-verbal "grunts and groans", facial expressions, snapping their fingers, scratching their heads, and so on. Some of these cues are idiosyncratic to the individual and need to be 'calibrated' to a particular person. Many of these cues, however, are associated with particular sensory processes"

- **a. Visual:** *High shallow breathing, squinting eyes, voice higher pitch and faster tempo.*
- **b. Auditory:** *Diaphragmatic breathing, knitted brow, fluctuating voice tone and tempo.*
- **c. Kinesthetic:** *Deep abdominal breathing, deep breathy voice in a slower tempo.*

3. Gestures.

People will often touch, point to or use gestures indicating the sense organ they are using to think with. Some typical examples include:

- **a. Visual:** *Touching or pointing to the eyes; gestures made above eye level.*
- **b. Auditory:** *Pointing toward or gesturing near the ears; touching the mouth or jaw.*
- **c. Kinesthetic:** *Touching the chest and stomach area; gestures made below the neck.*

4. Eye movements

Automatic, unconscious eye movements often accompany particular thought processes indicating the accessing of one of the representational systems. NLP has categorized these cues into the following pattern:

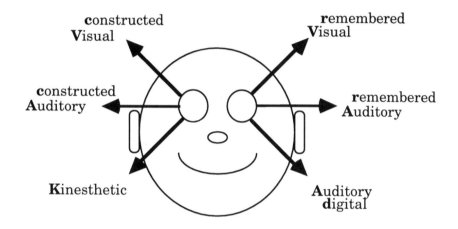

constructed
Visual

remembered
Visual

constructed
Auditory

remembered
Auditory

Kinesthetic

Auditory
digital

NLP Eye Movement Patterns

5. Language Patterns

A primary method of Neuro-Linguistic analysis is to search for particular linguistic patterns, such as 'predicates', which indicate a particular neurological representational system or sub-modality, and how that system or quality is being used in the overall program of thought. Predicates are words, such as verbs, adverbs and adjectives, which indicate actions or qualities as opposed to things. This type of language is typically selected at an unconscious level and thus reflects

the underlying unconscious structure which produced them.
The following is a list of common sensory based predicates:

VISUAL	AUDITORY	KINESTHETIC
"see"	"hear"	"grasp"
"look"	"listen"	"touch"
"sight"	"sound"	"feeling"
"clear"	"resonant"	"solid"
"bright"	"loud"	"heavy"
"picture"	"word"	"handle"
"hazy"	'noisy"	"rough"
"brings to light"	"rings a bell"	"connects"
"show"	"tell"	"move

Internal States

NLP focuses on identifying, using and changing patterns in the thought processes and physiology that influence people's behavior as a means of improving the quality and effectiveness of their performance. The basic premise of NLP is that the human brain functions similarly to a computer - by executing "programs" or mental strategies that are composed of ordered sequences of instructions or internal representations. Certain programs or strategies function better for accomplishing certain tasks than others, and it is the strategy that an individual uses that will to a great extent determine whether his performance is one of mediocrity or excellence.

The efficacy and ability to carry out a particular mental program is to a large degree determined by the physiological state of the individual. Clearly, if a computer has a bad chip or power surges in its electrical supply its programs will not be able to execute effectively. The same is true for the human brain. The level of arousal, receptivity, stress, etc., of the individual will determine how effectively he can carry out his own mental programs. Heart rate, breathing rate, body posture, blood pressure, muscle tension, reaction time and galvanic skin response are examples of physical measures that effect and accompany changes in overall physiological state. NLP uses these measures to identify, model and train physiological states of excellence in individuals so that these states may be purposefully reproduced and used to achieve optimal performance.

Thus, an individual's internal state has important influences on his or her ability to perform in any situation.

Anchoring

Anchoring is a process that on the surface is similar to the "conditioning" technique used by Pavlov to create a link between the hearing of a bell and salivation in dogs. By associating the sound of a bell with the act of giving food to his dogs, Pavlov found he could eventually just ring the bell and the dogs would start salivating, even though no food was given. In the behaviorist's stimulus-response conditioning formula, however, the stimulus is always an environmental cue and the response is always a specific behavioral action. The association is considered reflexive and not a matter of choice.

In NLP the term *"anchoring"* refers to the establishment of links between R.O.L.E. Model elements and has been expanded to include other logical levels than environment and behavior. A remembered picture may become an anchor for a particular internal feeling, for instance. A touch on the leg may become an anchor for a visual fantasy or even a belief. A voice tone may become an anchor for a state of excitement or confidence. A person may consciously choose to establish and retrigger these associations for himself. Rather than being a mindless knee-jerk reflex, an anchor becomes a tool for self empowerment. Obviously, anchoring can be a very useful tool for helping to establish and reactivate the mental processes associated with creativity.

Most often anchors may be established through simply associating two experiences together in time. In behavioral conditioning models, associations become more strongly established through repetition. Repetition may also be used to strengthen anchors as well. For example, you could ask someone to vividly reexperience a time that she was very creative and pat her shoulder while she is thinking of the experience. If you repeat this once or twice the pat on shoulder will begin to become linked to the creative state. Eventually a pat on the shoulder will automatically remind the person of the creative state.

Strategies

1. **Definition of *"Strategy"* :**
   a. From the Greek word *"strategos"* meaning *"general."*
   b. *"A detailed plan for reaching a goal or advantage."* (Random House Dictionary)
   c. In NLP, the term *"strategy"* is used to mean the steps of a mental process or program (in the sense of a computer program) that leads to a particular goal or outcome. Each step in the strategy is characterized by the use of one of the five senses or *"representational systems."*

2. **Classes of Strategies**
   a. Memory
   b. Decision Making
   c. Learning
   d. Creativity
   e. Motivation
   f. Reality
   g. Belief (or Convincer)

3. **Strategy Procedures**
   a. Elicitation
   b. Utilization
   c. Design
   d. "Installation" - Reorganization

4. **Structure of a Strategy**
   a. General Systems Model

b. NLP Strategy Structure

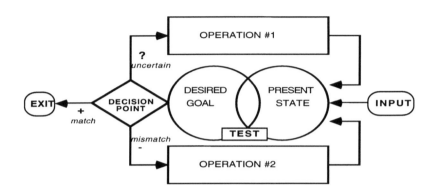

Appendix B:
Presuppositions of NLP

The Map is not the Territory

1. People respond to their own perceptions of reality.

2. Every person has their own individual map of the world. No individual map of the world is any more "real" or "true" than any other.

3. The meaning of a communication to another person is the response it elicits in that person, regardless of the intent of the communicator.

4. The 'wisest' and most 'compassionate' maps are those which make available the widest and richest number of choices, as opposed to being the most "real" or "accurate".

5. People already have (or potentially have) all of the resources they need to act effectively.

6. People make the best choices available to them given possibilities and the capabilities that they perceive available to them from their model of the world. Any behavior no matter how evil, crazy or bizarre it seems is the best choice available to the person at that point in time - if given a more appropriate choice (within the context of their model of the world) the person will be more likely to take it.

7. Change comes from releasing the appropriate resource, or activating the potential resource, for a particular context by enriching a person's map of the world.

Life And 'Mind' Are Systemic Processes

1. The processes that take place within a person, and between people and their environment, are systemic. Our bodies, our societies and our universe form an ecology of systems and subsystems all of which interact with and mutually influence each other.

2. It is not possible to completely isolate any part of a system from the rest of the system. People cannot not influence each other. Interactions between people form feedback loops - such that a person will be effected by the results that their own actions have on other people.

3. Systems are 'self organizing' and naturally seek states of balance and stability. There are no failures, only feedback.

4. No response, experience or behavior is meaningful outside of the context in which it was established or the response it elicits next. Any behavior, experience or response may serve as a resource or limitation depending on how it fits in with the rest of the system.

5. Not all interactions in a system are on the same level. What is positive on one level may be negative on another level. It is useful to separate behavior from "self" - to separate the positive intent, function, belief, etc. that generates the behavior from the behavior itself.

6. At some level all behavior is (or at one time was) "positively intended". It is or was perceived as appropriate given the context in which it was established, from the point of view of the person whose behavior it is. It is easier and more productive to respond to the intention rather than the expression of a problematic behavior.

7. Environments and contexts change. The same action will not always produce the same result. In order to successfully adapt and survive, a member of a system needs a certain amount of flexibility. That amount of flexibility has to be proportional to the variation in the rest of the system. As a system becomes more complex, more flexibility is required.

8. If what you are doing is not getting the response you want then keep varying your behavior until you do elicit the response.

Appendix C:
Glossary of NLP Terminology

ACCESSING CUES - Subtle behaviors that will both help to trigger and indicate which representational system a person is using to think with. Typical types of accessing cues include *eye movements, voice tone and tempo, body posture, gestures and breathing patterns.*

ANCHORING - The process of associating an internal response with some *external trigger* (similar to classical conditioning) so that the response may be quickly, and sometimes covertly, reaccessed.

AUDITORY - Relating to *hearing* or the sense of hearing.

BEHAVIOR - The specific physical actions and reactions through which we interact with the people and environment around us.

BEHAVIORAL FLEXIBILITY - The ability to vary one's own behavior in order to elicit or secure a response from another person.

BELIEFS - Closely held generalizations about 1) cause, 2) meaning and 3) boundaries in the (a) world around us, (b) our behavior, (c) our capabilities of and our (d) identities. Beliefs function at a different level than concrete reality and serve to guide and interpret our perceptions of reality often by connecting them to our criteria or value systems. Beliefs are notoriously difficult to change through typical rules of logic or rational thinking.

CALIBRATION - The process of learning to read another person's unconscious, non-verbal responses in an ongoing interaction by pairing observable behavioral cues with a specific internal response.

CALIBRATED LOOP - Unconscious pattern of communication in which behavioral cues of one person triggers specific responses from another person in an ongoing interaction.

CAPABILITY - Mastery over an entire class of behavior - knowing **HOW TO** do something. Capabilities come from the development of a mental map that allows us to select and organize groups of individual behaviors. In NLP these mental maps take the form of cognitive strategies and maps.

CHUNKING - Organizing or breaking down some experience into bigger or smaller pieces. *"Chunking up"* involves moving to a larger, more abstract level of information. *"Chunking down"* involves moving to a more specific and concrete level of information. *"Chunking laterally"* involves finding other examples at the same level of information.

CONGRUENCE - When all of a person's internal beliefs, strategies and behaviors are fully in agreement and oriented toward securing a desired outcome.

CONTEXT - The framework surrounding a particular event. This framework will often determine how a particular experience or event is interpreted.

CRITERIA - The values or standards a person uses to make decisions and judgments.

DEEP STRUCTURE - The neurological maps (both conscious and unconscious) that people use to organize and guide their behavior.

ENVIRONMENT - The external context in which our behavior takes place. Our environment is that which we perceive as being "outside" of us. It is not part of our behavior but is rather something we must react to.

FOUR TUPLE (or **4-tuple**) - A shorthand method used to notate the structure of any particular experience. The concept of the four tuple maintains that any experience must be composed of some combination of the four primary representational classes - **<A,V,K,O>** - where A = *auditory*, V = *visual*, K = *kinesthetic, and O = *olfactory/gustatory*.

FUTURE PACING - The process of *mentally rehearsing* oneself through some future situation in order to help insure that the desired behavior will occur naturally and automatically.

GUSTATORY - Relating to *taste* or the sense of taste.

IDENTITY - Our sense of who we are. Our sense of identity organizes our beliefs, capabilities and behaviors into a single system.

INSTALLATION - The process of facilitating the acquisition of a new strategy or behavior. A new strategy may be installed through some combination of anchoring, accessing cues, metaphor and futurepacing.

KINESTHETIC - relates to *body sensations*. In NLP the term kinesthetic is used to encompass all kinds of feelings including *tactile, visceral* and *emotional*.

LOGICAL LEVELS - An internal hierarchy of organization in which each level is progressively more psychologically encompassing and impactful. In order of importance (from high to low) these levels include 1) identity, 2) beliefs, 3) capabilities, 4) behavior and 5) environment.

META MODEL - A model developed by John Grinder and Richard Bandler that identifies categories of language patterns that can be problematic or ambiguous.

META PROGRAM - A level of mental programming that determines how we sort, orient to, and chunk our experiences. Our meta programs are more abstract than our specific strategies for thinking and define our general approach to a particular issue rather than the details of our thinking process.

METAPHOR - The process of thinking about one situation or phenomena as something else, i.e. *stories, parables* and *analogies*.

MODELING - The process of observing and mapping the successful behaviors of other people.

NEURO-LINGUISTIC PROGRAMMING (NLP) - A behavioral model and set of explicit skills and techniques founded by John Grinder and Richard Bandler in 1975. Defined as *the study of the structure of subjective experience.* NLP studies the patterns or *"programming"* created by the interaction between the brain (*"neuro"*), language (*"linguistic"*) and the body, that produce both effective and ineffective behavior in order to better understand the processes behind human excellence. The skills and techniques were derived by observing the patterns of excellence in experts from diverse fields of professional communication including psychotherapy, business, health and education.

OLFACTORY - Relating to *smell* or the sense of smell.

OUTCOMES - Goals or desired states that a person or organization aspires to achieve.

PACING - A method used by communicators to quickly establish *rapport* by matching certain aspects of their behavior to those of the person with whom they are communicating - a *matching* or *mirroring* of behavior.

PARTS - A metaphorical way of talking about independent programs and strategies of behavior. Programs or "parts" will often develop a persona that becomes one of their identifying features.

PERCEPTUAL POSITIONS - A particular perspective or point of view. In NLP there are three basic positions one can take in perceiving a particular experience. *First position* involves experiencing something through our own eyes *associated* in a first person point of view. *Second position* involves experiencing something as if we were in another person's 'shoes'. *Third position* involves standing back and perceiving the relationship between ourselves and others from an observer's perspective.

PREDICATES - Process words (like *verbs, adverbs* and *adjectives*) that a person selects to describe a subject. Predicates are used in NLP to identify which *representational system* a person is using to process information.

QUOTES - A pattern in which a message that you want to deliver can be embedded in quotations, as if someone else had stated the message.

RAPPORT - The establishment of *trust, harmony* and *cooperation* in a relationship.

REFRAMING - A process used in NLP through which a problematic behavior is separated from the *positive intention* of the internal program or "part" that is responsible for the behavior. New choices of behavior are established by having the part responsible for the old behavior take responsibility for implementing other behaviors that satisfy the same positive intention but don't have the problematic by-products.

REPRESENTATIONAL SYSTEMS - the five senses: *seeing, hearing, touching (feeling), smelling, and tasting.*

REPRESENTATIONAL SYSTEM PRIMACY - Where an individual systematically uses one sense over the other to process and organize his or her experience. Primary representational system will determine many personality traits as well as learning capabilities.

SECONDARY GAIN - Where some seemingly negative or problematic behavior actually carries out some *positive function* at some other level. For example, smoking may help a person to relax or help them fit a particular self image.

STATE - The total ongoing mental and physical conditions from which a person is acting.

STRATEGY - A set of explicit mental and behavioral steps used to achieve a specific outcome. In NLP, the most important aspect of a strategy is considered to be the representational systems used to carry out the specific steps.

SUBMODALITIES - Submodalities are the special sensory qualities perceived by each of the senses. For example, visual submodalities include *color, shape, movement, brightness, depth, etc.,* auditory submodalities include *volume, pitch, tempo, etc.,* and kinesthetic submodalities include such qualities as *pressure, temperature, texture, location, etc.*

SURFACE STRUCTURE - The *words* or *language* used to describe or stand for the actual primary sensory representations stored in the brain.

SYNESTHESIA - The process of *overlap* between representational systems, characterized by phenomena like *"see-feel circuits,"* in which a person derives feelings from what he or she sees, and *"hear-feel circuits,"* in which a person gets feelings from what he or she hears. Any two sensory modalities may be linked together.

T.O.T.E. - Developed by Miller, Galanter and Pribram, the term stands for the sequence *Test-Operate-Test-Exit,* which describes the basic feedback loop used to guide all behavior.

TRANSDERIVATIONAL SEARCH - The process of *searching back* through one's stored memories and mental representations to find the reference experience from which a current behavior or response was derived.

TRANSLATING - The process of *rephrasing* words from one type of representational system predicates to another.

UTILIZATION - A technique in which a specific strategy sequence or pattern of behavior is *paced* or *matched* in order to *influence* another's response.

VISUAL - Relating to *sight* or the sense of sight.

WELL-FORMEDNESS CONDITIONS - The set of conditions something must satisfy in order to produce an effective and ecological outcome. In NLP a particular goal is well-formed if it can be: *1) stated in positive terms. 2) defined and evaluated according to sensory based evidence. 3) initiated and maintained by the person who desires the goal. 4) made to preserve the positive by-products of the present state. 5) appropriately contextualized to fit the external ecology.*

Bibliography

Applications of Neuro-Linguistic Programming, Dilts, R., Meta Publications, Capitola, Ca., 1983.

Aristotle, *Britannica Great Books*, Encyclopedia Britannica Inc., Chicago Ill., 1979.

The Art of Walt Disney ; Finch, C.; Harry N. Abrahms Inc., New York, New York, 1973.

Beethoven: Letters, Journals and Conversations; Hamburger, M.; Pantheon Books, 1952.

Beliefs: Pathways to Health and Well-Being, Dilts, R., Hallbom T. & Smith, S., Metamorphous Press, Portland, OR, 1990.

Change Your Mind, Andreas, S., Andreas, C., Real People Press, Moab, Utah, 1987.

Changing Beliefs With NLP, Dilts, R.; Meta Publications, Capitola, California, 1990.

Chunking in SOAR; The Anatomy of a General Learning Mechanism; Laird, J. E., Rosenbloom, P., and Newell, A., *Machine Learning*, 1:11-46, 1986.

The Complete Sherlock Holmes, Sir Arthur Conan Doyle, Doubleday & Company, Inc., Garden City, New York, 1979.

A Composer's World: Horizons and Limitations, Harvard University Press, 1952.

The Creative Process, edited by Brewster Ghiselin, Mentor Books, New American Library, New York, New York, 1952.

Disney Animation; The Illusion of Life ; Thomas, F. & Johnson, O.; Abbeyville Press, New York, New York, 1981.

The Encyclopedia Britannica, Encyclopedia Britannica Inc., Chicago Ill., 1979.

The Encyclopedia Sherlockiana, Jack Tracy, Avon Books, New York, NY, 1979.

Frogs into Princes, Bandler, R. and Grinder, J.; Real People Press, Moab, Utah, 1979.

The Game of Business, McDonald, J.; Doubleday, Garden City, New York, 1974.

Great Inventors & Discoveries, edited by Donald Clarke, Marshall Cavendish Books Limited, London, 1978.

The Great Psychologists: Aristotle to Freud; Watson, R., J.B. Lippincott Co., New York, NY, 1963.

Growing Pains (1941), Disney, W., reprinted in *SMPTE Journal*, July 1991, pp. 547-550.

Imagined Worlds: Stories of Scientific Discovery; Andersen, P., and Cadbury, D., Ariel Books, London, 1985.

The Life of Mozart Including His Correspondence, E. Holmes, Chapman & Hall, 1878, pp. 211-213.

Listening Skills in Music; O'Connor, Joseph; Lambent Books, London, 1989.

Moshe Feldenkrais; NLP of the Body, Dilts, R., Dynamic Learning Publications, Ben Lomond, CA, 1990.

Neuro-Linguistic Programming: The Study of the Structure of Subjective Experience, Volume I ; Dilts, R., Grinder, J., Bandler, R., DeLozier, J.; Meta Publications, Capitola, California, 1980.

Ninety Nine Percent Inspiration; Mattimore, B.; American Management Association, New York, New York, 1994.

Organizations in Action, Thompson, J., McGraw Hill Inc., New York, NY, 1967.

Plans and the Structure of Behavior, Miller, G., Galanter, E., and Pribram, K., Henry Holt & Co., Inc., 1960.

Principles of Psychology, William James, *Britannica Great Books*, Encyclopedia Britannica Inc., Chicago Ill., 1979.

Productive Thinking, Max Wertheimer, Greenwood Press, Westpoint, Connecticut, Enlarged Edition, 1959.

Roots of Neuro-Linguistic Programming, Dilts, R.; Meta Publications, Capitola, California, 1983.

Skills for the Future: Managing Creativity and Innovation, Dilts, R. with Bonissone, G. ; Meta Publications, Capitola, California, 1993.

SOAR: An Architecture for General Intelligence; Laird, J. E., Rosenbloom, P., and Newell, A., *Artificial Intelligence*, 33:1-64, 1987.

Steps To an Ecology of Mind, Bateson, Gregory; Ballantine Books, New York, New York, 1972.

Strategies of Genius, Volume II: Albert Einstein, Dilts, R. B.; Meta Publications, Capitola, California, 1994.

Strategies of Excellence; Typing Strategy, Dilts, R., Behavioral Engineering, Scotts Valley, CA, 1982.

The Structure of Magic Vol. I & II, Grinder, J. and Bandler, R.; Science and Behavior Books, Palo Alto, California, 1975, 1976.

Synergetics of Cognition, H. Haken & M. Stadler (Ed.), Springer-Verlag, Berlin, Germany, 1989.

The Syntax of Behavior, Grinder, J. & Dilts, R., Metamorphous Press, Portland, OR, 1987.

Time Line Therapy, James, T., Woodsmall, W., Meta Publications, Capitola, CA, 1987.

Tools for Dreamers: Strategies for Creativity and the Structure of Invention, Dilts, R. B., Epstein, T., Dilts, R. W., Meta Publications, Capitola, CA, 1991.

Toward a Unifying Theory of Cognition, M. Waldrop, **Science,** Vol. 241, July 1988.

Turtles All The Way Down: Prerequisites to Personal Genius, J. DeLozier & John Grinder, Grinder DeLozier & Associates, Santa Cruz, CA, 1987.

Using Your Brain, Bandler, Richard; Real People Press, Moab, Utah,1984.

Walt Disney's Fantasia ; Culhane, J.; Harry N. Abrahms Inc., New York, New York, 1983.